The Distorted Image

THE DISTORTED IMAGE

German Jewish Perceptions of
Germans and Germany, 1918–1935

Sidney M. Bolkosky

ELSEVIER

New York/Oxford/Amsterdam

ELSEVIER SCIENTIFIC PUBLISHING COMPANY, INC.
52 Vanderbilt Avenue, New York, N.Y. 10017

ELSEVIER SCIENTIFIC PUBLISHING COMPANY
335 Jan Van Galenstraat, P.O. Box 211
Amsterdam, The Netherlands

© Elsevier Scientific Publishing Co., Inc., 1975

Library of Congress Cataloging in Publication Data

Bolkosky, Sidney M
    The distorted image.

    Bibliography: p.
    Includes index.
    1. Jews in Germany—History—1800–1933.
    2. Germany—Politics and government—1918–1933.
    I. Title.
DS135.G33B65   943'.004'924   75-8270
ISBN 0-444-99014-3

Manufactured in the United States of America

Designed by Loretta Li

To Lorraine, Miriam, and Gabriel

[Narcissus] fell in love with an insubstantial hope, mistaking a mere shadow for a real body. Spellbound by his own self, he remained there motionless, with fixed gaze.

Ovid

Contents

Acknowledgements

It is difficult to "acknowledge" or thank all those who contribute or assist in the creation of a project such as this. But acknowledge one must—and hope to include those most responsible for at least the successful parts of a book.

I would first express my feelings of respect and concern for those whom this book is about: German Jews who so proudly and honorably clung to and defended a view of themselves, Germany and the world that was humane and noble. My warmest thanks go to Professor Alexis Goldenweiser and the people who in 1966 and 1967 graciously granted interviews in New York. The efficient librarians at the Wiener Library in London facilitated—indeed, almost compelled—efficient research. Their aid was invaluable. Along with them, I thank the many members of the London German Jewish community, both those who did and did not work at the Wiener Library, who patiently discussed with me their feelings and thoughts about Germany and Germans, and who described the atmosphere in the Weimar Republic and under the Nazi Regime in very personal ways.

To those who, often laboriously, read and commented on the various drafts of the manuscript, I owe special thanks. They included: Professor John Weiss of Lehman College, Professor Peter Loewenberg of U.C.L.A., and Professor Peter Amann of the University of Michigan-Dearborn, all of whom made incisive and constructive criticisms; the late Professor Melvin Hill of Hobart and William Smith Colleges, who spent many hours reading and warmly discussing the form and content of the book with me in Geneva, New York and London; and Professor George Stein of the State University of New York at Binghamton, whose criticisms, both stylistic and contextual, were pertinent, and whose suggestions were always helpful. My thanks, too, to Bill Gum of Elsevier, for his encouragement and editorial assistance.

Two special notes of gratitude that can only insufficiently approximate my deep appreciation and feeling go to Professor Marvin Bram of Hobart and William Smith, whose genius and sensitivity helped to break through some depressing stalemates, and who pointed to Melanie Klein as a sympathetic theorist; and to my wife, Lorraine, who read and reread an indeterminable number of times, corrected and discussed the manuscript, patiently edited and re-wrote, and who tolerated what often seemed to be a total and insufferable preoccupation with German Jews.

The Distorted Image

I

Introduction

The regime confronting German Jewry in 1933 was of a type unprecedented in German history. Yet German Jewish responses were, on the whole, consistent with their responses to former regimes. There was little resistance, relatively little emigration until 1935 to 1938, pledges of loyalty to the new government, and virtually no organized political opposition. Some historians have posited purely material or economic motivations for these responses to the rise and triumph of National Socialism: to emigrate was to lose one's personal possessions—money, home, business.[1] By imposing taxes and fees, Nazi legislation made emigration difficult, if not impossible, for many Jews.[2]

But economic explanations do not provide reasons for the alleged lack of German Jewish resistance to National Socialism, which had been substantial before 1933. It stopped after Hitler's seizure of power. Fear, suppression, and despair reduced and stopped opposition after 1933. But to a significant degree, explanations founded on physical suppression rationalize early Jewish reactions to the

Nazi seizure of power by projecting the conditions of 1935–1938 back to the first two years of the new regime.[3] In 1933 and 1934 the racial atrocities and attempted genocide that followed were still inconceivable.[4]

Until 1935–1936 many Jews felt that Hitler was only a temporary burden, a necessary evil to bring Germany out of depression, but an evil that would disappear as soon as he fulfilled his purpose.[5] Many more Jews believed that Hitler's anti-Semitism was largely campaign rhetoric. Adolf Eichmann used the proverb that many Jews used: "Nothing's as hot when you eat it as when it's being cooked."[6]

Such answers to questions about German Jewish reactions to Nazism explain only in part why German Jews did not emigrate en masse or oppose the Nazis in an organized fashion after Hitler's ascension to power. The disposition of most German Jews toward the Nazis may more easily be understood if the Jews are studied not as Jews but as Germans. If the reactions of German Jews to Nazism were not as exceptional as one would have expected, perhaps it was because German Jews would not accept or believe that they were outsiders who were shunned by Germans—even by National Socialist Germans.

In an interview lasting two hours, a once-prominent German Jewish émigré, the former president of the Dresden Bank in Berlin, repeated the phrase "sehr gute Deutschen" some ten times in responding to questions about the depth of assimilation and the nature of the German Jewish population before (and after) 1933.[7] The essence of German Jews, he said, was Deutschtum, Germanness. Deutschtum as he knew it had died between 1933 and 1945—inexplicably. He did not recognize and sense the "otherness" of Jews in Germany that German anti-Semites had postulated. He could not envision Jews as strangers, foreigners, or outsiders in Germany. He believed that until 1933 or 1935 Ger-

4

man Jews and German non-Jews had been alike—all "sehr gute Deutschen."[8]

His testimony affirms Karl Jaspers statement that from 1933 to 1945 the Jews in Germany were robbed of "their home, origin, their fatherland, and their real and recognized unity with the German spirit."[9] The issue raised here is the nature and degree of German Jewish assimilation with German culture and society. Philosophers like Jaspers and historians and sociologists like Golo Mann, Leon Poliakov, and Franz Oppenheimer have argued that assimilation in Germany was more complete, that contributions to German life and history were greater, that adherence to German interests was more complete than anywhere else.[10]

One German Jewish historian has written that Germanism and Judaism reached their highest fulfillments in Heine, Marx, and Freud; men who, he believed, were children of the epoch of assimilation and emancipation.[11] Innumerable examples were given by German Jews in the Weimar Republic as evidence that the two peoples complemented each other and that their spirits blended perfectly and productively. Assimilation was seen to be a natural process,[12] and the ties that bound German Jews to other Germans seemed to be so firm that they were unbreakable. Walter Rathenau could respond to the "accusation" that he was a Jew with: "My people are the Germans, nobody else."[13]

German Jews in the Weimar Republic claimed that the "facts" of complete assimilation set them apart from all other Jews, especially from East European Jews. They maintained that there was no relevant comparison between themselves and the *Ostjuden* with whom they felt they held only religion in common. Religion allegedly was not the basis of modern anti-Semitism and also did not exclude German Jews from being assimilated in the twentieth century.[14] While Jews in Eastern Europe and even in other western lands were still separate from their host cultures,

5

V WDTN SSG

German Jews were one with German culture, rooted in that culture, in love with it, and inseparable from it.[15] Even some anti-Semites voiced these sentiments.[16] In 1934 a German Jewish Scholar in America, Jacob Marcus, agreed with Hitler that Germany's borders should be closed to East European Jews because "an invasion by East European Jews," by what he termed "culturally alien" and "intellectually inferior" Jews, would be a threat to Germany."[17]

In 1912 a leading member of the German Jewish community enumerated differences that he claimed existed between German and other Jews. He concluded that the problem for East European Jews was political and national. Such problems were to be solved by emigration and resettlement in Palestine.[18] But German Jews were successful in Germany; they were Germans "who [were] able to dine with the Kaiser."[19]

German Jews in the Weimar Republic, like those of the later years of the monarchy, insisted that, unlike East European Jews, they no longer needed to strive to be at home. Because they believed that only Germany could be their home, most German Jews seemed to feel that there was little or no room for a Zionist movement in Germany. Bitter arguments were carried on throughout the 1920s between German Zionists and other German Jews.[20] The most extreme opponent of Zionism in Germany was the Verband nationaldeutscher Juden (Union of National German Jews), a small group founded in 1921 by a Berlin lawyer, Max Naumann. In 1933 they hoped for a reconciliation with the Nazis. Their program began with a denunciation of East European Jews and an appeal to the government for the disenfranchisement of German Jewish Zionists. With black-uniformed "Jewish Storm Troopers" standing guard at its meetings, until its dissolution in late 1933, the VndJ claimed to speak for the German (Aryan) Jew.[21]

But Naumann's extremists were not the only or the most important German Jewish enemies of Zionism. As late as

6

1934 members of the largest German Jewish organization, the Centralverein für deutsche Staatsbürger jüdischen Glaubens (Central Association for German Citizens of the Jewish Faith; hereafter referred to as the CV) exhorted German Jews to say "No to Zionism and Yes to Germany."[22] During the Weimar years the CV asserted that if there was any role for Jews in Germany to play in the Zionist movement, it was only a philanthropic and financial one.[23] Most East European Zionists acknowledged this, and their activities in Germany were often confined to fund-raising, relegating recruiting to a secondary function.[24]

Most German Jews rejected Zionism in Germany because they believed that they were fully and successfully assimilated. But how they viewed their assimilation involves a consideration of what they deemed Germanism, of what it meant to be a "good German." The key to German Jewish life and culture is the German Jewish image of the archetypal German. To be German really meant to think, act, and live like the Germans. Consequently, the German Jewish perception of the "typical" German was crucial, since the image thus perceived was to be emulated. German Jews firmly believed that they were true Germans because they had conformed their patterns of living to their German models. National Socialists and other German anti-Semites labeled German Jews outsiders and non-German, because they did not conform to conservative considerations of true German models, racial or other. Most German Jews called anti-Semites and Nazis un-German for the same reasons.

In 1890 one patriotic German Jew wrote that "the homeless, wandering Jew is a product of national and social causes. These have ceased [to operate] in Germany."[25] Jews and Germans, he continued, had blended together to fulfill the dream of a German nation. Emancipation had facilitated assimilation; and assimilation, in turn, had fostered "the same pride in German heroes . . . German classics . . . ideals and art" in all Germans.[26] Who were the common

7

heroes? What were the classics and ideals, belief in which German Jews emphatically claimed made them German, made their identity as Germans self-evident to themselves and to foreigners?[27] On what basis did German Jews and some German non-Jews posit a *Gemeinsamkeit,* an organic sense of communal unity between German Jews and German non-Jews?[28] How could they continue to insist on such unity not only in the face of rising anti-Semitism and Nazism, but also in the first years of the National Socialist government?

> It is because of the eighteenth century and its demands for humanitarian thoughts and idealism, plus the activities of Mendelssohn and his followers that the Jews took part in the accomplishments and ideals of the western cultural world beyond the boundaries of Germany.[29]

So wrote H. G. Adler, German Jewish historian and defender of total assimilation in Germany.[30] It is significant that Adler began his history of Jewish assimilation with Germany in the age of the Enlightenment. The first mass encounter that Jews had with Germany came during the Enlightenment as they fled west from oppressive East European governments and persecutions. From this meeting, writes Gershom Scholem, was formed a lasting "great illusion" of everything German.[31]

From the eighteenth century on, German Jews fixed upon the Enlightenment as a formative age for German culture. They seemed to believe that the men of that age had irrevocably stamped Germany with their values. In the face of a growing threat from National Socialism in the last years of the Weimar Republic, German Jews continued to insist that Hitler and his followers were not in the mainstream of German history. They perceived Enlightenment figures like Schiller, Lessing, Goethe, Kant, and Herder—men who were objects of the initial perceptions of Jews in Germany—as the norms of German culture, as the originators and articulators of a German tradition that had lasted since the eighteenth century.

German Jews worshipped these Enlightenment masters as if they were Old Testament patriarchs. Their praise of Lessing's ideals echoed praise of Old Testament ideals. The ways they interpreted Schiller's plays and poetry recalled traditional rabbinical commentaries on biblical passages.[32] The renowned German Jewish sociologist, Franz Oppenheimer, seemed to intuit the equation of German and Old Testament traditions when he wrote:

> "I have been fortunate to have been born and educated in the land of Kant and Goethe, to have their culture, their art, their language and their knowledge as my own. My Germanism is as sacred to me as my Jewish forefathers ... I combine in me the German and Jewish national feeling.[33]

In short, Oppenheimer and most German Jews identified with Enlightenment Germans and saw the traditions and ethics of the Old Testament mirrored in the ethics of men like Lessing, Kant, and Goethe.

By thus identifying the two traditions, German Jews then concluded that they were utterly assimilated to Germany— physically and spiritually. Few doubted the physical assimilation; indeed, anti-Semites did not cease to point it out, but "spiritual" assimilation was the crux of the Jewish Question in Germany. If German Jews had the same heroes, ideals, and allegiances as German non-Jews, however, the question was answered: they were culturally, spiritually, and psychologically assimilated. No one denied that Goethe and the others were absolutely German in their ideas and ideals. By holding ideals of good and evil in common with other Germans, German Jews considered themselves an integral part of German culture.[34]

Although there were exceptions such as Kurt Tucholsky, Julius Leber, and several Socialist leaders, during the Weimar years most German Jews believed that Germany and most Germans were characterized by the values of the Enlightenment: tolerance, reason, cosmopolitanism combined with nationalism, understanding, and liberal humanism. They adhered to that belief even in the initial years of the Nazi government. By believing as they did, German Jews ignored the dangerous growth of anti-Semitism among more than just uneducated Germans and the existence of a large part of Germany that was anti-Enlightenment, racist, and irrational. That German Jews in the Weimar Republic acted as if all Germans were rational and enlightened indicates a peculiar type of blindness to growing, real threats to their well-being.

Unyieldingly affirming themselves at home in Germany, at home with German values, at home with German heroes, at home with German patriotism, and at home with German tradition "grounded" German Jews by providing what they perceived to be a common background for *all* Germans. The distinguished social psychologist, Kurt Lewin, pointed out in 1935 that all actions have some specific "background" related to the existential situation, and are at least in part determined by that background. "Background," he continued, is of crucial importance for the perception of reality and is intimately bound to the need for security. "Firmness of action and clearness of decision" depend upon the "stability of this 'ground.'" All people, but especially minority groups, need "some ground to stand upon."[35] Those who desperately need and create security are often sensitive to threatening encroachments upon it, yet they can be obstinately impervious to real danger because of the strength of that psychosociological indispensability.

. One constituent of "ground" is belonging, and social myths provide it by integrating, ordering, and adjusting desires and external reality; they allow the manipulation of a disorderly world so that it is transformed into an orderly one. In short, they provide security and hope without which action would be at best difficult. For German Jews,

10

those myths that afforded "background" were often at odds with what many non-Jewish Germans characterized as "tradition."

At least since German unification by Bismarck and the so-called Prussification after 1871, many conservative Germans, men who held power positions and social status, identified being anti-Semitic, promilitarism, antirepublican and antiliberal with being "German." German Jews, therefore, in the nineteenth century and until the founding of the Weimar Republic, were fighting triumphant conservatism when they opposed anti-Semitism. Jews in nineteenth-century Germany were caught in an environment of rising nationalism, in a state whose leaders, unlike France's or England's, were from the preindustrial, conservative, Junker class.[35] Until the Weimar Republic, most German Jewish writing identified Jews in Germany as conservative, or at least denied the equation of Jewish and liberal. Yet only through liberal reform had they gained some sort of emancipated, equal civil status.

When German Jews rejoiced in the Weimar Republic, they did so claiming that it represented a continuity of moral values, of ethics that marked German history from the Enlightenment. But to identify German Enlightenment values as truly German was to ignore that fact that although the values of the Enlightenment were liberal in the main, in nineteenth-century Germany the liberal generation of the Stein-Hardenberg reforms and of 1848 lost at every turn. The Weimar Republic, therefore, was not a logical, natural product of historical continuity; it was not rooted in pre-World War I political, social, and moral principles, as German Jews claimed. Rather, it was a break with the past, rooted in defeat. Weimar was the product of the temporary weakness of nineteenth-century conservative (and anti-Semitic) classes who slipped from leadership in 1918.[36]

To prove themselves deserving of civil rights and social equality, German Jews would have to prove themselves

German. The tragic dilemma of German Jews was that to achieve these German rewards they had to identify with those elite, conservative groups who denied that liberal ideals of social equality, civil rights, and emancipation were German. Yet German Jews seemed to repress much of this dilemma and to live their lives according to the more pleasant illusions they manufactured by keeping alive the ideals and heroes of the German Enlightenment.

For all that, German Jews could not and did not completely block out or ignore the reality of German anti-Semitism. They were, of course, aware not only of contemporary anti-Semitism but of a history of hostility to Jews that was traceable at least as far back as Luther and further to the First Crusade.[37] But for all the notable anti-Semites—Luther, Lagarde, Treitschke, Chamberlain, Stòcker, and Hitler—German Jews found opposite numbers in Lessing, Schiller, Goethe, Kant, Herder, Fichte, Humboldt, and Mommsen.[38] Even Luther's and Treitschke's anti-Semitism was seen as a "minor deviation" from their overall philosophies of tolerance and positive feelings for Jews.[39] The dominant tradition that best characterized Germans of the past and present, at least in the eyes of German Jews, was tolerance and reason. When that belief—that ground, that myth—was shaken and began to give way, they were profoundly affected, as Lewin had suggested happens under such circumstances; and as anthropologists, historians, sociologists, and psychologists have described as happening when myths, ideas, world-views, or philosophies are exposed as false. One of the many German Jewish suicides in 1933, Fritz Rosenfelder, left a note that pathetically testified to the belief in German reason. Unable to understand the National Socialist victory, Rosenfelder wrote, "I leave without any feelings of hatred. I have only one burning desire: that reason may return."[40]

Men like Rosenfelder and Oppenheimer who believed in equating the essence of *Deutschtum* with the essence of

Judentum also experienced a sort of schizophren\
tion that came from living in two worlds. In *Die Juo*\
Zirndorf (1894), and most clearly in his autobiogr\
Mein Weg als Deutsche und Jude (1921), Jakob Wass\
mann, one of the most famous of German Jewish novelist\
in the Weimar Republic, described pressures he felt as a
result of being forced daily to play the dual role of German
and Jew that was often contradictory.[41] Eugen Fuchs, president of the CV, had voiced similar conflicting feelings in
1919 when he said:

> We are German and want to remain German, and achieve here,
> in Germany, on German soil, our equal rights, regardless of our
> Jewish characteristics. . . . Also, we want inner regeneration, a
> renaissance of Judaism, not assimilation. And we want proudly
> to remain true to our characteristics and our historical develop-
> ment. Here on German soil we want to fight for our equal rights
> as citizens.[42]

Yet there is no contradiction or conflict if German and
Jew are defined by the same values, life-styles, and intellectual traditions, if "inner regeneration" means only religious, or confessional, separateness. Assimilation is then a
self-evident phenomenon. Those traditions of reason and
tolerance, which German Jewish scholars found were alike
in both the Old Testament and the German Enlightenment,
seemed to reach their peak and fulfillment in the institutions of the Weimar Republic. Ernst Toller, the revolutionary opponent of the Republic, was at first elated by the
possibilities of the change from monarchy to republic and
of the realization of the dream of humanitarian internationalism.[43] The reason for hopes as high as Toller's was the
Weimar constitution, which German Jews believed typified
the spirit of eighteenth-century Germany as well as of the
Weimar Republic. It was now, in fact, the official spirit and
ideology of twentieth-century Germany and seemed to
demonstrate that Germany and Germans were, and always

13

had been, the land and people of the Enlightenment.

Ernst Berg, a "moderate" anti-Semite, might have been responding to these ideas when he wrote that German Jews tried "to read [themselves] into German things."[44] He agreed with the Jews in Germany that they were united with other Germans, but he saw that union as one of persecution: after World War I Germans were persecuted, he said, in the same way that Jews had been for ages.[45] But to believe German Jews were like Germans in any other ways, he continued, was a serious mistake.[46] His prescription for the solution to the "Jewish problem" in Germany was total assimilation, by which he meant the death of Judaism and the submission of Jews in Germany to true German ways as he saw and defined them—true German conservative ways. In less abstract terms, Berg demanded that Jews cease projecting their values onto Germans, withdraw from leadership in intellectual and cultural life, and thereby stop the harm they were unintentionally doing Germans.[47]

German Jews in the Weimar Republic did not see themselves as Berg saw them. They did not think of themselves as doing harm to Germans or Germany Gershom Scholem wrote that "the unending longing to be at home was changed [in Germany] to the ecstatic illusion of being at home,"[48] of being insiders, not intruders. German Jews did not recognize differences between true Germanism and Judaism. They did not think of themselves as outsiders alienated from the mainstream of German history and culture. Scholem compassionately recognized the tragic dilemma of Jews in Germany when he added that "only today [1966], after so much blood and tears, can we say that it was only illusory?"[49]

Because of their firm convictions, because of this illusion of acceptance and acculturation and their identification with eighteenth-century German *philosophes*, German Jews (as well as some German liberals) manifested symptoms

14

that might be called neurotic—especially their repression of harsh segments of reality and the substitution of illusions for reality. This psychological and intellectual disposition motivated their actions in the Weimar Republic and determined how they responded to the rise of Nazism and the fall of the Republic. Understanding the origins and functions of these beliefs, and the mechanisms that perpetuated them, is crucial to understanding the historical acts of German Jews as a group.

German Jews were a most diverse and divided group. At least one sociologist has described the diversity in historical and regional terms, pointing out cultural, social, economic, and intellectual differences.[50] The plethora of German Jewish organizations and unions in the Weimar Republic offers other evidence of this diversity.[51] Zionists and members of the Union of National German Jews (Naumann's group) were at opposite ends of the spectrum. Yet it was the CV, with its public, explicit policy of assimilation without complete denial of Judaism, that had the greatest following among German Jews. With its 60,000 members belonging to over 550 sections and 21 "rural offices," the CV also was affiliated with most of the other organizations,[52] and by 1930 it claimed to speak for some 300,000 German Jews (about one half the German Jewish population) and to represent the opinions of nearly 90 percent of all Jews in Germany.[53] The NSDAP viewed the CV as its major organized Jewish opponent before 1933, and after the Nazi seizure of power, they dealt with the Jewish population through CV leaders[54]

In the following pages, therefore, I have chosen to deal primarily with the CV through its weekly and monthly newspapers, the *C. V. Zeitung* (hereafter *CVZ*) and the *C. V. Zeitung Monatsausgabe* (hereafter *CVZ Monthly*), and its other educative publications, such as *Blütlugen, Marchen und Tatsachen*, edited by the CV; *Zur Ritualmordbeschuldigung*, edited by the CV; and *Deutsches Judentum und*

15

Rechtskrisis, edited by the CV. There are no Zionist publications in this bibliography. Because of the CV's bitter opposition to Zionism in Germany, I have largely omitted those Jews who supported the Zionist movement. The CV leaders believed that they and their ogranization spoke for the overwhelming majority of German Jews. They made this claim often, and took it for granted by 1925. I have accepted this somewhat egocentric view, but only because of membership statistics and the apparent support the CV received from virtually all other Jewish organizations in Germany save the two extremes. Phrases like "most German Jews" or "German Jews" generally, then, refer to those who echoed the CV assimilationist point of view.

This may risk too narrow a focus. An expansion of views would perhaps aid in understanding the CV attitude. That there were alternative attitudes, myths, or ideals should be clear. In 1917, the German Jewish philosopher Franz Rosenzweig, referring to his criticism of his mentor Hermann Cohen's assumption of the German "grand tradition" of the Enlightenment as his own and German Jewry's, wrote:

> To be a German means to *fully* undertake responsibility for one's people, not just to harmonize Goethe, Schiller, and Kant, but also the others and above all with the inferior and average, with the assessor, the fraternity student, the petty bureaucrat, the thick-skulled peasant, the pedantic school master; the real German must lock all these in his heart, or suffer from them. ... Cohen confuses that which he as a *European* finds in German culture with what a German finds in it. Of course: "German philosophy and music" are European phenomena ... but with Cohen only the European exists, a genuine Germanism with which it could cross-fertilize is missing.[55]

Rosenzweig, however, was unusual among German Jews in this realistic, candid appraisal. That this is so is apparent from the position of such a man as Cohen—an avowed assimilationist—as well as other prominent spokesmen of the German Jewish community, intellectual and nonintellectual alike, and the testimonies of a multitude of not-so-prominent people from virtually every stratum of German society.

The Zionists, German Jewish Socialists, and Socialist-Zionists presented what can be seen in retrospect as a more "realistic" analysis of Germany and Germans. Zionism is, of course, the antithesis of assimilationism. Socialism denied that Germany had rediscovered its semi-holy tradition of the Enlightenment. Both positions were unacceptable to members of the CV and to the majority of German Jews. Although these alternative movements were vocal and obvious, they were nevertheless small in Germany. Unquestionably, German Jews would have been wiser to have accepted these alternatives. Yet, most did not. The question that should haunt scholars therefore remains: why accept a lethal ideal, a self-destructive myth, an illusion, madness? Why was the CV so defensive in its absolute rejection of Zionism for German Jews in the 1920s?

No doubt comparative psychoanalytic studies of Zionists and anti-Zionists would reveal considerable psychological differences. That is not my purpose here. It remains a fact that at least until 1933, the overwhelming majority of German Jews clung tenaciously to a myth of Germans and Germany that gave them a secure position, a seemingly solid ground to stand upon, in German culture. What that myth was and why it existed is the subject of this book. Siegfried was transubstantialized into Nathan the Wise because German Jews could live normal, secure lives with that dream-reality; an "illusion" but one that dispelled a wakeful reality that was deeply hostile and irrational to them. Thus, a wakeful illusion reflected a normative, saner reality in their eyes. Few would choose differently. This "neurotic" stance seems paradoxically normal, completely human; and because of this, German Jews should not be condemned, but their acts should be explained; they must not be accused, but understood.

17

I have tried to examine the questions of how and why German Jews from the end of World War I to 1935 reacted to anti-Semitism and specifically to the rise of National Socialism. This involved other questions in which the "how" and the "why" are equally implicit: the ways German Jews viewed Germans, themselves, and other Jews; what they considered German actions and thoughts in the Republic; what they considered were truly German values and ideals; what they believed were the dominant themes and figures in German history.

There is a continuity in German history that makes distinctions between 1932 and 1933 misleading, distorting, even fatuous. Yet to liberal Germans and to the German Jews with whom we are here concerned, the Nazi victory was a monumental event, an event that symbolically and literally heralded a total break with the past. Theirs is the perspective that matters here, not the "objective" historian's. The question of the logical progression of events is a problem of the nature of German history, its conservative tradition, and the nature of Nazism. These were crucial questions for German Jews, yet questions most of them idealized, denied, or distorted for purposes I hope to show were psychically necessary.

To have accepted "reality," the conservative and anti-Semitic tradition of Germany that ironically triumphed at the close of the Weimar Republic, would have openly acknowledged a dooming dilemma for German Jews: their alienation, dispensability, false contact, their aloneness, which contrasted so sharply with their conviction of their oneness with Germany. Surely reality crept into their lives, forcing them to ponder silent warnings like nightmares. Yet, in order to retain equilibrium in their lives, they dismissed those warnings in the rational light of day—a light that blinded them to an increasingly obvious truth. Few could distinguish between the dark reality that *seemed* illusory as it intruded into their illusion, and the illusion that seemed real because it allowed life to continue with hope.

These are historical issues. The "hows" are answerable through examination of the documents and observation of German Jewish actions. But the "whys" need understanding of psychological as well as historical motivations. Motivations of this sort are not simply products of political and economic forces, but products of cultural conditions and traditions that mold psychological predispositions to certain beliefs that are held collectively. In the case of German Jews, their cultural attitudes, education, and beliefs can be analyzed as being similar in form to those of primitive or archaic cultures; the mechanisms and structures that ordered their lives can be described in terms of myths, heroes, and archetypes.

The conception of the German *philosophe* in the minds of German Jews took on an aura that resembled the aura attached to heroes and prophets in primitive worship. And just as do primitive myth-believers, German Jews tried to emulate the life-styles of their German heroes. By that emulation they believed that they were reliving the lives of their archetypes and reanimating their values and ethics. German Jewish literature that so often and so religiously discussed German Enlightenment figures was readily adaptable to comparisons with mythical accounts of mythical heroes or archetypes.

NOTES

[1]Leon Poliakov, *Harvest of Hate* (Syracuse: Syracuse University Press, 1954), pp. 3, 10.
[2]Raul Hilberg, *The Destruction of the European Jews* Chicago: Quadrangle Books, 1961), pp. 55–60.
[3]Cf., for example, Jacob Robinson, *And the Crooked Shall Be Made Straight. The Eichmann Trial, the Jewish Catastrophe, and Hannah Arendt's Narrative* (New York: Macmillan Co., 1965).

19

[4]Hilberg, *The Destruction of the European Jews;* Hannah Arendt, *Eichmann in Jerusalem. A Report on the Banality of Evil* (New York: Viking Press, 1965) p. 43, passim.

[5]See Chapter viii

[6]Arendt, *Eichmann,* p. 39.

[7]Interview with the former director of the Dresden Bank of Berlin, November 1966.

[8]Ibid.

[9]Karl Jaspers, in *Deutsche und Juden. Beiträge von Nahum Goldmann, Gershom Scholem, Golo Mann, Salo W. Baron, E. Gerstenmaier, und Karl Jaspers* (Frankfurt am Main: Suhrkamp verlag, 1967), p. 118.

[10]Poliakov, *Harvest of Hate,* p. 9; Sidney Osborne, *Germany and Her Jews* (London: Soncino Press, 1939), pp. 8, 35–37, passim; C. A. Stonehill, *The Jewish Contribution to Civilization* (London: C. A. Stonehill, Ltd., 1940); Jaspers, *Deutsche und Juden;* Golo Mann, *Deutsche und Juden.*

[11]H. G. Adler, *Die Juden in Deutschland von der Aufklärung bis zum Nationalsozialismus* (Munchen: Kösel-Verlag, 1960), p. 160.

[12]"Der Streit um die 'wahre Kunst' im preussischen Landtag. Gibt es eine 'negroide jüdische Kultur'?" *CVZ,* IX (April 11, 1930).

[13]Arnold Brecht, "Walter Rathenau and the Germans," *Journal of Politics,* X (February 1948), 20–48.

[14]Heinrich Stern, *Warum sind wir Deutsche? Sechs Aufsätze für die deutsche-jüdische Jugend* (Berlin: C. V. Landesverband Ostwestfalen und Nachbargebiete, 1926), p. 28.

[15]Jacob R. Marcus, *The Rise and Destiny of the German Jew* (Cincinnati: Union of American Hebrew Congregations, 1934), p. 29.

[16]Friedrich Hiebscher, "Reich und Israel," *Klärung. 12 Autoren, Politiker über die Judenfrage* (Berlin: Verlag Tradition Wilhelm Kolk, 1932), pp. 33–42; Ernst Berg, *Wohin treibt Juda?* (Leipzig: Diskus-Verlag Emil Krug, 1926), p. 16 et passim; Graf Ernst Reventlow, "Deutsche—Juden," *Süddeutsche Monatschefte,* XXVII (September 1930), 846–852; Theodor Fritsch, "Zur Geschichte der anti-semitischen Bewegung," *Süddeutsche Monatschefte,* XXVII (September 1930), 852–856.

[17]Marcus, *Rise and Destiny,* p. 101.

[18]Eugen Fuchs, *Um Deutschtum und Judentum* (Frankfurt am Main: Verlag von J. Kauffmann, 1919), p. 9.

[19]Ibid.

[20]"Volksgemeinde und nationale Autonomie. Ein kritische Betrachtung von Spektator," *CVZ,* IV (January 23, 1925).

[21]Poliakov, *Harvest of Hate,* p. 11; Marcus, *Rise and Destiny,* pp. 203, 295–296; Max Naumann, "Grüne Fragen und gelbe Antworten," *Klärung,* pp. 70–85.

[22]Alfred Hirschberg, "Der Centralverein deutscher Staatsbürger jüdischen Glaubens," *Wille und Weg* (Berlin: Vortrupp Verlag, 1935), pp. 12–29.

[23]Interview with a Russian Zionist (who had "served" in Germany from 1923 to 1932), November 1967; Gerhard Holdheim. "Der Zionismus in Deutschland," *Süddeutsche Monatshecte,* XXVII (September 1930), 814–817.

[24]Interview with a Zionist, November 1966.

[25]Civis Germanus Sum, von Einem Juden deutscher Nation (Berlin: Verlag von Richard Wilhelm, 1890), p. 16.

[26]Ibid., pp. 3, 14–15, 18; Caro Leopold, Die Judenfrage. Eine ethische Frage (Leipzig: Grunow, 1892), pp. 24, passim.

[27]Ismar Elbogen, Die Geschichte der Juden in Deutschland (rev. ed.; Frankfurt am Main: Europäische Verlaganstalt, 1966), p. 297; Arnold Paucker, Der jüdische Abwehrkampf gegen Antisemitismus und Nationalsozialismus in der letzten Jahren der Weimarer Republik (Hamburg: Leibniz Verlag, 1969), p. 15.

[28]Jakobe Fromer, Das Wesen des Judentums (Berlin; Leipzig, Paris: Hüpeden & Merzyn, 1905), p. 104; Berg, Wohin treibt Juda?, p. 65.

[29]Adler, Die Juden in Deutschland, p. 107.

[30]Ibid., p. 115, passim.

[31]Scholem, Deutsche und Juden, p. 31.

[32]Ernst Lissauer, "Der deutsche Jude und das deutsche Schriftum," CVZ, XII (June 22, 1933).

[33]Franz Oppenheimer, Erlebtes, Erstrebtes, Erreichtes. Erinnerungen (Berlin: Welt-Verlag, 1931), p. 214.

[34]Group Psychology and the Analysis of the Ego, The Standard Edition of the Complete Psychological Works of Sigmund Freud, ed. James Strachey, Anna Freud, Alix Strachey, and Alan Tyson. (24) Vols. London; Hogarth Press and The Institute of Psycho-Analysis, 1954-, XVIII, p. 116. Hereafter, Works.

[35]Kurt Lewin, Resolving Social Conflicts: Selected Papers on Group Dynamics (New York: Harper & Row, 1948), pp. 145–146. It should be noted that in a later essay (1942) Lewin contrasted the high morale of the German Zionists with that of non-Zionists. Their ground had not been shaken because it was based upon more realistic evaluations of the German situation and their hopes had remained alive. Ibid., pp. 104–105.

[36]A. J. P. Taylor, The Course of German History (New York: G. P. Putnam's Sons, 1962), pp. 189ff.

[37]The CV was, after all, founded as a defensive organization for the purpose of combating German anti-Semitism. Cf. Arnold Paucker, Der jüdische Abwehrkampf.

[38]Baron, Deutsche und Juden, p. 86.

[39]Julius Bab, Lieben und Tod des deutschen Judentums (Paris, 1939), p. 20.

[40]Poliakov, Harvest of Hate, p. 12.

[41]Jakob Wassermann, Mein Weg als Deutscher und Jude (Berlin: S. Fischer Verlag, 1921), p. 118; Hugo Bieber, "Jews and Jewish Problems in German Literature," Jewish People Past and Present (New York: Central Yiddish Culture Organization, 1952), III, 239–256; J. G. Robertson, A History of German Literature, 3d ed., ed. Edna Pardie; (Edinburgh & London: William Blackwood & Sons, 1959), p. 554.

[42]Fuchs, Um Deutschtum und Judentum, p. 133.

[43]Ernst Toller, Briefe vom Gefangnis (1935), pp. 19, 24, 39.

[44]Berg, *Wohin treibt Juda?*, p. 41.

[45]Ibid., p. 9.

[46]Ibid., p. 49.

[47]Ibid., p. 54.

[48]Scholem, *Deutsche und Juden*, p. 34.

[49]Ibid., p. 31.

[50]Werner J. Cahnman, "The Three Regions of German-Jewish History," *Jubilee Volume Dedicated to Curt C. Silberman*, ed. Herbert A. Strauss and Hanns G. Reissner (New York: American Federation of Jews from Central Europe, Inc., 1969), pp. 1–14; interviews with two former CV members, November 1966. A quick perusal of the literature makes the divisions and rifts among German Jews immediately apparent. See also Hans Lamm, *Über die innere und aussere Entwicklung des deutschen Judentums im Dritten Reich*, pp. 1–22.

[51]Among the many associations, which were not necessarily at odds with each other, but often disagreed on matters of German Jewish life, were: The Jewish Women's Bund, The Association for Liberal Judaism, The Jewish Conservative Association, The Union of German Jews, Union of Eastern Jewish Organization in Germany, along with the Zionists, National German Jews, CV, and the Reichsbund jüdischen Frontsoldaten.

[52]Eva Reichmann-Jungmann, "Der Centralverein deutscher Staatsbürger jüdischen Glaubens," *Süddeutsche Monatshefte*, XXVII (September 1930), 818–824.

[53]Arendt, *Eichmann in Jerusalem*, p. 59; Hans Martin Klinkenberg, "Zwischen Liberalismus und Nationalismus," *Monumenta Judaica*, ed. Konrad Schilling (Koln, Published by the City of Koln 1963), p. 324; Ismar Schorsch, *Jewish Reactions to German Anti-Semitism, 1870–1914* (New York: Columbia University Press, 1972), pp. 117–148.

[54]Max Gruenwald, "Der Anfang der Reichsvertretung," *Deutsches Judentum: Aufsteig und Krise. Veröffentlichung des Leo Baeck Instituts* (Stuttgart: Deutsche Verlags-Anstalt, 1963, pp. 315–325; interview with former vice-president of CV, November 1966.

[55]Rosenzweig to his parents, September 20, 1917, *Briefe* (Berlin: Schocken Verlag, 1935), pp. 231–232.

II

The Illusion of
Assimilation

The Jew had come to believe that his interests and those of the
German nation were, in all respects, one and the same—that
German culture, German nationality, the German past and future
were his own.

ARTHUR COHEN

In his popular novel of 1922, *Stadt ohne Juden*,[1] Hugo
Bettauer concocted a hypothetical expulsion of all Jews
from "Christian" Austria. The fictitious criteria for expulsion anticipated those of the National Socialist Aryan Paragraph and Nuremburg Laws of 1934 and 1935, and they
repeated earlier church criteria for expulsion and persecution of Jews.[2] The resulting situation in the novel was
unbearable for Christian Austrians. Jews, it seemed, had
become indispensable because of their roles in the economy, the arts, the government, and the total culture. The
unsubtle moral of the novel was that Jews in Austria were
totally assimilated into their host German (Austrian) culture.

Stadt ohne Juden was an endorsement and description of
assimilation. Although the setting was Austria and not
Germany, Jews in Germany also endorsed the book, the
idea of assimilation, and the cultural position of Jews in
both Austria and Germany. Despite the differences in political, economic, and social status that existed between Aus-

23

trian and German Jews, Jews in Germany identified with the completely assimilated Jewish characters of *Stadt ohne Juden*. In á book published as recently as 1970, a German Jewish historian treats Austrian Jews—indeed, almost all Central and East European Jews—as if they were German Jews. The title, *Deutschland ohne Juden*, ironically imitates Bettauer's title.[3] In its position on assimilation, and in its portrait of Jews as devoted, psychologically and physically, to their host culture, *Stadt ohne Juden* was typical of much German Jewish literature of the 1920s.

Bettauer's Jewish characters were completely Austrian and suffered as much by being torn from their beloved fatherland as did their Christian neighbors whose economy and culture were thrown into chaos. The happy ending, the return of the Jews on Christian request, is the salvation of Austria. The Austrian Jewish hero and his Austrian non-Jewish fiancée rejoice with the crowds for the mass return and reunion: bells peal, laughter rings, tears of happiness flow, Austria and her culture flower and prosper because of the complete reassimilation that unites Jews and non-Jews in perfect harmony.

Assimilation, as Bettauer portrayed it, is rarely a one-dimensional phenomenon. It is "the process by which the identity of groups is fused."[4] Assimilation exceeds the process known (among sociologists) as "accommodation," which is a mutual adjustment of groups that retain their own identities and interests.[5] Assimilation that manifests itself externally through political, economic, and social activity may be termed external or "profane" assimilation, in the sense that it is based upon "everyday facts including those of social organization and many other aspects of external life."[6]

Ferdinand Tönnies implied in *Gemeinschaft und Gesellschaft* that full-fledged membership in a cultural *community (Gemeinschaft)* required intellectual or spiritual communion.[7] *Internal* features of total assimilation include

24

assumption of the same values, goals, and ideals of the assimilating culture. "Sacred" assimilation involves psychic factors that allow an emotional fusion which must incorporate a *"Gemeinschaft* of the mind."[8]

Acculturation is perhaps a more precise term than assimilation. Acculturation is not a fusing of identities (assimilation) or an accommodation of one group by another. It is a form of complete "culture change in which one people takes on the cultural forms, beliefs, values, and practices of another."[9] Acculturation irrevocably blends all the elements of a *Gemeinschaft*, external and internal, in an organic unity. It is based upon a spiritual as well as a physical bond.

Were German Jews externally assimilated, a part of the economy and the "society"? By 1925 Jews constituted 0.9 percent of the total population of Germany, yet they held more than 3.5 percent of all positions in the so-called bourgeois occupations.[10] Nowhere else were so many Jews so strongly a part of the middle class, at least in terms of professions such as medicine, law, academics, civil service, banking, and business.[11] Although the role of German Jews in the German economy has been exaggerated by both anti-Semites and Judaeophiles, there can be no question that Jews contributed heavily to the German economy between 1848 and 1933.[12] This is not to imply, as some German Jews have, that German Jews were indispensable to Germany's economic development in those years. Most German Jews, however, were gainfully employed in productive service professions that ranged from merchants to jurists. The overwhelming majority were involved in the German economy, not in a separate German Jewish economy.[13]

The origins of the professional, economic assimilation, an example of external assimilation, were primarily political. Since "assimilation is the goal of emancipation,"[14] emancipation was the source, the sine qua non, of assimilation. Certain basic civil and economic rights were granted in the nineteenth-century drive for emancipation. Assimilation and emancipation were viewed by those seeking both as two sides of the same coin, as standing "in an unmitigated reciprocity ... the inner and the outer of the same phenomenon."[15] Jews in Germany had expressed their desire to be assimilated as Germans in their endorsement of the 1812 Hardenberg Edict, which offered them civil rights by reclassifying them from "Fremde" (foreigners) and "Schutzjuden" to "Einlandern" (residents) and "Staatsbürger" (citizens).[16] The edict provided only limited rights and was lengthy because of the qualifications it demanded for Jewish citizenship. But in the eyes of Germany's Jews (and other Jews as well), "nowhere else was there [even] a limited emancipation"[17]; this despite the French emancipation. The Prussian legislation was only the first in a series of civil legislation which German Jews perceived to be representative of the trend toward emancipation in the nineteenth century.[18] It seemed to presage a more complete and intimate relationship between Germans and Jews.

Such deeper intercourse seemed on the brink of realization in 1848. In the revolutions of that year in Germany, the demands of Jews were often identical with those of non-Jewish liberals and revolutionaries.[19] German Jews began active participation in German politics. Some, like Ludwig Bamberger, even went so far as to man the barricades.[20] Other Jews led the parliamentary fight for equal rights: Gabriel Riesser, the liberal vice-president of the Frankfurt Parliament, whose eloquent words were said to have convinced that assemblage to offer the leadership of Germany to the Prussian king; and Moritz Veit, spokesman for Berlin Jewry, also elected to the National Assembly, were only two of many.[21] As a consequence of this increased involvement, German Jews began to perceive Germany as a liberal land and themselves as living in harmony with German non-Jews.

Emancipation of the Jews was coupled to liberal demands for separation of church and state, for equality before the law, for economic freedom, and for universal human freedom. Only one deputy raised his voice against Jewish emancipation in the National Assembly of 1848.[22] Jakob Wassermann's father could say with considerable conviction and some truth at that time that "we live in the age of tolerance."[23]

Despite the triumph of reactionary forces, several of the liberal achievements survived and furthered the assimilation process. Tolerance meant the removal of walls, of physical and psychological boundaries. Employment opportunities increased for German Jews, as free residence laws stimulated new urban migration. The German Jewish population grew, and assimilation simply in terms of residence, a type of "physical" assimilation, was an indisputable fact.[24] Economic assimilation accompanied it. Jews were needed, said Moritz Veit,[25] and philanthropy in this case would yield a social as well as an economic profit.

Even before 1848 Ludwig Philippson, in an editorial for the *Allgemeine Zeitung des Judentums*, had called for the "dissolution of [Jewish] communities" and a reorganization along new guidelines that would allow freer communication with Christian communities.[26] Religious ties began to dissolve with the growth of Reform Judaism, and with them the age-old physical and spiritual walls of the ghetto communities gradually disintegrated. The once "total" ghetto communities *(Gemeinschaft)* became fragmented and lost the "organic unity" similar to the type Tönnies had described.[27] Secular cosmopolitanism and liberalism in the form of political activity filled the newly created religious gap. Because that political activity provided a substitute for religion,[28] it was carried on with a religious enthusiasm and fervor. Most Jews did not cease to practice their religion, but many adjusted that practice to a more secular lifestyle. The new generation of German Jews wanted the "burden of Jewish existence," that is, the burden of disenfranchisement and unequal opportunity, lifted from them.[29] In its stead they desired a sense of community based upon liberal ideals of nonsectarian cooperation.

Many German Jewish intellectuals thought that the religion of their forefathers, practiced and applied the same way for centuries, was useless in the nineteenth century. Through the support of liberal and social movements they turned to what was later called a "modernized Judaism."[30] Men like Eduard Lasker and Ludwig Bamberger belonged to the National Liberal Party and then were instrumental in the founding of the Progressive Party,[31] both parties composed of liberals, and both combining ideals of *Freiheit und Einheit*, liberty and unity, ideals that were construed as utterly German and not identified as "Jewish." Bamberger returned from Swiss exile to enthusiastically support Bismarck's liberal plans. Lasker, "the liberal in the liberal decade,"[32] received praise from virtually all segments of German political opinion, including Bismarck, who credited him with "civil courage."[33] Both Bamberger and Lasker were symbolic of the German Jewish abandonment of traditional Judaism for social and civil causes. Lasker claimed he was neither a Christian nor a Jew, but a "humanitarian," while Bamberger showed a marked antipathy toward all organized religion.[34]

Secularization meant assimilation, and both were attempts to wipe away the "mark of disenfranchisement"[35]—attempts not necessarily to dissolve group identity, but to allow individuals of that "marked" group to blend more freely into German society. Assimilation with the greater German community seemed especially feasible because the apparent essentials for acceptance seemed already achieved: common language, physical proximity, and what seemed to be the final necessity—intellectual union, a meeting of minds, morals, and purposes.[36]

The enthusiasm of liberal activity in 1848 produced an intensified rapprochement between Christian and Jewish groups and communities. Cooperation was rampant. After the first revolutionary successes, people were told by their respective leaders to forget the differences and to emphasize the similarities.[37] In Leipzig, such eminent Jewish scholars and rabbis as Zacharias Frankel, Adolf Jellinek, Samuel Holdheim, and Julilus Fürst collaborated in the founding of the Ecclesiastical Association for All Denomitions.[38] In Stettin a newly formed congregation of Free Christians intermittently used a local synagogue while its own church was being built.[39] In Karlsruhe Jewish leaders advocated a Free National Synagogue. In Hamburg the Hermann Heine Foundation, established by Salomon Heine to offer charitable loans to Jewish workers, now extended its philanthropy to needy Christians as well. Even the Orthodox Jewish *Voice of Jacob* proposed an international league of peoples and hinted at a softer line on intermarriage.[40]

The 1848 liberal brand of assimilation meant fraternization, coexistence, conversion, and intermarriage. This revolutionary change in social circumstances owed a great deal not only to Jewish efforts but also to a marked change of attitude among non-Jewish Germans. The wave of assimilation was a direct response to, indeed a part of, the liberal political revolution of the time.[41] The new attitude did not mean that Germans had suddenly developed deeper love for Jews. Nor was there a sudden and simple love for Germans on the part of Jews.[42] Jews like Bamberger and Lasker, and even Moritz Veit and Zacharias Frankel, believed that they could both help and be helped by cooperation and assimilation. Germany's salvation, they felt, lay in liberalism. And they were intensely committed to the creation of a liberal Germany.[43] Non-Jewish German liberals held similar beliefs. They valued the use of German Jews.[44] As early as the 1780s, Christian Dohm's landmark statement, *Über die bürgerliche Verbesserung der Juden* (1781), promoted emancipation of Jews on pragmatic grounds.[45]

29

Minor legislation throughout the nineteenth century dealing with such subjects as education, military service, and admission into arts and crafts guilds in small German states, was calculated both to make Jews happier and, more important to the governments, to use them for the state.[46] Civil liberties were useful, and liberal appeals to German and Jewish unity were practical and aimed at unifying Germany. The primary motivation was functional, pragmatic nationalism, and it was intertwined with pragmatic liberalism.

Jews in Germany were therefore increasingly identified with liberalism. The rising influence of Jews in trade, politics, finance, and literature dates from the liberal revolutions of 1848 and the "Liberal Summer" of the 1860s.[47] The so-called liberal press originated with the easing of government censorship in 1848. It was during this period of liberal ascendency that Jews, no longer feeling the need for special Jewish journals, entered the German journalistic profession in relatively large numbers.[48] Systematic complaints of Jewish domination of the press began just after 1848.

There is some truth in the claim that political anti-Semitism was a reaction to liberalism.[49] It is also true that there was a logical and factual connection between nineteenth-century bourgeois liberalism and Jewish emancipation: "In general, the German Jew ... [was] the prototype of the *Bürger*."[50] Overtly or covertly, as with most *Bürgers*, German Jews were bourgeois liberals.[51]

The influx of Jews into the Christian community that accompanied the rise of bourgeois liberalism was intensive and thorough. Through intermarriage, conversion, and religious disavowal, an increasing number of German Jews identified with non-Jewish Germans. Those who chose to continue as Jews, defined by religion, contributed creatively and energetically to German communities.[52] Even anti-Semites and ultraconservative nationalists reluctantly

30

admitted the apparent thoroughness of German Jewish assimilation to German life. The conservative *Kreuzzeitung* noted in 1910 that Jews were a vital element in the German economy.[53] Ernst Berg concluded from his study of German history that German Jews were fully emancipated, were not strangers to Germany, and had equal claim to the communal position of citizen—that "holy right"—"with all their *fellow countrymen*."[54] The ardent anti-Zionist and extreme conservative, nationalistic German Jew, Max Naumann, believed firmly in the indissoluble bond between German and German Jew. It was absolutely necessary, he wrote, in light of German history, to engage in collective work with non-Jews "toward the formation of a better German future."[55]

Such statements that demonstrate the link between German liberalism and German Jewish emancipation also demonstrate German Jewish nationalistic loyalty. Liberalism in the first half of the nineteenth century in Germany was synonymous with nationalism. The beliefs of conservative superpatriots, from Naumann to Hitler, display a paradoxical strain of European (not only German) liberalism. Although their loyalties to the German nation were group-oriented, they were also firmly founded on the liberal value of the sanctity—or at least the safety and security—of the individual within the group. What was good for one could only be good for all. German unity offered German Jews economic opportunity along with the hope of an end to arbitrary rule and civil inequality. What would benefit Jewish individuals, however, would also benefit the nation. "Jüdischer-deutscher Nationalismus" was a form of liberalism whose tenets were somehow equally balanced between individualism, nationalism, and universal humanitarianism.

Liberal nationalism sought to redress civic injustice. German Jews seeking to escape the "mark" of disenfranchisement considered the path to be a civic one. The road

31

to end the old injustices seemed to be the law. Because of this perception of the way out—or in—the large number of Jews in the legal profession was logical and understandable. German Jewish lawyers and jurists sought individual betterment while fulfilling a social, moral, humanitarian, national, and even biblical, obligation.

Whatever the reasons, the solid involvement of German Jews in the legal profession further projected the image of external assimilation. By 1925 some of the finest and most successful lawyers in Germany were German Jews.[56] German Jewish apologists alleged that the battle for civil rights came naturally to German Jews as a defense against anti-Semitism. They had to go beyond words, theories, and intellectual weapons to active, legal, real defenses. And still the fight was theoretically grounded in religion: "The Jewish religion affirms that justice is not simply an abstract idea. . . . Jewish jurists require just *lives*, i.e. reality in the world . . . in practice."[57] The list of leading German Jewish legal theorists is both lengthy and impressive. Virtually all of them—Georg Jellinek, Eduard Lasker, Eduard Gans, Hugo Preuss, to name only a few—dealt with the rights of individuals in a state or nation. They were adherents of the liberal and nationalistic legal theories.[58]

"It was no accident," wrote Fredrich Meinecke in *Weltbürgertum und Nationalstaat*, "that the land of individual princes and personalities became a nation through the philosophy of individualism."[59] Meinecke went on to say that with the awakening of national consciousness in Germany, the Jews became citizens, individuals, human beings.[60] But since the liberal ideal was *individual* freedom, the "emancipation" was not of the group but of each individual. This seemingly inconsequential, semantic distinction assumed grave significance in the 1880s and on into the twentieth century with the question of group assimilation.[61]

Even enlightened non-Jews who had fought for emancipation since the eighteenth century "counted on the disappearance of Jews qua Jews."[62] Liberals in general held the hope of the dissolution of Jewish communal life. Christian Dohm seemed to have set the pattern: he had believed that emancipation and education of Jews would not only shape them into useful citizens, but transform and convert them into non-Jews. Educating Jews would direct them away from Judaism and make them moral and ethical Christian citizens.[63]

This philosophy confronted and reversed a process begun with the French Revolution that continued to the 1840s. As the Jewish comunities broke apart, Jewish collectiveness during that period gradually became more exclusively spiritual. After 1848 this sublimation of communal feeling to religion allowed German Jews to identify more strongly with German sympathizers and citizens.[64] The meaning of even the token emancipation of 1848 and of the more effective emancipation laws of 1869[65] became clear in Germany in the 1870s and 1880s. German Jewish influence had gained a prominence disproportionate to the Jewish population. In its wake came a new, secular, political, economic, and finally racial, anti-Semitism.

The entrance of Jews into the German economy had already caused alarm before 1848. In 1842, for example, Johann Hoffmann, in "Zur Judenfrage," expressed his fears of Jewish domination of law and political science if German Jews were allowed more freedom. His warning appeared before Jews were permitted to enter the civil service. Hoffmann cautioned that Jews must not be seen as individuals, as liberals would see them, but as eternal members of Jewry.[66]

Hoffmann's line of attack focused on the crux of the German Jewish goal: German identity. The question of Jews in Germany was one of their identity. If Hoffmann and other anti-Semites of his ilk were correct, Jews could have only Jewish identity. Not only religious but socioeconomic

33

and national differences were the grist of this anti-Semitism and its concomitant "question." Hoffmann had expressed a fundamental disagreement with the liberal and individualistic conceptions that individuals, not groups, constituted citizens of states and members of nations. German liberals could accept loyal individuals as citizens. But they were plagued by the persistent, haunting anti-Semitic tradition of characterizing Jews as an identifiable group with a clear and separate group identity.[67] To question the possibility of German Jewish German identity in this way was to question at the same time the possibility of real assimilation.

Jews who identified with legal, economic, and political liberalism had gained a political identity. They seemed to have found that their main hope for equal rights was with the Left. This attraction to the Left created a type of political identity that evoked a political anti-Semitism, primarily of the Right. German Jews were perceived as "the embodient of all equalizing, egalitarian-democratic, revolutionary spirits."[68] Jews were stamped as antiestablishment revolutionaries and retained this stigma even after liberalism was acknowledged as opposition but not treason. Political anti-Semites perceived Jews to be "destructive elements."[69]

As historians like P. G. Pulzer, George Mosse, and Fritz Stern have pointed out, a virulent, embittered, political and economic anti-Semitism was produced by a combination of liberal reforms, industrialization, and the identification of "liberal" with "Jewish." Jews were held responsible for the changes in society and the attendant economic impoverishment of guild members, artisans, peasants, and aristocrats.[70] The new anti-Semitism flourished because, to many, liberalism was in fact evil and dangerous, since it had proven economically and socially harmful.[71]

In the eyes of those displaced victims of liberalism and liberal "modernization," and in the eyes of anti-Semitic ultranationalists, emancipation was only surface assimilation. Nationalists like Heinrich von Treitschke and anti-Semites like Johann Hoffmann denied that individual Jews could be free of age-old, inherited group characteristics. But unlike Hoffmann, Treitschke called for "total assimilation": the individual could and must completely renounce the group and divest himself of its characteristics. For if these group traits existed, they infected all the individual members who claimed membership in the Jewish religious community. To Germans, emancipation began to mean assimilation, or making Jews completely like "the Germans."[72] In short, assimilation was necessary for emancipation, not the reverse.[73] In these terms the situation presented a seemingly hopeless dilemma, since obviously assimilation was at best difficult without emancipation, yet the prerequisite for emancipation was now to be the degree of assimilation.

Such self-contradictory ideologies elicited new responses from the German Jews in their defense against anti-Semitism. Part of the *jüdische Abewhrkampf*, the Jewish defense struggle, was continuing the struggle for equal rights, for social equality, and for political liberalism. Legislation had been passed, and German Jews turned to the law as their first line of defense. The first active organization for combating anti-Semitism in Germany was formed in 1891. Its founders were not Jews but liberal intellectuals who spoke for emancipation.[74] In 1891 and 1892 the Conservative Party officially adopted an anti-Semitic plank, charges of ritual murder were lodged, and by 1893 an ultraconservative, openly anti-Semitic movement seemed to be gaining strength. Partly as a response to these occurrences of public and political anti-Semitism, a number of prominent German Jews founded the Comite zur Abwehr antisemitischer Angriffe (Committee for the Defense Against Anti-Semitic Attacks).[75] Shortly thereafter, the Committee established the CV, urged by a pamphlet by Raphael Löwenfeld entitled, *Schutzjuden oder Staats-*

bürger?, which exhorted Germans to adhere faithfully to the Religious Law of July 3, 1869.[76] After the passage of that law, Löwenfeld said, Jews should no longer need protection from the Kaiser or anyone else.

Members of the CV conceived of Jews solely as a religious group.[77] Their first public statement firmly asserted that "the Verein will call upon all its strength for self-defense." Löwenfeld's brochure and the CV boldly demanded protection of Jews from anti-Semites, based not upon privileged status but upon "civil self-help," which was due *all* German citizens.[78] The CV would consecrate itself to bridging the gap between Germans and Jews, between *Deutschtum* and *Judentum*. Its goal was synthesis of the German and Jewish cultures,[79] and its pivotal idea was emancipation.[80] Its weapon was rational discourse wielded in the public arena: in politics, the media, and the courts.

Defense against anti-Semitic attacks was two-pronged. As long as Germany was a *Rechstaat*, Jews, like all citizens, had constitutional rights. The CV considered its initial and major task to be legal defense in cases where Jews were attacked and defamed as Jews.[81] Defense was to be based upon the civil rights of German Jews as citizens who "stand upon the soil [*Boden*] of German nationality."[82] Accompanying the legal procedures were public, didactic ones. The early written material from the members of the CV were relatively mild polemics against anti-Semitism in general. They were apologetics, which attempted to answer accusations of ritual murder and the *Protocols of the Elders of Zion*. They tried to explain the human need for scapegoats and to examine the historical reasons for the Jews being cast in that role.[83] Even nonreligious, apostate Jews denounced such anti-Semitic fantasies.[84]

If irrational anti-Semitism had existed for ages in Europe, it had to be fought and destroyed in the new era, "especially in the land of the greatest poets and thinkers." The

CV intended to preserve religious, political, civil, and social rights for *all* Germans as German citizens. Equality was the concern of the "German attitude" as the CV perceived it, the German attitude or nature which, according to prominent CV members, had confirmed equality for centuries.[85]

The new method of defense prescribed in the modern age was "More devotion! More sacrifice! Strengthen the organization!" to expose the lies of anti-Semites who would argue that German Jews were not Germans.[86] Part of that defense was devoted to denials of charges that German Jews were strangers or had about them a kind of foreignness that denied their German identity. Members of the CV methodically argued that German Jews were not strangers, nor were they *eingedeutscht*, made into or nationalized as Germans, but rather *eingeboren*, or born Germans. This argument entailed marshaling of historical evidence that Jews in Germany "for more than 1600 years have been rooted in the German soil, breathed the German air, loved the German forests, seas, and rivers, and have grown with the German culture."[87] The campaign against anti-Semitism was one based on allegedly objective evidence revealing that German Jews' history could be traced to pre-Roman times in the Rhineland.[88] Löwenfeld's conscious or unconscious choice of the word "Boden" in his statement spoke for a sense of earthly rootedness in the German soil and the German past. How, then, Weimar's Jews asked, could descendants of German Jews be defamed as immigrants or strangers? The CV's defense program categorically denied such "uninformed" and "unhistorical" assertions.

That defense was marked by its explicit aversion to direct political action. Liberal non-Jews recognized the nonpolitical character of the Jewish defense.[89] Even in 1930 the CV was denouncing those who accused it of political partisanship.[90] "Defense by education" was the *Aufklärungsarbeit* of the CV.[91] The *CVZ Monthly* was written and published expressly for the education of non-Jews, "to instruct them in the nature of Judaism and German Jews." Public meetings and membership drives were held regularly in attempts to gain support from enlightened non-Jews.

With the monthly issues came scholarly brochures and books refuting the traditional accusations in highly intellectual and academic fashion. These works were directed at non-Jews and included contributions by well-known German non-Jewish scholars and eminent citizens.[92] In all this there was deliberate avoidance of political partisanship.

The use of the word *Aufklärung* is significant in the CV's fight against anti-Semitism. It reveals a strong attraction of German Jews for that period of German history and its values. CV authors combated anti-Semitism, firm in the belief that it represented an "attack on culture in general, on morality, reason, and humanity."[93] The assault on the Jews was an assault on all civil rights, on democracy, and on freedom: on all that the Enlightenment had represented in Germany. Anti-Semitism was a "sickness of German politics," and curable through a strong dosage of reason. By the Weimar period, "the activity of the CV was that of a respected, middle-class [*bürgerlich*], republican organization." From the middle-class point of view of most if its members, all that was needed to defeat anti-Semitism was to illuminate, enlighten, and expose its irrational and mendacious roots.

As wielded by the CV, *Aufklärungsarbeit* was a double-edged sword. Along with the older, negative responses denying anti-Semitic accusations of ritual murder, the Elders of Zion, the existence of a mythical Sanhedrin, or worldwide economic and political conspiracies,[94] came the "new" responses which were positive, assertive, and affirming: German Jews insisted they were Germans. Contributions of German Jews to German history and culture became the focus of an official CV policy of "enlightenment."

It was the first time that German Jews based their defense on their claims to German identity.

Consequently, submission of "proof" of Germanness was an integral part of the educational side of the *Abwehr-kampf*. German Jews delineated and catalogued specific historical evidence of their patriotic nationalism. The devotion to the unification of Germany, quite apart from the self-interest and the liberalism, became evident through the large number of exemplary famous individuals, like Gabriel Riesser, who had played major roles in the nationalist movement.[95]

In a review of a book entitled *Juden in der deutschen Politik*, the CVZ praised the author for demonstrating Jewish contributions to intellectual and political life in Germany. It showed, the review continued, "how they [German Jews] *shaped* the fate of the German *Volk* . . .[and] created the German Fatherland."[96] Although Treitschke had been reviled as an anti-Semite, German Jewish liberals favorably referred to him again and again for his "solution" to the Jewish question—total assimilation—and for his unbounded praise of Gabriel Reisser as "brave, noble, devoted to the fatherland,"[97] and of Heinrich Heine as one of the greatest of Germany's national poets.[98] Treitschke was the archetypal German nationalist. He had praised Gabriel Riesser, the archetypal German Jew, and Moses Mendelssohn, the "first German Jew,"[99] both of whom were considered by many Jews and non-Jews to be the symbols of German Jewish devotion to Germany and all things German.[100]

Nationalism became a political force in Germany during and after the Napoleonic Wars. The German Jewish *Abwehr-kampf* boasted of German Jews who fought and died for the cause of German nationalism from 1813 to 1815,[101] of the nationalistic assiduity that continued in the "national movement" of 1848 when Germans, the grandfathers of the anti-Semites of the 1920s, "stood side by side with the grandfathers of their Jewish neighbors ... for the Black, Red, and Gold."[102] Weimar German Jewish literary critics like Arthur Eloesser discerned a political nationalism emerging in the literature and in the historical works of German Jews. In 1814, for example, Ludwig Börne proclaimed: "We want to be free Germans." Eloesser writes that Börne sought to befriend ultranationalist leaders like Father Jahn and Wolfgang Menzel,[103] as if to display his feeling of assimilation and emancipation as a patriotic phenomenon. Heinrich Heine's "patriotic" poems, with their expression of exiled yearning for the mysterious enchantment of his lost home, were cited in support of German Jewish deep patriotic loyalty. The significance of such historical activities of famous German Jews is partly in their achieving personal advancement and respectability. To their German Jewish encomiasts of the twentieth century, their collaboration in the national achievement was equally significant. The resounding conclusion, despite the controversies surrounding them, was that they remained German poets.

Despite the resoluteness of historical patriotism, men like Theodore Wolff, Jewish editor of the *Berliner Tageblatt*, seemed to substantiate anti-Semitic claims that Jews were unpatriotic when they criticized Wilhelmian foreign policy.[104] To counter the relentless stigma of antigovernment, unpatriotic attitudes, German Jews enumerated key figures in conservative policy-making positions. According to defenders of German Jewish nationalism, Jews did not support only liberals or left-wing politics. This contention was an essential ingredient of the nationalistic assertions of German Jews. Moritz Veit was offered as only one example: in 1848 and after, he was a member of the Right Centre Party.[105] From Bismarck's chancellorship on, some Jews supported anti-Semitic parties that were radically patriotic, like the National Liberals, and later showed their

40

love of the German Fatherland by supporting conservative candidates against Social Democrats.[106] To prove their true national devotion, German Jews pointed to their past conservatism as well as their liberalism.

Prussian ministers Heinrich Friedberg and Rudolf Friedenthal, both German Jews, had served the Kaiser as advisers for a total of eighteen years. Paul Karper had directed the Colonial Office from 1890, while Bernhard Dernberg was cabinet officer in charge of German colonies; positions that were clearly tied to conservative, nationalistic ideologies. Dernberg became Minister of Finance in 1919, but quickly resigned, protesting the Republic and the signing of the Versailles Treaty. In attempts to belittle or even deny German Jewish participation in left-wing organizations and movements, several German Jewish writers point out that other "high-ranking Jews" had followed Dernberg's example.[107]

The CV did not escape the tendency to assert German Jewish conservative nationalism. Eugen Fuchs, once president of the CV, proudly spoke of the "phenomenal success" of Jews who were personal friends of the Kaiser."[108] Before 1918, *Im Deutschen Reich*, the forerunner of the *CVZ*, emphatically stated it was "*kaisertrue* and represented a Judaism of a *German* past and a *German* future."[109] Max Naumann voiced opinions as right wing as the most *völkisch* of the conservative parties—including the NSDAP.[110] What distinguished Naumann from other individual German Jewish conservatives like the historian Ernst Kantorowicz, who had joined a Freikorps group, or the poet Karl Wolfskehl, a member of the conservative Stefan George Circle, was his loud insistence upon his affiliation with other Jews in Germany. To Naumann, Jews as a group in Germany had been firm German patriots for generations. In a similar vein, Jakob Marcus went so far as to claim that the coordination of the German states by National Socialists "was an idea which German Jewish patriots in 1848 did

41

much to further. In this respect Adolf Hitler is their testamentary legatee."[111]

Marcus and Naumann were obvious extreme examples of a desire to demonstrate national policy. The majority of German Jews, however, did not find it necessary to assume such exaggerated postures. Nor did they hold such conservative beliefs. Most felt satisfied with the CV position and accepted the organization as public spokesman for their feelings.[112] The founding of the CV, based on the principles set forth in Löwenfeld's pamphlet, was meant to be a public event. Löwenfeld's words openly announced the beliefs and intentions of the CV and its supporters: "Are we closer to French Jews than to German Catholics?" Löwenfeld's answer to that trenchant question placed German Jews firmly "on the soil of German nationality." *National* identity was the organizational goal. German Jews, he contended, had "for years . . . been willing to sacrifice [their] strength and blood." In the eyes of German Jews, the battles of 1815, 1848, and 1871 had proved German Jewish loyalty. Some 6000 Jews fought in the Franco-Prussian War; 448 died, and 327 were decorated with the Iron Cross. Religion, like the choice of political party, was an individual decision, and Löwenfeld insisted that neither of those choices determined nationality.[113]

The CV organization began, then, with Löwenfeld's pamphlet, by insisting on its physical contributions to the German nation in emotional, patriotic language. When it grew to some 300,000 "affiliates" by 1926, it still espoused those convictions. Such attitudes parallel the first, external level of assimilation in the economic, material sense; they bolstered the belief that assimilation was achieved, that the facade accurately reflected the inner conditions.

World War I was a turning point for German Jews. Any number of historians, sociologists, and philosophers have documented a mood of ennui and despair that spread from a handful of intellectuals before the war to "lower levels"

42

after it.[114] One historian, paraphrasing Thomas Mann, has characterized the postwar period as marked by an "erosion of the liberal, bügerlich feelings" which had underscored the previous era, and which had been besieged by conservative forces since the 1870s.[115]

The anti-Semitism of the 1880s grew as a reaction to changes in the social, economic, and political situtation that many considered a result of the "rule of liberalism." That legendary reign brought economic and social hardships that struck non-Jews harder than Jews.[116] The ensuing economic and psychological depression heralded a renewed, reenergized anti-Semitism, which made life for European Jews unusually precarious. It was in the defeated nation, however, that anti-Semitism waxed strongest.[117]

But if anti-Semitism became more vehement, vicious, open, and widespread, so too did opportunities multiply for expression of patriotism by German Jews. Emancipation seemed complete when non-Jews were forced by circumstances to treat Jews as equals.[118] German Jews now had the opportunity to increase their acceptance by Germans through identifying with them in time of stress and trouble. Their patriotism had been tested, they later declared, and they had responded by sacrificing themselves for Germany. Lowenfeld's words of "sacrifice our blood and strength" took on a more intense, a more literal meaning. Spilling their blood gave German Jews the impression of purifying their identity as Germans—of creating a nationalism that was chaste because of its physical dedication.

That baptism by blood reenforced German Jews' assertions of their German identity. Those most deserving of German acceptance seemed to be Jewish veterans. In 1918 the Reichsbund jüdische Frontsoldaten (RjF) was founded by German Jewish veterans. Its purpose was "to defend aganst anti-Semitic reproaches," but more specifically to defend against the accusation "that the German Jews had not performed to the extent that other German servicemen had in the World War."[119] It opposed the anti-Semitism that accused German Jews of cowardice and lack of love for the Fatherland.[120] Leo Löwenstein, one of the RjF's founders, wrote of his continuing devotion to German nationalism even in 1935: "We have and *will* always fight for our German home and teach our children the same thing."[121]

The first task of the RjF in that fight was to publish a list of the 12,000 "fallen on the field of honor." One hundred thousand had served, 2000 of whom were officers. In minute details, with complete statistics, the RjF documented the contention that in "the Great War" German Jews had fulfilled their duty to their German home.[122] Its ultimate, unspoken goal was to alter the image of the Jew in Germany.[123]

Emphasis on physical sacrifice and allegiance to Germany increased and spread from the RjF. By 1933, partially as a response to National Socialism, even the *Israelitisches Familienblatt*, a more sophisticated journal aimed primarily at intellectuals, filled its last issues with references to German Jewish Olympic champions, athletes, artists, and craftsmen. The drive incorporated interviews, capsule biographies, and action photographs.[124] In a special publication by the *Israelitisches Familienblatt*, a painting by Max Liebermann entitled *Mother of 12,000* was dedicated to the RjF. The painting portrayed a shadowy, mourning, despairing mother wailing over an endless field of German Jewish graves.[125]

Virtually every history of German Jewry written after World War I by all but the most anti-Semitic historians praised the loyal participation of German Jews for the Fatherland in the war. Ismar Elbogen was a peaceful and peaceloving scholar, yet he defended that militaristic patriotism with statistics of dead, wounded, distinguished, and promoted.[126] The youngest enlistee, Elbogen noted, was a thirteen-year-old German Jew, Joseph Zippes; and the first member of the Reichstag to enlist was the Jewish

44

Social Democrat Ludwig Frank. Frank's emotionally nationalistic letters from the front were allegedly typical of the intensity of German Jewish nationalism.[127] Even Ernst Toller, the radical revolutionary of the postwar years, shared the mood of Frank and Zippes; when he heard of Germany's entrance into World War I he rejoiced and chorused "Deutschland über Alles" with other Germans. His heart glowed as he read beneath the Kaiser's picture his lord and idol's words: "I recognize no parties, only Germans." The budding poet, the latent revolutionary, reveled in his brotherhood with the Kaiser, a brotherhood based upon one language, "one mother: Germany."[128]

Proofs of German Jewish patriotism incorporated homefront patriots as well as those who served in the field. In the 1920s and 1930s German Jewish spokesmen gave endless acclaim to those German Jewish bankers, financiers, industrialists, and scientists who had aided the war effort.[129] German Jewish chemists and physicists, they said, developed glycerine and perfected artillery; Wassermann prevented tetanus in the trenches with his vaccine;[130] Ricard Willstatter's invention of the gas mask saved an estimated 100,000 German lives; and Rathenau organized raw material maintenance, which received high praise from Bethmann-Hollweg in 1916 for "saving Germany" from premature disaster.[131] Max Warburg and Carl Melchior served as financial advisers during the war. Warburg also had stood firmly for the army command and Ludendorff at the time of the armistice, thereby proving, to some, his "patriotism" or at least his conservatism.[132] At the close of the war Albert Ballin, the financier, economic adviser, and friend of the Kaiser, committed suicide rather than accept German defeat.[133] These Jews, and many more, had apparently devoted their talents to the national cause. That devotion was continually stressed by German Jewish defenders in the Weimar years.

In addition to their military service in World War I

(which includes behind-the-lines efforts), there was perhaps no greater example of their fidelity to Germany than the German Jews' united (or seemingly united) voice for a German Posen after the war. This, too, was stressed in the Weimar years. Jewish support for the Posen *Anschluss* was "overwhelming."[135] Posen Jews spoke German. They had come to Posen in the Middle Ages with German colonists and crusaders. They had suffered the Black Death with Germans there. "They were as German as Posen itself." That Posen and Posen Jews were German was a "simple fact of history."[136]

Ernst Toller wrote of his childhood memories in Samotschin, where his grandfather had been the first Jew. Toller recalled that his German nationalism and that of his family and their Jewish neighbors bordered on fanaticism. He remembered his boyhood excitement and love for "Kaisercards" (a series of animated portraits of the Kaiser with different romantic backgrounds, something like contemporary American sports-figure cards); the portrait of the Kaiser that was worshipped in his household in Poland; and childhood games and dreams of blond Teutons with spears and shields, and of their blond women. What troubled his later recollections was the memory that Poles did not discriminate between Jews and Germans, but that Germans did. As a boy, he had been unable to understand German anti-Semitism because of the deep reverence his family had held for all things German.[137]

His feelings had troubled Toller. He later confronted his childhood and past and renounced it, along with what he later regarded as his near-fanatical nationalism. Other German Jews, however, clung tenaciously to those feelings. Again they combined the experience of the war with desires to annex Posen; suffering by Posen Jews during the war was German suffering, because they were imprisoned as Germans who refused to renounce their Germanism and their German nationality.[138] In 1919 the most eloquent

46

spokesmen in the Posen parliament were German Jews who demanded union with Germany as a concession to what they called their already existing "inner unity with the German *Volk.*" Many Germans emigrated to Poland and denounced or denied their German language and customs, along with their nationality. But not Posen Jews. Instead, they continued to "love it, identify with it, cry out to it, embrace it."[139] Such historical arguments—tinged with emotionalism, somewhat exaggerated—were nonetheless factually sound; and they lay at the heart of the contention that German Jews had a legitimate claim to German nationality.

From 1815, German Jews had been offering their bodies and minds in service to a national ideal. The conclusion of this amassing of names and numbers was that German Jews had made Germany strong before the war, had kept her alive and powerful during the war, and had fought to keep her unified and honorable after the war. The minds and blood of German Jews, commented the CVZ in 1932, had made Germany strong economically and nationally. Throughout the Weimar Republic years, CV statements fostered the German Jewish "unflagging care for a German attitude" among German Jews. On behalf of all the CV members and supporters, Alfred Wiener proudly proclaimed that "Fatherland is no empty word for us."[140] To the end, it seemed, CV editors who spoke for the majority of German Jews would talk of their love for Germany, of how German Jews had "loved her and love her even in their misfortune. . . . They are more nationalistic than many for whom the word Fatherland has become only a phrase."[141]

As he grew into his revolutionary mold, Toller encountered the most fanatical patriotism among German Jews. He related his experiences with a Jewish doctor who refused him proper care in prison because he had deprecated the Imperial Government. For the same reason, a Jewish noncommissioned officer had spat upon him. He recalled his

confrontation with Rathenau, who symbolized to Toller
German Jewish nationalistic militarism when he pleaded
for continued national resistance at a public meeting as late
as October 1918.[142] Toller's examples can serve to illustrate
the strong German Jewish beliefs that such blood sacrifices
as they suffered in the war would "make us German."[143]
German Jews after World War I believed with redoubled
feeling Riesser's words that "Whoever contests my claim to
my German Fatherland, my right to my own ideas, my own
feelings . . . I must defend myself against him as I would
against a murderer."[144]

German anti-Semites could not deny with any credibility
the physical, material assimilation of German Jews. They
recognized it, and some acknowledged it as a positive
augmentation of German progress. In light of German Jewry's deep affiliation with and glorification of Germany,
how could German anti-Semites shun German Jews as
"outsiders"? How could they still deny Jewish assimilation? Conversely, how could German Jews, in the face of an
advancing, intransigent anti-Semitism, continue to identify
themselves as German? The second dimension of assimilation or acculturation, beyond the physical or material, is
the spiritual, psychological, and cultural one. Culture,
Volk, and Geist were the grounds of anti-Semitic exclusion
of Jews from Germanism. Paradoxically, they were also the
grounds on which German Jews identified themselves as
Germans.

The concept of "total" assimilation, of acculturation,
involved more than physical, that is, economic, political,
or social integration. "Total" meant body and soul. It was
not simply becoming a member of a state, but of a Volk or
a Volksgemeinschaft. Total assimilation or total acculturation moves beyond external manifestations to emotion,
feeling, and the murky, mystical, even arcane, realm of
spiritual oneness. It includes identification with a particular culture, but also with a psychology unique to a given

culture or nation, a mythology, a *Geist*. Acculturation or total assimilation means existence deeply rooted in the soil of all these or in a collective soul or psyche.

From 1925 to 1929 German Jews were increasingly on the defensive in newspapers, essays, and various argumentative collections. There was a gradual increase in literature on the "Jewish Question," the "Jewish Problem," anti-Semitism, "Deutschtum und Judentum."[145] After 1928, because of the more powerful and serious attacks by *völkisch* groups—primarily the National Socialists—discussions of the subject became openly defensive. The mood of German Jews seemed to grow silently frantic. More than seven hundred books dealing with the "Jewish Question" were written by anti-Semites from 1929 to 1932. The number of replies from German Jews easily doubled that figure.[146] Included among these were rebuttals to both the accusations of ritual murder and the infamous *Protocols of the Elders of Zion*. Until 1929 the percentage of books dealing with such archaic elements of anti-Semitism had been minimal. It is indicative of both the new defensiveness and the frequency and virulence of the attacks that German Jews returned to refutations of those old themes in their books and newspapers.[147] The most consistent theme in all these responses, however, was cultural harmony; German Jewish cultural and material unity with German non-Jews. There was a vigorous, implacable insistence upon the synthesis, the oneness of *Deutschtum* and *Judentum*.

Definitions of German and of Jewish seemed to appear in almost every publication. Attempts to characterize German Jew, Germany, Jews, Germans, were juxtaposed in argumentative *Festschriften* on the position of Jews in Germany or the "Jewish Question" that included articles by German Jews and National Socialists, at public meetings, and in the organs of the various German Jewish associations.[148] Responses to anti-Semitic verbal outrages had often been assertive and sometimes cynical because of the contempt

49

held by German Jews for anti-Semitic, irrational, archaic superstitions and hatreds. But a tone of desperation became discernible beneath the confident veneer of their rational, logically reasoned responses. After 1929, physical abuse in forms of beatings, vandalism, and desecrations by S.A. men seemed to make the eloquent arguments of German Jews in the *CVZ, Der Schild, Die Israelit*, and the like, pathetically ineffective and academic. Yet they continued.

N O T E S

[1]Hugo Bettauer, *Die Stadt ohne Juden. Ein Roman von Übermorgen* (Wien: Gloriette-Verlag, 1922).

[2]Cf. Raul Hilberg, *The Destruction of the European Jews* (Chicago: Quadrangle Books, 1961), pp. 5–7.

[3]Bernt Engelmann, *Deutschland ohne Juden. Eine Bilanz* (München: Franz Schneekluth Verlag, 1970), pp. 1–65, passim.

[4]Leonard Broom and Philip Selznick, *Sociology. A Text with Adapted Readings*, 3d ed., (New York: Harper & Row, 1963), p. 34; also, see Chap. vi.

[5]Ibid.

[6]John Layard, "Identification with the Sacrificial Animal," *Eranos Jahrbuch*, XXIV (1955), 341–406; Ferdinand Tönnies, *Community and Society (Gemeinschaft und Gesellschaft)*, ed. and trans. Charles P. Loomis (New York: Harper & Row, 1965), pp. 33–35, 64, passim.

[7]Tönnies, *Community*, pp. 42, 48, 64–102.

[8]Layard, "Identification."

[9]Broom and Selznick, *Sociology*, pp. 84, 499; Robert A. Nisbet, *The Quest for Community* (New York: Oxford University Press, 1953), pp. 23–52; Tönnies, *Community*, pp. 35, 39, 192.

[10]Ismar Elbogen, *Die Geschichte der Juden in Deutschland*, 3d ed. rev. by Elenore Sterling; (Frankfurt am Main: Europäische Verlaganstalt, 1966), p. 251; Esra Bennathan, "Die demographische und wirtschaftliche Struktur der Juden," *Entscheidungsjahre 1932*, rev. ed. (Tuebingen, J.C.B. Mohr [Paul Siebeck], 1965), pp. 87–131; A. Marcus, "Jews as Entrepreneurs in Weimar Germany," *YIVO Annual of Jewish Social Science*, VII, 175–203; cf. also the classic if jaded studies by Werner Sombart and H. Silbergleit.

[11]Kurt Zielensiger, "German Jews in the German Economy," *Der Jud ist schuld. Diskussionbuch über die Judenfrage* (Basel, Berlin, Leipzig, Wien: Zinnen-Verlag, 1932), pp. 225–270, also reprinted with revisions

in CVZ Monthly, XV (November 1932); Zielensiger, Juden in der deutschen Wirtschaft (Berlin: Heine Bund, 1930), pp. 94–96, passim; cf. also Sidney Osborne, Germany and Her Jews (London: Soncino Press, 1939), pp. 14–21, 22–29, 30–34; Arthur Ruppin, The Jews in the Modern World (London: Macmillan & Co., Ltd., 1934), pp. 183–185, 218–221; Daniel Bernstein, "Wirtschaft: Handel und Industrie," Juden im deutschen Kulturbereich, rev. ed., ed. Siegmund Kaznelson (Berlin: Judischer Verlag, 1959), pp. 760–797; Bernstein, "Finanzsen," Kaznelson, pp. 720–759.

[12]Erich Rosenthal, "Trends in the Jewish population of Germany, 1910–1939," Jewish Social Studies, VI (1944), 233–274; Osborne, Germany and Her Jews, pp. 30–34; Bennathan, "Die demographische"; Marcus, "Jews as Entrepreneurs."

[13]Bennathan, "Die demographische."

[14]Rudolf Kaulla, Der Liberalismus und die deutschen Juden. Das Judentum als Konservatives Element (Leipzig: Verlag von Duncker-Humboldt, 1928), p. 90.

[15]Alfred Hirschberg, "Der Centralverein deutscher Staatsbürger jüdischen Glaubens," Wille und Weg des deutschen Judentums, ed. Joachim Schoeps (Berlin: Vortrupp Verlag, 1935), pp. 12–29.

[16]Ernst Rudolf Huber, ed., Dokumente zur Deutschen Verfassungsgeschichte, 3 vols. (Stuttgart: W. Kohlhammer Verlag, 1961), Vol. I: 2Deutsche Verfassungsdokumente 1803—1850, 45–47; Heinz Cohn, "Die jüdische Aufgabe des CV," CVZ, XI (January 15, 1932).

[17]Kaulla, Der Liberalismus, p. 5; H. G. Adler, Die Juden in Deutschland von der Aufklärung bis zum National-sozialismus, rev. ed. (Munchen: Kösel-Verlag, 1960), p. 17.

[18]Dokumente, I, 80, 147, 204; II (1851–1918), 288, 356.

[19]Adolf Kober, "Jews in the Revolution of 1848 in Germany," Jewish Social Studies, X (1948), 135–164; Siegfried Erasmus, Die Juden in der ersten deutschen Nationalversammlung, 1848–1849 (Weimar: Fink, 1941), pp. 22, 27, passim.

[20]Carl Misch, "Politik," in Kaznelson, pp. 531–589. See appendix for biographical information on Bamberger and other German Jews.

[21]Erasmus, Die Juden, p. 59; Elbogen, Die Geschichte der Juden, p. 235; Salo Baron, "The Jewish Communal Crisis in 1848," Jewish Social Studies, XIV (1952), 99–114; Heinrich Stern, "Der Aufmarsch der Parteien zur Verbandswahl," CVZ, IV (January 16, 1925).

[22]Elbogen, Die Geschichte der Juden, p. 238.

[23]Wassermann, Mein Weg als Deutscher, p. 10.

[24]Elbogen, Die Geschichte der Juden, p. 242; Baron, "The Jewish Communal Crisis"; Howard Morley Sacher, The Course of Modern Jewish History (New York: Dell Publishing Co., 1958), p. 67; Bennathan, "Die demographische"; Hilde Ottenheimer, "The Disappearance of Jewish Communities in Germany, 1900–1938," Jewish Social Studies, III (1941), 189–206; Rosenthal, "Trends in the Jewish Population."

[25]Baron, "The Jewish Communal Crisis."

26Ibid.

27Tönnies, Community, p. 38.

28Stanley Zucker, "Ludwig Bamberger and the Rise of Anti-Semitism in Germany, 1848–1893," Central European History, III, No. 4 (Decembei 1970), 332–352; Jakob Toury, Die Politischen Orientierengen der Juden in Deutschland von Jena bis Weimar (Tübingen: J. C. B. Mohr [Paul Siebeck], 1966), pp. 80–84, passim.

29Elbogen, Die Geschichte der Juden, p. 242.

30Paul Nathan, "In Memory of Ludwig Bamberger," CVZ, IV (June 22, 1925).

31Elbogen, Die Geschichte der Juden, p. 251; Zucker, "Ludwig Bamberger."

32Misch, "Politik."

33Kaulla, Der Liberalismus. p. 7; Max Pinn, "Rechtswissenschaft," in Kaznelson, pp. 590–672.

34J. Levy, "Um was geht es?" CVZ, IV (January 2, 1925); Zucker, "Ludwig Bamberger."

35Klinkenberg, "Zwischen Liberalismus."

36Tönnies, Community, p. 47; Broom and Selznick, Sociology, p. 493.

37Baron, "The Jewish Communal Crisis."

38Ibid.

39Dr. Meisel, Die jüdische Synagoge und die freie christliche Gemeinde. Eine Beleuchtung ihres Verhaltnisses zu einander (Nordhausen, 1850).

40Baron, "The Jewish Communal Crisis."

41Kaulla, Der Liberalismus, p. 89.

42Ibid., p. 16.

43Zucker, "Ludwig Bamberger."

44Kaulla, Der Liberalismus, p. 16; Uriel Tal, Christians and Jews in Germany. Religion, Politics, and Ideology in the Second Reich, 1870–1914, trans, Noah. Jonathan Jacobs (Ithaca and London: Cornell University Press, 1975), pp 31–80.

45Christian Wilhelm Dohm, Über die bürgerliche Verbesserung des Juden (Berlin, 1781); Fritz Friedlander, "Ein Charakterbild in der Geschichte. Zu Wilhelm Grau: 'Wilhelm von Humboldt,' " CVZ, XIV (July 11, 1935). German Jews later developed an ambivalent attitude to Dohm's position. He had voiced the liberal creed of individual service based on merit. Yet his campaign for emancipation of Jews was cold and calculated; its thrust was political emancipation for citizens, not for human beings. Cf. Kaulla, Der Liberalismus, p. 11.

46Jacob Toury, "The Jewish Question—A Semantic Approach," Leo Baeck Yearbook, XI, ed. Robert Weltsch (London, East and West Library 1966), 86–106; Kurt Zeilensiger, "German Jews in the German Economy," CVZ Monthly, IV (November 1932).

47Peter G. J. Pulzer, The Rise of Political Anti-Semitism in Germany and Austria (New York: John Wiley & Sons, Inc., 1964), p. 9.

48Ibid., p. 4; B. Poll, "Jüdische Presse in Deutschland," Joodse Pers in de Nederlanden en in Duitsland, 1674–1940. Jüdische Presse in den Niederlanden und in Deutschland, 1674–1940 (Amsterdam: Nederlandsch Persmuseum, 1969), pp. 49–128.

49Pulzer, The Rise of Political Anti-Semitism, p. 11, passim.

50Zielensiger, "German Jews in the German Economy."

51Elbogen, Die Geschichte der Juden, p. 349; cf. Pulzer, The Rise of Political Anti-Semitism; Bernstein, "Finanzwesen"; Wischnitzer, "Jewish Emigration from Germany, 1933–1938"; Marcus, "Jews as Entrepreneurs"; Ruppin, The Jews, pp. 218–221.

52Cf. Rosenthal, "Trends in the Jewish Population"; Ludwig Karpe, "Technology," in Kaznelson, pp. 710–719; Hadrian Stahl, "Physics," in ibid., pp. 401–419, and other essays in Kaznelson's monumental anthology.

53Berg, Wohin treibt Juda?, p. 14.

54Ibid., pp. 7, 13.

55Max Naumann, Sozialismus, Nationalsozialismus und nationaldeutsches Judentum (Berlin: Self-Published, 1932), p. 1.

56One of the most successful Berlin lawyers, for example, was Maximilian Kempner, a prominent German Jew. Cf. Pinn, "Rechtswissenschaft"; Marvin Lowenthal, The Jews of Germany (New York: Longmans, Green, 1936), pp. 333–335; Stonehill, The Jewish Contribution to Civilization.

57Pinn, "Rechtswissenschaft."

58Ibid.; Osborne, Germany and Her Jews, pp. 35–37.

59Quoted in Zielensiger, "German Jews in the German Economy."

60Ibid.

61Werner Cahnmann's scholarly article, "Deutsche Tradition," CVZ Monthly, IV (July 1932), is one of the better examples of the countless articles dealing with the meaning and significance of emancipation in Germany.

62Gershom Scholem, "Jews and Germans," Commentary, XLII (November 1966), 31–38, points out that men like Humboldt and Herder espoused the cause of the Jews only because they hoped for the disappearance of Jews as an ethnic group.

63George L. Mosse, Germans and Jews. The Right, the Left, and the Search for a "Third Force" in Pre-Nazi Germany (New York: Howard Fertig, 1970), pp. 39–50.

64Bennathan, "Die demographische"; Rosenthal, "Trends in the Jewish Population."

65The famous Religious Law of July 3, 1869, theoretically eliminated all restrictions of civil rights based on differences of religion. Dokumente, II, 248.

66Toury, "The Jewish Question."

67Ibid.

68Werner Mosse, "Der Niedergang der Republik und die Juden," Yearbook of the Leo Baeck Institute, Entscheidungs-jahre 1932, pp. 3–50; George L. Mosse, "Die deutsche Rechte und die Juden," Entscheidungsjahre 1932, pp. 183–246; Kaulla, Der Liberalismus, p. 21.

[69]Mosse, "Der Niedergang der Republik."

[70]Pulzer, *The Rise of Political Anti-Semitism;* cf. Fritz Stern, *The Politics of Cultural Despair* (Garden City: Doubleday, Inc., 1965); George Mosse, *The Crisis of German Ideology* (New York: Grosset & Dunlap, 1964); Theodore Hamerow, *Restoration, Revolution, Reaction* (Princeton: Princeton University Press, 1967), for some of the better examples of this thesis. Also, Wilhelm Treue, "Zur Frage der wirtschaftlichen Motive im deutschen Antisemitismus," *Deutsches Judentum in Krieg und Revolution 1916–1923,* ed. Werner E. Mosse (Tübingen: J. C. B. Mohr [Paul Siebeck], 1971), pp. 387–408.

[71]George Mosse, "Die deutsche Rechte"; Pulzer, p. 31.

[72]Kaulla, *Der Liberalismus,* p. 90.

[73]Adler, *Die Juden,* p. 103.

[74]Marcus, *The Rise and Destiny of the German Jew,* p. 201; Elbogen, *Die Geschichte der Juden,* p. 265; Schorsch, *Jewish Reactions,* p. 80 f.

[75]Klinkenberg, "Zwischen Liberalismus"; Schorsch, *Jewish Reactions,* pp. 103–105, 113.

[76][Raphael Löwenfeld], *Schutzjuden oder Staatsbürger?* (Berlin: Schweitzer & Mohr, 1893), pp. 7ff; Schorsch, *Jewish Reactions,* p. 115.

[77]Marcus, *The Rise and Destiny of the German Jew,* p. 202; Löwenfeld, *Schutzjuden,* p. 26.

[78]Löwenfeld, *Schutzjuden,* pp. 26–27; Klinkenberg, "Zwischen Liberalismus."

[79]Fuchs, *Um Deutschtum und Judentum,* p. 133.

[80]Hirschberg, "Der Centralverein."

[81]Klinkenberg, "Zwischen Liberalismus"; Paucker, *Der jüdische Abwehrkampf,* p. 74; Paucker, "Der jüdische Abwehrkampf," *Entscheidungsjahre 1932,* pp. 405–499.

[82]Löwenfeld, *Schutzjuden,* p. 26.

[83]Paucker, *Der jüdische Abwehrkampf,* pp. 62–63.

[84]Naumann, *Sozialismus,* p. 11.

[85]Ludwig Hollander, *Deutsche-Jüdische Probleme der Gegenwart. Eine Auseinanderung über die Grundfragen des Central-Vereins deutscher Staatsbürger jüdischen Glaubens* (Berlin: Philo-Verlag, 1929), p. 31.

[86]Bruno Glaserfeld, "Mehr Optimismus! Mehr Hingabe! Mehr Opfer!", *CVZ,* X (July, 10, 1931).

[87]CV, *Wir Deutschen Juden, 321–1932* (Berlin: CV, 1932), pp. 3, 6, passim

[88]Paucker, "Der jüdische Abwehrkampf."

[89]"Offen Brief am die deutschen Juden," *Deutsche Republik,* IV, No. 39 (1930), 1189–1192.

[90]Eva Jungmann, "Brief," *CVZ,* IX (March 14, 1930), rejecting the idea of German Jewish "partisanship" in any form other than "unity with Germans and . . . German *Volkstum.*" (Reply to "Offen Brief am die deutschen Juden," cf. n. 89).

[91]"Aus der Arbeit des CV. Aufklärung unter Juden und Nichtjuden," *CVZ,* IX (March 21, 1930); "Aufklärungsarbeit des CV in Nahalt. Versammlungen in Köthen, Bernburg, Dessau." *CVZ,* IX (April 4, 1930);

54

"Gewaltige Aufklärungsversammlung des CV in Düsseldorf," *CVZ*, IX (March 21, 1930); Karl Löwenstein, "Nationaljuden und Abwehrkampf," *CVZ*, IX (July 11, 1930).

[92]Alfred Wiener, "Mehr Kleinarbeit! Keine grossen Worte," *CVZ*, IX (January 3, 1930).

[93]Elbogen, *Die Geschichte der Juden*, p. 300.

[94]See Norman Cohn, *Warrant for Genocide. The Myth of the Jewish World-Conspiracy and the Protocols of the Elders of Zion* (London: Eyre & Spottiswoode, Ltd., 1967).

[95]Gabriel Riesser (1806–63) was vice-president of both the Hamburg Bürgerschaft and the National Assembly at Frankfort in 1848. He was an eloquent spokesman for both national unity and liberalism.

[96]Review of Rudolf Schah's *Juden in der deutschen Politik*, *CVZ*, IX (February 14, 1930).

[97]"1831–1931," *CVZ*, X (August 7, 1931).

[98]Ibid.; Heinrich von Treitschke, *Politics*, ed. Hans Kohn (New York: Harcourt, Brace & World, 1963), p. 133.

[99]Treitschke, *Politics*, p. 127.

[100]"1831–1931."

[101]Sachar, *The Course of Modern Jewish History*, p. 66; J. Levy, "Um was geht es? Ein Wahlruf," *CVZ*, IV (January 2, 1925).

[102]Hans Reichmann, "Dem inneren Frieden. Deutsche 'und' Juden," *CVZ Monthly*, IV (December 1932).

[103]Arthur Eloesser, "Literatur," in Kaznelson, pp. 1–67.

[104]The confinement of the "critical attitude" to the "Jewish Press" was satirically lampooned by Hugo Bettauer, when criticisms leveled against the government in his novel were labeled evidence of a "Jewish spirit," despite their Christian authorship. See Bettauer, *Stadt ohne Juden*, p. 63; cf. also Werner Mosse, "Die Niedergang der Republik"; Werner Becker, "Die Rolle der liberalen Presse," *Deutsches Judentum in Krieg und Revolution 1916–1923*, pp. 67–136; Poll, "Jüdische Presse."

[105]Misch, "Politik"; Toury, *Die politischen Orientierungen*, pp. 75–77, 114–117, *passim*.

[106]Toury, *Die politischen Orientierungen*, pp. 261–275; Werner Mosse, "Die Niedergang der Republik."

[107]Marcus, *The Rise and Destiny of the German Jew*, p. 15; Wolfgang Heine, "Damals in Wiemar," *CVZ*, VIII (August 9, 1929).

[108]Fuchs, *Um Deutschtum*, p. 122.

[109]"Umwälzung und Kriegsende," *Im Deutschen Reich*, XXIV, No. 11 (November 1918), 417–427; Werner Kienitz, "Das jüdische Gemeindeleben und die politische Situation der deutschen Juden," *Monumenta Judaica*, pp. 385–418.

[110]Among other themes, Naumann did not tire of railing against the "false socialism" of the Republic perpetrated by the "November criminals." See Naumann, *Sozialismus*.

[111]Marcus, *The Rise and Destiny of the German Jew*, p. 73.

[112]Membership by 1925 was over ten times that of the Zionist organization and more than 10 percent of the total Jewish population of Germany. Lamm, *Über die innere und aussere Entwicklung*, pp. 19, 30.

[113]Löwenfeld, *Schutzjuden*, p. 10; Klinkenberg, "Zwischen Liberalismus"; Elbogen, *Die Geschichte der Juden*, pp. 274–275.

[114]H. Stuart Hughes, *Consciousness and Society*, and George L. Mosse, *The Culture of Western Europe*, are among the better overviews of the *Zeitgeist* of the period.

[115]Werner Mosse, "Die Krise der europäischen Bourgeoisie und das deutsche Judentum," *Deutsches Judentum in Krieg und Revolution 1916–1923*, pp. 1–27.

[116]Cf. Pulzer, *The Rise of Political Anti-Semitism*; Felix Theilhaber, *Der Untergang der deutschen Juden* (Berlin, 1928), p. 79.

[117]Werner Mosse, "Die Krise der europäischen Bourgeoisie."

[118]Anti-Semitism did not, of course, die during the war. There are several accounts of anti-Semitic acts in the front lines in memoirs and autobiographies like Frederick Perls, *In and Out of the Garbage Pail* (Lafayette, California: Real People Press, 1969), and Ernst Toller, *I Was a German*. trans. Edward Crankshaw (London: Lane, 1934).

[119]Kienitz, "Das jüdische Gemeindleben"; Paucker, *Der jüdische Abwehrkampf*, p. 61; Schorsch, *Jewish Reactions*.

[120]Paucker, *"Der jüdische Abwehrkampf."*

[121]Leo Löwenstein, "Des Linie des Reichsbundes jüdischen Frontsoldaten," *Wille und Weg des deutschen Judentums*, pp. 7–11.

[122]Ibid.

[123]The RjF was concerned, through its organ *Der Schild* and its youth groups, with fostering physical fitness and with such efforts as resettling German Jewish veterans as farmers—closer to the soil. Cf. Kienitz, "Das jüdische Gemeindleben"; "Gesprach mit dem deutschen Tennismeister Prenn," *CVZ*, VIII (July 26, 1929).

[124]Cf. *Israelitisches Familienblatt*, XXXI, No. 19 (May 11, 1933), entire issue.

[125]"Mother of 12,000," *Blatter für Erziehung und Unterricht*, special publication by *Israelitischen Familienblatt*, May 1933.

[126]Elbogen, *Die Geschichte der Juden*, p. 282.

[127]Ibid., p. 283; Marcus, *The Rise and Destiny of the German Jew*, p. 81.

[128]Ernst Toller, *I Was a German*, trans. Edward Crankshaw (London: Lane 1934), p. 53.

[129]Bernstein, "Wirtschaft: Handel und Industrie"; *Wir deutschen Juden*, pp. 10ff. The phenomenon of Jews asserting their national loyalty and patriotism during and after World War I was of course not unique to Germany. The same was true in most Western nations. Accounts of the contributions of famous Jews to the various nations in the past were also like those of German Jews. Thus, Riesser's American counterpart, for example, was Haym Solomon, alleged by American Jews to have been the financier of the American Revolution.

56

[130]Martin Gumpert, "Medizin," in Kaznelson, pp. 461–527; Ludwig Karpe, "Technologie," in ibid., pp. 710–719; Theilhaber, Der Untergang, p. 12.

[131]"Deutsche oder völkische Erziehung," CVZ Monthly, IV (October, 1932); Wir deutschen Juden, p. 13.

[132]Osborne, Germany and Her Jews, p. 10.

[133]Ibid.; Marcus, The Rise and Destiny of the German Jew, p. 15.

[134]"Deutsche oder völkische Erziehung"; "Jewish Hatred Is the Same as German Hatred," CVZ Monthly, IV (January 1932); "Vom jüdischen Handwerk," CVZ Monthly, IV (October 1932); Zielensiger, "German Jews in the German Economy," which includes some eighty-five names of German Jews who distinguished themselves during the war.

[135]Stern, Warum sind wir Deutsche? p. 18. Posen (Poznan) was part of the territory taken by Prussia in the partitions of Poland at the end of the eighteenth century. The city became a center for German commerce, and Germans considered it a truly German province. Having been lost to Germany because of the Versailles Treaty, Posen became a rallying issue for German nationalism. It was one of the few nonpartisan issues in the Weimar Republic.

[136]Berthold Haase, "Die Posen Juden," CVZ, IV (January 9, 1925).

[137]Toller, I Was a German, p. 50; psychological conflicts of this type have been described in other minority groups: Albert Memmi, in The Colonizer and the Colonized, discusses the dilemma of Tunisian and Algerian Jews; Frantz Fanon, in Black Skins, White Masks, and E. Franklin Frazier, in Black Bourgeoisie, consider the positions of self-deceiving black minorities.

[138]"Die jüdische Abwehr," Die Israelit, LXXI, No. 26 (June 26, 1930). Toller may not be typical of German Jews, but because of his antipathy toward the German nation and his negative feelings about German Jews, his confessions of loyalty to Germany in his early years reveal much about the character of an educated, intellectual Jewish elite in Germany. Although he does not speak for poor, rural or working-class Jews, his views ironically reflect again the ideas of the CV. That organization claimed to speak for all German Jews, regardless of class or level of education.

[139]Haase, "Die Posen Juden."

[140]Alfred Wiener, Das deutsche Judentum in politischer, wirtschaftlicher und kultureller Hinsicht (Berlin: Philo-Verlag, 1924), p. 3.

[141]Zielensiger, "German Jews in the German Economy."

[142]Toller, I Was a German, pp. 117, 121, 136.

[143]Zeilensiger, "German Jews in the German Economy."

[144]Klinkenberg, "Zwischen Liberalismus."

[145]See Adolf Kober, "Die Geschichte deutschen Juden in der historischen Forschung der letzten 35 Jahre," Zeitschrift für die Geschichte die Juden in Deutschland, I, No. 1 (1929), 13–23; Heinrich Loewe, ed., "Die Juden in Deutschland. Bibliographischen Notizen," Zeitschrift für die

Geschichte die Juden in Deutschland, I, No. 1 (1929), 75–87; also issues of the same journal from 1930–1933, esp. "Bibliographischen Notizen" in each volume. In 1928 alone the following were published: *Anti-Anti* (C.V. Verlag); H Stern, *Angriffe und Abwehr*; Julius Goldstein, *Raase und Politik und Deutsche Volksidee und deutschvölkische Idee*; Alfred Wiener, *Das deutsche Judentum*; B. Segal, *Die Protokolle der Weisen von Zion*; and M. Guttmann, *Die Juden und seine Umwelt*. These are the better known, more publicized and "popular" works that flooded Germany in response to the rising tide of anti-Semitic literature.

[146]See n. 145; also *German Jewry: Its History, Life and Culture*, Wiener Library Catalogue Series No. 3 (London, Vallentine, Mitchell & Co. Ltd., 1958).

[147]Ernst von Aster, "Über allem der Mensch," *CVZ*, IX (February 21, 1930); Paucker, *Der jüdische Abwehrkampf*, p. 49.

[148]At the same time, anti-Semitic groups were defining those same categories in a different manner.

III

The Search for a Home

Être ailleurs, le grand vice de cette race [Jews], la grande vertue
secrète, la grande vocation de ce peuple. (Being elsewhere, the great
vice of this race, the great secret virtue, the great vocation of this
people.)

CHARLES PÉGUY

One of the more thoughtful books dealing with the topic of cultural and national assimilation was Felix Goldmann's, *Deutschtum und Judentum*.[1] He paused, even more rationally and thoroughly than his colleagues, to ask openly a question that lurked at the bottom of the public issue: "What *is* culture?"[2] The question seems to be one that especially plagued German intellectuals. It is of particular importance in an analysis of what constitutes total assimilation, of whether one can claim to be acculturated.

The question is, of course, not uniquely German, despite the apparent German fixation. Scholars from different disciplines and nationalities, men as varied as Sigmund Freud and Bronislaw Malinowski tried to deal with the problem of understanding culture. From Malinowski's functionalist school to Freud's followers in anthropology there is, despite bitter differences between them, agreement on culture as fulfillment of some human needs, organic or psychological. Eminent cultural anthropologists like Morton Fried, Clyde Kluckhohn, and Alfred Kroeber—men who are followers of neither Malinowski nor Freud, in the main, concur with these ideas.[3] They agree, too, on culture as the achievement of human cooperation; of people organized in groups delineated by a given ensemble of prerequisites that are historical as well as human.

Group effort, then, is among the fundamental prerequisites for a culture to exist. But before the group endeavor can be active, there must be "agreement on a set of traditional values for which human beings come together."[4] A system or pattern of traditional ideas and their attached values—what anthropologist A. R. Radcliffe-Brown called a "system of sentiments,"[5] what Freud labeled "regulations to adjust the relations of men to one another,"[6] what Malinowski termed "integrative imperatives"[7]—has been designated as the "essential core of culture." Culture then becomes the collective *acceptance* of the ideas behind certain political, social, economic, or moral institutions. Members of a given culture must agree on common purposes and interests as well as upon values. Conversely, an individual might be said to be assimilated into a culture if he accepts its systems of sentiments, deliberately assumes its convictions, its fundamental, comprehensive beliefs that "function as . . . orienting and integrating factors" in it.[8]

Within this framework of what is and is not a culture, of who is and is not acculturated into a given culture, and given the two complementary aspects of culture, and consequently of cultural assimilation—the physical and the psychological—what, then, was the status of German Jews in the twentieth century vis-à-vis German culture?

German Jews by 1920 were assimilated into the material or physical level of German culture. The "organized behavior" of German Jews was virtually indistinguishable from that of other Germans. The "organic needs" of German Jews were satisfied within German culture or society. Most German Jews agreed upon the nature of Germany, German culture, and Germans. They made common purpose with the dominant culture. Hugo Bettauer's didactic novel[9] again testifies to the important and presumably indispensable role that German Jews played in the German culture. After two years of life without Jews, the Vienna of *Stadt ohne Juden* was dying. Bettauer described his country without Jews as a cultural and economic wasteland.[10] The exiled Jews had to be summoned back because they were instrumental in the satisfaction of the physical or "organic" needs of Austrian non-Jews.

Bettauer's feelings were those of most German Jews. The strong assertions of devotion to monarchical Germany by German Jews in the nineteenth century served to affirm their agreement with non-Jews on German institutions. This affirmation was projected again in patriotic support of Germany in World War I. The contention of loyalty to traditional German institutions may have been difficult to make convincing in the nineteenth century, but it became considerably easier and more plausible in the twentieth century with the support of the Weimar Republic. The constitution and the Republic itself were institutions, cultural projections, to which German Jews readily and loyally pledged their allegiance.

Such confirmation of political institutions of German culture contributed to the feeling of physical assimilation on the part of Germany's Jews. But allegiance to the material projections of a given society is only one dimension of participation in its culture. If German culture encompassed physical tools to satisfy the physical needs of Germans, it also encompassed ideas to fulfill intellectual and spiritual needs. These internal factors address the ideals, the "core of culture," that underlie the institutions. How German Jews perceived and expressed what they believed were German beliefs, precepts, and values is a cardinal constituent in determining their rootedness in German culture, in examining their "Germanness."

Germanness for all Germans, but especially for Jewish

61

Germans, was measured in the nineteenth century in terms of nationalism, a phenomenon that is a product of a secularized era and a secularized culture. In a religious culture, religious conviction is the mainstay and the vehicle of cultural unity. But in nineteenth-century Europe, as historian Carlton J. H. Hayes and others have pointed out, nationalism became a substitute for religion, a surrogate that bestowed the same sense of unity earlier granted by religion.[11] As such, nationalism assumed a similar role in terms of fulfillment of certain cultural needs: security, belief, conviction, identity, communal unity, and cultural achievement.

In Germany, nearly all the early theorists of nationalism were theologians or students of theology. Friedrich Schleiermacher's *Speeches on Religion* were filled with national enthusiasm,[12] while Fichte's *Addresses to the German Nation* rang with religious fervor.[13] Herder's cultural nationalism was based on "religious" attitudes.[14] Hegel's *Philosophy of History* was in a sense a theological tract, which Hegel himself labeled a theodicy.[15] The group identity that had characterized a people was no longer transmitted through its religion, but through its sense of nationality. Culture was now firmly nation-bound rather than religion-bound.[16]

By the nineteenth century, religion in its traditional form was an inadequate source of identification for Jews in Germany. But the source of their being and their cultural existence did not die, it was transposed. Religion had taken on a different tone; a more temporal, secular orientation suited to a national identity. The values and ideals of Judaism had been retained and transposed to what German Jews now perceived as Germanism within the German nation. The function of religious convictions transplanted to a secular world was to support their continued identity as Jews, but at the same time, to broaden this identity to encompass their new identification with Germany. The "people of Israel" were now the "people of Germany," and virtually all the principles that had determined the one were active in their perception of the other.

In their quest for a definition of a German identity and a national home, German Jews paralleled German non-Jews. Herder, the "father of German nationalism,"[17] had developed his ideas of cultural nationalism, perhaps the first in a long line of explanations on the relationship between nation and culture.[18] Membership in a "nation" in the modern sense finally seemed, to national theorists, to have required a common language, a common land, a common will for political unity, and a common "culture."[19] There had to be, said Germans concerned with the problem of nationality after Herder, "an organic union" of all four elements to have a "nation."[20]

For German Jews, the study of history became the key to proving that they shared the organic unity of those four requisites with German non-Jews. History was the empirical and irrefutable discipline. A nation was not only a fact, but an *historical* fact. The thesis that assimilation was always at its highest in Germany[21] was no more than a subjective hypothesis until it was proven by what advocates of that thesis considered genuine, historical documentation. German Jews often described the historical affinity that Jews of other lands felt for eighteenth-century German philosophers, poets, and men of letters. Without investigating possible social or status motivations, they pointed out that Polish Jews, for example, had read and written of Goethe, learned and taught German in their schools;[22] that Galican Jews had established schools with German Jews as teachers;[23] and that East European Jews had studied in Germany and read and taught Schiller in their ghetto schools.[24]

German Jews continually enumerated these historical facts. With such evidence they simultaneously sought to demonstrate the broad appeal of German culture, its sympa-

63

thy with Judaism, and (somewhat paradoxically) the fundamental differences between themselves and East European
Jews. German Jews had, for centuries before the eighteenth
century, been a part of Germany's history, and they consequently identified themselves as culturally German from
the time of Charlemagne or the "benevolent reign of Kaiser
Heinrich IV," if not earlier.[25] German Jewish membership
in or identification with cultural Germany was, they
argued, a fact that could easily be substantiated by an
objective observation of history. In the face of heightening
anti-Semitism in the 1920s and 1930s, they believed that
educated, rational men had to denounce blood and race
theories of national, cultural traits and character. Tradition,
environment, and education determined cultural characteristics and were "a *product of life and history*."[26] These
were products of development, and they included language
and shared fate, both past and future.[27]

What German history revealed—when viewed "objectively" by German Jewish historians—was that "for one
thousand years Germans and Jews were so tightly tied to
each other they must appear to historians as identical
twins."[28] It seemed crucial to German Jews in the Weimar
years to demonstrate that the cultural bond was not simply
a product of the liberal, middle-class movement for Jewish
emancipation in the nineteenth century. Cultural participation might then be shown to reach beyond the liberal era,
even beyond political ideology. As long as anti-Semites
had anticapitalist, antiliberal, antimodern ideas as part of
their motiviation and arsenal, German Jews tried to deny
that their German identity was solely a consequence of the
nineteenth century, which had brought capitalism, liberalism, and modernity to Germany.

To substantiate these denials, German Jews fixed on the
Middle Ages as the origin of German Jewish cultural and
national assimilation. In retrospect, some serious accounts
by reputable historians to show the medieval origins of

64

cultural and national unity seem pathetically comic. H. G. Adler's contention that Germans and Jews lived in harmony under a united empire from the eighth century to 1096 typified a thesis expounded in numerous studies published until around 1935.[29] The Crusades, wrote Adler, signaled the breakup of the united German Empire, and "the hordes which devastated Germany and all the West with fire, hardship, and robbery and which destroyed the Jewish communities in the First Crusade came from France."[30] Adler concluded that both Jews and Germans suffered from persecution. Julius Bab, in 1938, called the end of the Middle Ages the "first death of Germanism."[31] With it, he added, died the Christian ethic and peaceful coexistence of Jews among Germans.[32] Already, in the Middle Ages, the "community of fate," the shared experience, shared language, and community of interest existed between Germans and Jews.[33] They were united in persecution; the result was a common goal of political unity (of the sort described by Tönnies) to reestablish the harmony of bygone imperial days.

In light of such genealogies, there could be no doubt that each Jew was culturally and nationally German, if only because of his ancestors.[34] Coupled with that primary, genealogical rationale were the philological studies proving that the language, *Mittelhochdeutsch*, was akin to Yiddish[35]—the teutonic language that German non-Jews had long forgotten—and that twelfth-century assumptions of German rather than Biblical names by German Jews had transformed Jews in Germany into secularized, nationalized Germans.[36]

There is considerable significance in an appeal to the Middle Ages. How ironic that both völkisch and, later, National Socialist theorists appealed to that epoch as the *illud tempus*, the edenic time when Germany was one in language, will, culture, and *Geist*.[37] It was a nationalistic myth. Cultural and national unity were alleged to have reached a peak in the Middle Ages. Nation and culture both bestowed identity to members of the *Volk*. Nonnationalistic historians have hypothesized that, in a sense, perhaps at no other time in history was there less crisis of identity or question of assimilation than during the European Middle Ages.[38]

The crisis of assimilation is a crisis of identity. Lack of assimilation and lack of identity are both psychological problems that arise from certain basic psychic needs. Freud believed that the drive for psychological security is one of the "instinctual demands" of civilized or cultured men.[39] From observation of his obsessional patients, he discovered that fear of isolation or solitude was a major cause of insecurity.[40] A sense of identity as a member of a group partially remedies the fear and insecurity of isolation.[41]

Although Freud's considerations about the nature and meaning of culture have been the source of considerable controversy and disagreement—not the least of which was with Malinowski[42]—it is important to note here that he saw culture as a creator of security, just as the ego created it.[43] His theories were elaborated more fully by Geza Roheim, who claimed to have proven that the chief function of culture was that it provides security by prescribing identities.[44] Culture, like the ego, "is the instrument whereby the individual adjusts to his total setting."[45] Psychologist and anthropologist could agree on this function of culture as the bestower of some type of security through identity.

Perhaps the major source of insecurity among German Jews was anti-Semitism. In an age of striving for national unity in Germany, any vestige of Jewishness might be perceived as grounds for isolation. The fear of isolation, the loneliness of bearing "the mark," grew to phobic proportions in the nineteenth and twentieth centuries. Anti-Semitism threatened not only physically but also psychologi-

66

cally, as an assault on the identity that German Jews possessed or could possess.

German Jewish reactions to anti-Semitism were obsessive assertions of German identity—national and cultural. Jewish identity by itself became untenable, and the contention of Germanness became the crucial defense—obsessive in nature—against anti-Semitism. Insecurity therefore was a fundamental element in an emotional confusion which became a group characteristic, and which fostered a single-minded preoccupation with Germanism.

Deutschjudentum (German Jewishness) was the name given to that preoccupation.[46] Shunning their original identity became a trait more intense in Jews in Germany than in Jews anywhere else. German non-Jews acknowledged this to a great extent. Those nationalists who conferred upon German Jews the "honor of Germanness" pointed to the great Jews who had thrown off their chains of tradition and achieved greatness because "they have ceased to be Jews."[47] German Jews alleged that "Jewishness" was an East European life-style, trait, and mystique that involved a language, style of dress, customs, superstitions, even religious beliefs that were different from their own. Contemporary Jewish culture was that of East European Jews and only they carried a "Jewish *Volkstum*."

German history and culture, on the other hand, was alive and belonged to the living in Germany.[48] The CV summoned Jews to strengthen their consciousness as Jews by reaffirming their *religious* ties to each other, since these ties were all that bound them together. The *Ostjuden*, East European Jews, were not a religious problem but a political one, and as such were aliens to German Jews.[49] Jewish culture in Germany was to be considered a religious culture and nothing more. Most certainly it was not national.[50]

Large numbers of Jews wandering from Poland and Russia had encountered German *Kultur* in the eighteenth century. For them and their descendants East European Jewishness had ceased. Germany became the "motherland of my tongue" as well as the "Geist of my people," said David Ben-Gurion.[51] The Geist of his people—in Germany. The idea of "one Volk . . . one fate and one cultural community" theoretically originated in the Middle Ages; but CV authors claimed that it had its practical renaissance in the eighteenth century.

As evidence of this rebirth, German Jews claimed that linguistic changes reflected changes in relationships between German Jews and German non-Jews in the nineteenth century. Until 1820, Jews were mentioned as "the Jewish nation in Germany." Gradually this nomenclature was transformed into phrases like "German citizens of the Mosaic persuasion" or "Jewish faith," phrases used by Jews and non-Jews alike.[52] As German Jews became more preoccupied with German culture and more involved in it, there seemed to have developed a consequent linguistic disavowal of Jewish identity as being national.

Until the eighteenth century, German influence had penetrated the ghettos by a "barely conscious process of osmosis."[53] But in the latter half of the eighteenth century, largely because of Moses Mendelssohn and those he inspired,[54] there began a "conscious process of turning towards the Germans."[55] The coming of the Crusades had unified medieval Germans in common suffering. The Jewish identification with medieval Germany was therefore one of a community of fate, of sorrow, and of disenfranchisement.[56] There is a marked hiatus of identification between the eleventh century and the eighteenth century. A positive bond between Jews and non-Jews in Germany seems to emerge with the German Enlightenment. According to some German Jewish historians, Germanness became more than the negative phenomenon it had been in the Middle Ages: to be German meant much more than to be divided, harassed, and downtrodden. The values, ethics, restrictions, or regulations that are the inner working of German culture seemed, at that time, to form a community of mind and ideals more than of only sorrow.

German Jewish and German non-Jewish newspapers and journals advocating assimilation never seemed to tire of stressing that Jews in other countries had retained their own language, actions, beliefs, and physical appearance.[57] In Germany the situation was quite the opposite: not only was the language of Jews and non-Jews the same, but so, too, were the loyalties, values, and goals identical.[58] Jews in other lands, noted a CVZ author, had suffered not as Jews but as Germans, especially during the war.[59] Even Treitschke had acknowledged that "the more honorable and serious men of Judaism have long seen that their position might be considered equal when they have entered, without hesitation, into German life."[60] And they had done it—had claimed Germany as their fatherland, German as their language. Like their non-Jewish neighbors, they were children of German culture and fathers of it as well.[61]

The drive for Germanism was cultivated throughout the nineteenth century and continued into the twentieth century. What "Germanism" meant, the definition of German culture, became psychologically crucial for German Jews in the Weimar Republic. Whatever the hallmarks of German culture, Jewish Germans identified with them. For to discover and define German culture would lead to a definition of German identity.

In other words, German Jews wanted desperately to be part of German culture. They willed it: "We *want* to be German! . . . We can be nothing else."[62] This meant, first of all, assimilation of values, morals, and ideals. The third of the four points of the CV charter read: "We have the same *morals* as our fellow citizens of different [religious] beliefs."[63] Hugo Bettauer's hero had clung tenaciously to what was clearly an Austrian (German) identity. In *Stadt* ohne Juden the salvation of Austrian culture had come with the salvation of the Jews (their return to Austria).[64] Paul Amann, an Austrian linguist, wrote Hugo Bergmann that Jewish literature, music, and economics were German, as Jews had penetrated universities and every fibre of the economy and culture of non-Jewish society.[65] Golo Mann claimed that he could consider German Jews he knew *only* as Germans.[66] He averred that his Jewish grandfather had been more loyal to Germany than most non-Jews.

The crux of cultural identity is how the ideal (and ideals) of a culture is perceived. If, as Golo Mann declared, German Jews *were* German and *felt* German, what German Jews considered "German" was the key to their actions in the twentieth century. German Jews did not seek to reject absolutely their Judaism or their "Jewishness." Rather, they attempted to redefine it in terms of Germanness.

NOTES

[1]Felix Goldmann, *Der Jude im deutschen Kulturkreise. Ein Beitrag zum Wesen des Nationalismus* (Leipzig, Philo-Verlag, 1930).

[2]Ibid., p. 24.

[3]See Morton H. Fried, *The Evolution of Political Society. An Esssy in Political Anthropology* (New York: Random House, 1967); Clyde Kluckhohn, "The Study of Culture," in *The Policy Sciences. Recent Developments in Scope and Method*, ed. Daniel Lerner and Harold D. Lasswell (Stanford: Stanford University Press, 1951), pp. 80–101; and *Culture. A Critical Review of Concepts and Definitions*, ed. A. L. Kroeber and Clyde Kluckhohn (New York: Vintage Books, 1952).

[4]Bronislaw Malinowski, *A Scientific Theory of Culture and Other Essays* (Chapel Hill: University of North Carolina Press, 1944), pp. 37, 39; Malinowski, "Culture," *Encyclopedia of Social Sciences*, 1935, IV, 625; Kluckhohn, "The Study of Culture"; Claude Levi-Strauss, *Structural Anthropology* (Garden City: Doubleday & Co., 1967), pp. 13, 19.

[5]A. R. Radcliffe-Brown, *The Andaman Islanders* (Cambridge: Cambridge University Press, 1933), pp. 233–234; Radcliffe-Brown, *Structure and Function in Primitive Society* (Glencoe: The Free Press, 1952), pp. 1–14.

[6]*Future of an Illusion, Works*, Vol. XXI, p. 6.

[7]B. Malinowski, *Sex, Culture, and Myth* (New York: Harcourt, Brace & World, 1962), pp. 202–204, 209; Malinowski, *Sex and Repression in Savage Society* (New York: Harcourt, Brace & World, 1925), p. 182.

[8]Cornelius Loew, *Myth, Sacred History, and Philosophy* (New York: Harcourt, Brace & World, 1967), pp. 3ff.

[9]See Chap. ii.

[10]Bettauer, *Stadt ohne Juden*.

[11]Carlton J. H. Hayes, *Nationalism: A Religion* (New York: Macmillan Co., 1960); Salo Baron, *Modern Nationalism and Religion* (New York: Harper & Row, 1947); and Koppel Pinson, *Pietism as a Factor in the Rise of German Nationalism* (New York: Octagon Books, 1968).

[12]Friedrich Schleiermacher, *On Religion: Speeches to Its Cultured Despisers*, trans. John Oman (New York: Harper & Row, 1958), pp. 4, 7, 24, 35, 45, 112, passim; see esp. second and fourth speeches and Epilogue; Jerry F. Dawson, *Friedrich Schleiermacher, the Evolution of a Nationalist* (Austin & London: University of Texas Press, 1966).

[13]See Johann Gottlieb Fichte, *Addresses to the German Nation*, trans. R. F. Jones and G. H. Turnbull (Chicago & London: Open Court Publishing Co., 1922), p. 130, passim.

[14]Johann Gottfried Herder, *God, Some Conversations*, trans. Frederick H. Burckhardt (Indianapolis: Bobbs-Merrill, 1940), esp. the "Fourth Conversation," pp. 131–161; *Herders Werke*, III, *Fragmente über die neuere deutsche Literatur*, ed. Hans Lambel (Berlin & Stuttgart: Verlag von W. Spemann).

[15]Georg Wilhelm Friedrich Hegel, *The Philosophy of History*, trans. J. Sibree (New York: Dover Publications, 1956), pp. 12, 15, 20, passim.

[16]See Hans Kohn, *The Idea of Nationalism. A study of Its Origins and Background* (New York: Macmillan Co., 1943); Hayes, *Nationalism*; Baron, *Modern Nationalism*.

[17]Carlton J. H. Hayes, "Contributions of Herder to the Doctrine of Nationalism," *American Historical Review*, XXXII, No. 4 (July 1927), 719–736.

[18]Georg G. Iggers, *The German Conception of History. The National Tradition of Historical Thought from Herder to the Present* (Middletown: Wesleyan University Press, 1968), pp. 9, 11 passim; Boyd C. Shafer, *Nationalism: Myth and Reality* (New York: Harcourt, Brace & World, 1955), pp. 40–56, 97; see also *Culture. A Critical Review* for evidence of German preoccupation with definitions of culture, civilization, and nation.

[19]Goldmann, *Der Jude*, p. 42; Tönnies, *Community*, pp. 39, 47, 48, passim; Treitschke, *Politics*; Fichte, *Addresses*, p. 69, passim; Eugen Diesel, *Germany and the Germans* (New York: Macmillan Co., 1931), p. 7; Schleiermacher, *Speeches*, pp. 2, 9, 230, passim.

[20]Goldmann, *Der Jude*, pp. 42–43; Schleiermacher, *Speeches*, p. 242; see nn. 16 and 18.

71

[21]See Chap. i.

[22]Adler, Die Juden in Deutschland, p. 108.

[23]Ibid.; CVZ, VIII (August 30, 1929).

[24]Adler, Die Juden in Deutschland, p. 108.

[25]See "Over 1600 Years on German Soil, in German Language and German Culture," CVZ Monthly, IV (March 1932); Stern, Warum sind wir Deutsche? pp. 4–6, passim; Wir deutschen Juden, pp. 3ff; Siegmund Salfeld, "Welt und Haus des deutschen Juden in Mittelalter," Jahrbuch für jüdische Geschichte und Literatur, XXIII (1920), 61–85; also the many histories of German Jews that begin with the Middle Ages or the Roman conquests of Gaul.

[26]Ernst von Aster, "Über allem der Mensch," CVZ, IX (February 21, 1930); Hollander, Deutsche-Jüdische Probleme, pp. 16, 19; "Deutschtum und Judentum" Der reichsdeutsche Jude im dritten Reich," CVZ, XII (June 29, 1933).

[27]See n. 26.

[28]Baron, Deutsche und Juden; Stern, Warum sind wir Deutsche? p. 3.

[29]Adler, Die Juden in Deutschland, pp. 13–14; Stern, Warum sind wir Deutsche? p. 9; Salfeld, "Welt und Haus."

[30]Adler, Die Juden in Deutschland, p. 14.

[31]Bab, Lieben und Tod, p. 11.

[32]Ibid., p. 10; Ludwig Rosenberg, "Jedoch als Deutscher schäm ich mich. Brief an einem Nichtjuden," CVZ Monthly, I (April 1928).

[33]Bab, Lieben und Tod, p. 10.

[34]Ludwig Hollander, "Klarheit und Wahrheit," CVZ, IV (January 16, 1925).

[35]"Over 1600 Years on German Soil."

[36]Ibid.; Wir deutschen Juden, pp. 3ff.

[37]Cf. Hans Kohn, The Mind of Germany (New York: Harper & Row, 1960); Peter Viereck, Metapolitics (New York; Alfred A. Knopf, 1941); Stern, The Politics of Cultural Despair; G. Mosse, The Crisis of German Ideology; G. Mosse, Nazi Culture, pp. 24–27, 34–35, 93f.; and Bill Kinser and Neil Kleinman, The Dream that Was No More a Dream. A Search for Aesthetic Reality in Germany, 1890–1945 (Cambridge: Schenkman Publishing Co., 1970).

[38]Mircea Eliade, Myth and Reality, trans. Willard R. Trask (New York: Harper & Row, 1963), p. 174; Nisbet, Quest for Community, pp. 80, 107.

[39]Moses and Monotheism, Works, Vol. XXIII, pp. 126, 127.

[40]Freud, "Obsessions and Phobias: Their Psychical Mechanisms and Their Aetiology," Collected Papers, 5 vols, trans. Joan Riviere (London: Hogarth, 1924–50), I, 129–136.

[41]Moses and Monotheism, Works, Vol. XXIII, p. 86.

[42]See Ernest Jones, "Mother-Right and the Sexual Ignorance of Savages," International Journal of Psychoanalysis, VI, Part 2 (April 1925), 109–130; Harold D. Lasswell, "A Hypothesis Rooted in the Preconceptions of a Single Civilization Tested by Bronislaw Malinowski," in Methods

in Social Science, ed. Stuart A. Rice (Chicago; University of Chicago, 1931), pp. 480–488; A. L. Kroeber, "Totem and Taboo in Retrospect," American Journal of Sociology, XLV, No. 3 (November 1939), 446–451.

[43]Future of an Illusion, Works, Vol. XXI, p. 18.

Moses and Monotheism, Works, Vol. XXIII, pp. 126, 172

[44]Geza Roheim, The Origin and Function of Culture (Garden City: Doubleday & Co., 1971), pp. 39, 106, 109.

[45]Kluckhohn, "The Study of Culture."

[46]Scholem, "Jews and Germans."

[47]Berg, Wohin treibt Juda? pp. 16–17.

[48]Stern, Warum sind wir Deutsche? p. 29.

[49]"Unsere Aufgehen im neuen Jahre," CVZ, IV (September 18, 1925).

[50]Hoffmann, "Gottes Volk," CVZ, IV (January 23, 1925).

[51]Quoted in Adler, Die Juden in Deutschland, p. 110.

[52]Scholem, "Jews and Germans"; Theilhaber, Der Untergang der deutschen Juden. Ein Volkswirtschaftliche Studie, 2nd ed. (Berlin: Judischer Verlag, 1921), p. 41; Toury, "The Jewish Question."

[53]Scholem, "Jews and Germans."

[54]Julius Guttmann, Philosophies of Judaism (New York: Holt, Rinehart & Winston, 1964), pp. 294–303. There are innumerable articles and monographs that concur with the thesis that Mendelssohn began the assimilation movement. See Chap. v.

[55]Scholem, "Jews and Germans."

[56]Ferdinand Lion, "Deutsches und jüdisches Schicksals," Der Neue Merkur, V, No. 5 (August 1921), 297–317.

[57]F. Wachsner, "Auch wir müssen von den anderen lernen!" CVZ, VIII (September 27, 1929).

[58]Ibid.; "The Jews of Bitola," CVZ, VIII (July 12, 1929), an article discussing the gradual disintegration of the Macedonian (Jugoslavian) Sephardic community in Bitola (Monastyr) which had retained a separate language, customs, dress, etc., unlike the German Jews.

[59]Rosenberg, "Jedoch als Deutscher schäm ich mich."

[60]"Before the Decision," CVZ, VIII (January 29, 1929); also Heinrich von Treitschke, Ein Wort über unserer Judentum (Berlin; Reimer, 1880).

[61]"Before the Decision"; Hugo Sonnenfeld, "Vote as Jews, Vote as Germans!" CVZ, VIII (January 29, 1929).

[62]Stern, Warum sin wir Deutsche? p. 18.

[63]Quoted in Klinkenberg, "Zwischen Liberalismus."

[64]Bettauer, Stadt ohne Juden, p. 109; cf. Karl Schwarz, "Kunstsammler," in Kaznelson, pp. 120–125.

[65]Klinkenberg, "Zwischen Liberalismus"; Thomas Mann, Letters to Paul Amann, 1915–1952, ed. Herbert Wegener (Middletown: Wesleyan University Press, 1959).

[66]Golo Mann, Deutsche und Juden, p. 49.

IV

The Mark

What bound me to Jewry was . . . neither faith nor national
pride. . . . But plenty of other things remained over to make the
attraction of Jewry and Jews irresistible—many obscure emotional
forces, which were the more powerful the less they could be
expressed in words, as well as a clear consciousness of inner
identity, the safe privacy of a common mental construction.

SIGMUND FREUD

On July 20, 1933, *Die Israelit*, newspaper of the
orthodox Jews of Germany, emphatically rejected the idea
that German Jews were a national minority.[1] Religion defined Jews as Jews. Religion was not political, and therefore
decidedly not the creator of nationality. To consider German Jews a separate nationality in terms of religion or race
was a "denial of historical truth and reality."[2] This statement of unity only in religion was a familiar theme. It was
a theme that had been expounded by German Jews since
the nineteenth century in Germany. but with increasing
intensity in the Weimar Republic.

Rarely did this theme become a denial of religious community. It was merely a firm denial of separate nationality
and was expressed most publicly in disaffiliation from
Zionism for German Jews. Industrialist and Foreign Minister, Walther Rathenau, perhaps the best known German
Jewish critic of Zionism, who "spent much of his time in
the company of writers and painters whom he believed to
embody the values of the age of Goethe," tried desperately

to harmonize Prussian traditions with Jewish ones in a "cult of the past." He adamantly renounced and abjured Zionism: "My people are the Germans and no one else. The Jews are for me a branch of the German nation. . . ." And later, on the connection between German and other Jews: "[it] does not extend beyond the sense of a common religious past."[3] Such comments are indicative of his and most German Jewish attitudes.

In the elections of 1925 in Berlin, for example, the CVZ political advertisements bore slogans like: "We must retain our community as a *religious* community"; and "A Zionist majority would change our religious community into a national community."[4] The CVZ Monthly expressed the "philosophy" of "synthesis of *Deutschtum und Judentum*" by asserting that German Jews were Jewish in religion and German in nationality.[5] They could not, wrote Eva Reichmann-Jungmann in July 1933, accept "minority rights," because they did not constitute a "national" minority. German Jews were not, she said, strangers or aliens in Germany and ought not be treated as such.[6] Felix Goldmann, with a critical, even cynical view of characterizing groups, conceded that "*if* Jews can be said to be marked by a specific cultural disposition, it is not from a common origin, but from a common *religion*."[7]

Perhaps the culmination of the attempts to define Jews (and consequently Germans) came not from German Jews but from the Nazis. Significantly, the final criterion in the Aryan Paragraph, which attempted to define Jews for the purpose of prohibition from various aspects of German life, was neither race nor nationality but religion.[8] But still the problem was not solved. How was the law to define adherence to the Jewish religion? Membership in a synagogue? Attitude? Self-regard?[9] If religion was what made Jews Jewish, there still remained the more difficult question of what constituted that religion. Aside from the obvious purposes of the National Socialist legislation, the confused attempts at definition are indicative of a perplexity ende-mic not only to anti-Semites or non-Jews but to German Jews perhaps even more.

For almost all German Jews and many German non-Jews it was a generally accepted fact that religion was what bound Jews together, what made them identifiable as a group with inner differences yet with a distinct external facade.[10] To German Jews and German non-Jews alike the question persisted: What, then, was the nature of that religion? What was the mark that Jews, and German Jews in particular, bore upon their heads or hearts or souls—the mark that made them both chosen and outcast? After the nineteenth century it was no longer simply the "mark of disenfranchisement." If it was the mark of Cain, perhaps it was redefined as Hermann Hesse had perceived it in *Demian:* a quality of difference, genius, heroism, even messianism—of chosenness.[11] What marked them as the "other"? What gave them the shadowlike, haunting yet hunted, demonic yet seraphic mien that inspired in some German non-Jews an uneasiness born of fear yet awe, of hatred yet respect, of contempt yet aspiration?[12] What was it in that religion and that people that the German philosopher Erwin Reisner claimed made the "chosen of the earth, the people of the German Reich" feel this discomfort in the presence of the chosen yet downtrodden of God?[13]

Whatever defined the group, by the 1920s it seemed futile to deny that some sort of commonality existed among Jews in Germany[14]—that they were at least viewed by others as a distinctive, sometimes mysterious, group. Most Jews did not seem to want to deny it. Instead, arguments were again marshaled in a logical, intelligent, and rational manner to explain what "German citizens of Jewish faith" meant. True to form, the German Jewish definers began with an historical premise. Also true to form, the CV was the leading popular educator. Through a myriad of lectures, articles in the weekly and monthly organs, special pamphlets, books, and meetings, members of the CV empirically demonstrated that *historically* the Jews were "the people of the Bible." Not the people of a particular brand of politics or a nationality, but the Bible, the people of a book and of God.[15] The role played by Jews in history was to carry the idea of God the creator to mankind.

In that avalanche of intellectual dialogue, Hegelian ideas of the torchbearer of the Spirit in history appear to have been of decisive influence. So, too, was the influence of Herder and even Treitschke upon particular presentations. The influence was not simply in the torchbearer concept, but in the conclusion and consequence of being the "people of the Bible": as such, they carry morality, values, and ethics, and therefore a particular culture. These remnants of an ancient but eternal living religion were the components of a "system of sentiments," of a "charter" for the content of a culture. How German Jews perceived that content was, in theory, the motivating fact in their lives.

Moreover, the ethical value of the religion was appraised as the basis of the modern state.[16] The love of justice bred in the legal religion *par excellence* became the rationale for the striving for equal rights; liberalism was nothing more than the religion of the Old Testament transferred to the secular realm.[17] Felix Theilhaber saw it as the tie that bound Jews to their environment.[18] The *CVZ* editors wrote that the religion of the Old Testament could only be realized, in modern times, through the experience of freedom, human kindness, and equality in a national group.[19] Jakob Wassermann considered it the foundation of all liberalism.[20]

Not only was the Jewish religion transferred to politics; it was portrayed as the basis of culture as well. Eminent theologian-philosophers like Hermann Cohen, noted historians like Ismar Elbogen, Jewish and Christian clergymen, scholars from every discipline, all attributed the foundation of European culture and morality to that religion—the keeper of the word of the Talmud and the Torah.[21] German Jews turned to the study and teaching of nineteenth-century philosophers and theologians like Schleiermacher, who had recognized that religious consciousness carried cultural consciousness.[22] Just as had Schleiermacher, German Jews in the 1920s contended that as a moral, ethical value system, religion—their religion—was a cultural force. To many of them it had been *the* cultural force in Western Europe, and especially in Germany.

Many twentieth-century intellectuals pursued studies similar to those of Schleiermacher on the nature of religion as a cultural product and force. Among those not concerned with such aspects of religion was Freud who, for a number of reasons, both personal and professional, was disturbed by what seemed to be a peculiar Jewish psyche. His considerations led him to postulate that the dominant character trait among Jews was "a compulsion to monotheism."[23] That compulsion to monotheism meant the belief in one united humanity.[24] It was this concept of the unity of mankind that became the focus of a flurry of literature in the Weimar Republic about the nature of German Jews. The authors of that literature affirmed that the practice of organized, formal religion had declined, but they alluded to the influence and the memory of religion that continued in the form of general ethical principles.[25]

German Jews incessantly described those ethical principles as the moral ideals and principles that they claimed as "the heritage of our fathers." When Ludwig Philippson called for collaboration with the Christian community,"[26] he said it was in the spirit of the Old Testament's call for the harmony of mankind. As Jews became politically free, he believed, "the more freely [they] must cultivate and refine [their] faith."[27] One God, one humanity; one morality for one mankind. Judaism was the bearer of these ideals to other cultures. That was the heritage. That was their burden, their mark, their pride, and their joy. Theodore Lessing claimed he was a "hard-core" Marxist-Socialist.[28] Yet in 1933 he called himself a "Zionist" simply because he considered himself a Jew who wanted the fulfillment of the international rights of men based on the principles of the Old Testament.[29] He believed that religion created a "cosmic community." It bound men together in the Eternal. To him, the statement "God is One" meant transcendence of arbitrary labels like Aryan and Semitic, German and Czech, Jewish and Arabic. "One logic and one ethic" was for him and, he claimed, for all Jews, a "spiritual conviction."[30]

The dominant attitude of apostate Jews like Lessing and of orthodox or observant Jews like Elbogen and Leo Baeck was that Judaism dealt with world culture and world history as did "true" Christianity. Such religions were supranational and based upon the oneness of man in God, on the concept of "mankind as the larva of all *Völker* . . . of all 'nations.' "[31]

In what was perhaps the most massive, verbose, and overwritten of the many expositions of the substance and temper of Judaism, theologian Michael Guttmann tried to create a moral for German non-Jews that would guide their actions as they perceived and encountered German Jews.[32] His goal was to rebut anti-Semitic defamations of Jews by again showing that Jews in Germany were not a nation.

In the Bible, Guttmann noted, no *Volk*, no individual man or nation is free from the obligation to the moral and ethical principles of God.[33] Like Freud after him, Guttmann began his study with monotheism: "Along with monotheism comes the proclamation of pure ethics and pure humanism. One morality, one justice for all mankind."[34] The Jews were the first people, wrote Guttmann, to see this oneness of the human race and it has marked them forever. They could never forget that fundamental lesson.

Guttmann's emphasis was on the first book of the Torah. Genesis, he said, had transcended the interest of any one people. Rather than in the commandments of Moses, the essence of Judaism rested in "the four commandments of Noah," which spoke to all people.[35] Abraham in Genesis signified the spiritual father not only of Israel but of all men. The biblical story of the creation denies fundamental (racial) splits within the human race. With one prevalent idea, Guttmann seemed to destroy the grounds for denial of Jews as Germans. He did not explicitly approach the problem of German Jews, but this was clearly his aim. His reviewers and probably his readers recognized it.[36]

Virtually all German Jews had contended that there were religious differences, but nothing more, between themselves and German non-Jews. Guttmann now argued that even those differences were only in ritual form, and that there was an affinity and a harmony between Judaism and Christianity: the "harmony is on the universal soil of ethics," but is not political or confessional.[37] Paul, Guttmann wrote, had recognized the common fatherhood of Abraham and the consequent brotherhood of man.[38] Prophets and apostles had borne the same universal message and differed only because the prophets did not proselytize or propagate any specific cult or confessional form. The commandments of Noah were cultural, legal, moral, and humanitarian. They were not geographic, political, national, or historical.[39]

Christian apostles had recognized the universalism of the content of these four commandments. Since both religions assented to the universal truth of the ethics of the Old Testament, they did not constitute "strangers" to each other. Political and ethnic differences, according to the laws of the Old Testament (Deuteronomy), do not make for the categorization Fremde, stranger. Only moral and ethical differences could carry that legal designation in ancient Israel.[40] Egypt was Moses' home, and in remembrance of that came the law: "And judge with justice between a man, his brother and his stranger" (Deuteronomy). Guttmann noted that brother was placed with stranger. Love the

80

stranger, he said, is an implicit extension, in the Old Testament, of the basic command to love all men as brothers.[41] There could then be no strangers, only brothers.

Die Juden und seine Umwelt was well received by those reviewers who grasped its importance for the Jews in Germany in 1927. The *CVZ* review began with the lesson that World War I had supposedly taught the world: all peoples are part of one organism, each depending upon the others for life.[42] The reviewer, G. Ksinski, noted that this idea had been dominant in Western society until the Christian late Middle Ages and then had declined. Its source, however, was not Christianity but the Talmud and the Old Testament.[43] Guttmann's book was, to Ksinski, Truth revealed and retold.

Aside from Guttmann and his admirers, there were countless others who also held that Judaism was the source of all that was good and noble in the modern world. Hermann Cohen had written earlier of the Judaic foundation of Christianity and Western culture.[44] Felix Goldmann acknowledged the contribution of Jewish ideas to human ethics.[45] Freud saw Judaism as a step forward for civilization.[46] The *CVZ* quoted German scholars and philosophers like Nietzsche in order to demonstrate that the Old Testament was generally considered by great non-Jews to be the foundation of Western culture, justice, and civilization.[47] Guttmann had carefully, *objectively* rediscovered, or rather restated, the same truths in precise, nonpolitical, nonpsychological, allegedly noncontroversial terms, and with no apparent ulterior motive.

Jews, then, were identifiable as Jews only through the ethical universalism of their religion. There was no other mark. It made them obvious in cultural life because it influenced and motivated their profane activities as well as their sacred ones. Adherents of the religion of law could not simply preach justice and equality in the abstract; they had to practice it as well.[48] The principles of equality of

81

men were made real by political, social, and cultural deeds, not theories. Judaism contained ideas of the maintenance of individual national characteristics and cultures, "but united under the banner of justice, human love, and freedom,"[49] and Jews were forced by religious conviction to strive for the achievement of that goal. To strive for that goal would be "a confirmation of [Judaism's] ancient, biblical-traditional conception of allowability of differences of confession among residents of one and the same land."[50] Tolerance and allowability of differences was the message; religion was the medium. It was hardly necessary to include the admonition that Germans should "go and do likewise."

In his classic study of religion and magic, *The Golden Bough*, James G. Frazer defined religion as that which motivates from love or fear of God. Action sparked by love or fear of man is moral or immoral, but not necessarily religious. However, religion was not complete, in Frazer's observation, without moral or ethical content. He further noted that "it was the ethical side of religion which the Hebrew prophets, inspired with the noble ideal of God's goodness and holiness, were never weary of inculcating."[51] German Jews of the Weimar Republic never seemed to weary of inculcating it either. Like Frazer, they saw that if religion was incomplete without its moral content, it was also incomplete without the practical application of that morality in life. Judaism's God was a God of ethics, of man. He was a model, an Ideal for individuals and for the human race. Love of God became also love of man and assumed the unity of mankind. Based on this assumption, belief and practice had to go together.

Frazer was not the only student of religion to discuss it in terms of practice based on belief. In *Moses and Monotheism*, Freud concluded his characterization of the Mosaic doctrine by saying that it "demands only belief and a life of truth and justice."[52] Guttmann also had finally concluded that the core of Judaism was love of God and his principles, but that the love must stimulate teaching and living of these principles.[53] One of the most frequent themes of Hermann Cohen's philosophical writings is the relationship of religion to life, that is, to living deeds.

Cohen throught of religion as an active unifier of life within culture.[54] The great impact of Judaic thought, he said, was its emphasis on the deed as an expression of the moral attributes of God.[55] Judaism required, in absolute, unequivocal commandments, the application of its principles in the present by means of a "more social morality and . . . more cosmopolitan humanity."[56] Cohen was perhaps the leading German Jewish philosopher of his time.[57] The primary consideration of the Old Testament religion as perceived by him and many German-Jewish intellectuals was its directive power in culture, in real, active life.[58]

Theoretically, then, the "return of the original (ürsprünglichen) Jewish teachings" manifested itself not in religious terms but in profane, cultural life.[59] Although modern culture was allegedly formed by Judaism and its teachings, secularized and nationalistic German Jews claimed to be aware of a need for a new interpretation of those sources to make them more relevant to the twentieth century.[60] The eternal truths hidden in the ancient Hebrew texts had to be shown applicable to the contemporary scene by stripping away the old confessional trappings and traditional religious forms by which most non-Jews seemed to define Judaism. German Jews wanted to convey Judaism as a modern, ethical system rather than as an antiquated, ritualistic cult.

That process of deritualizing Judaism involved a particular type of intellectualizing. In a recent study of Germans and German Jews, George L. Mosse attempts to describe the process as he considers the position of Jews vis-a-vis Germans in the Weimar Republic.[61] The longest chapter in

Mosse's book is entitled "Left-Wing Intellectuals in the Weimar Republic."[62] Mosse builds his thesis with numerous, specific examples that might serve to typify the *Zeitgeist* of Weimar Germany: a Kantian revival swept the left-wing intellectuals during the Weimar years; in opposition to Hegelian theory, Neo-Kantians posited the categorical imperative for all men at all times.[63] For Hermann Cohen, for example, there existed an eternal ethical ideal that unites mankind. That ideal was embodied in the law "founded on correct ethical premises . . . the anchor of ethics."[64]

Cohen's "Kantian" belief in the basic equality of man created his respect for law, not simply civil law, but "an 'objective law' which is not of human invention."[65] Cohen's followers preached the formation of an elite of cultured, educated men whose duty was to bring about the actualization of ethical idealism. Leonard Nelson, a Cohen disciple, called this group "the true invisible church"[66] made to serve society. Education was of primary importance, and Mosse writes that Nelson called for socialist education on the basis of Kantian ethics.[67]

After pointing out the significance of the large number of German Jews in the left-wing, Neo-Kantian, idealist-socialist movement,[68] Mosse mentions the possible influences religion may have exerted upon these men and their ideologies. He notes Hermann Cohen's testament of his debt to monotheism, and that he equated the categorical imperative with his monotheistic God.[69] He notes, too, the shift from traditional religion to ethical idealism that accompanied the secularization of Jews and Judaism in Germany; that for a few of the Jewish left-wing intellectuals, Judaism manifested itself in a social concern for liberty. And he concedes the possible impact of Judaism upon the *religious* feelings of some of those men.[70]

These brief inferences about the determinative impact of religion on Neo-Kantian philosophers can be expanded by observing the parallels between Old Testament Judaism and new, humanitarian, idealist socialism. A mountain of literature by German Jews exists to confirm these parallels. Cohen's call for ethical universalism and his consistent appeal to the Old Testament crystallizes the hidden ties between religion and philosophy. Words like "ethical ideal," "objective law," and "true invisible church" had their roots in the Old Testament religion—at least for these men. Certainly Cohen was not talking simply of civil law, but of the Law. His innumerable articles, books, and lectures instructed Germans in the religious sources of Kantian ethics and Western culture.[71] An educated elite whose duty it is to lead mankind toward the realization of an ideal is a striking parallel to the concept of the Chosen, the bearers of Truth and God to humanity. It echoes the call of a CVZ author in 1933 "to remain true to the 3000-year-old command of Moses" admonishing Jews to lead the way for humanity and all mankind.[72]

Along with Cohen, Alfred Döblin and Gustav Landauer were also steeped in philosophical Judaism. When Döblin spoke of "spiritual value" in Kantianism, and Landauer of his "Jewish . . . concern for humanity at large," they were endorsing the universalism of the Old Testament that men like Guttmann were also describing. There can be little doubt that the left-wing intellectuals of Weimar, like their nineteenth-century liberal precursors, felt themselves unbound by class, with "everyone's interest at heart."[73] Ernst Toller wrote that Landauer was the symbol of Germany,[74] with a "holy duty" to announce the truths of mankind and altruism.[75] In 1919, before his disillusionment with Germany, Toller believed that Landauer had "shown the essential humanity of the German people."[76]

Having secularized their religious beliefs and transformed them to a liberal humanism, by the 1920s most of the German Jewish organizations and their organs were asserting that there was no conflict between *Deutschtum* and *Judentum*.[77] Along with the large organizations like the CV, German Jewish "extremist" movements of Zionism and National German Jews confronted the meaning of *Deutschtum* as well as *Judentum*. Both Zionists and National German Jews, antithetical in ideology and purpose, agreed upon the need to settle the question of Jews in Germany on Germain soil.[78]

Robert Weltsch (a leading German Jewish Zionist)[79] and Max Naumann asserted that a fundamental sympathy existed between German and Jewish communities in Germany. Naumann called for a blending into a collective productive life—for total assimilation[80] So, too, did *Der Israelit*, the *CVZ*, and virtually all German Jews. It was perhaps the only point of agreement among them. This demand for assimilation was also perhaps the most telling and important point of agreement. German Jews were above all, despite differences among them, Germans.

Regardless of economic or social success or failure, political involvement or noninvolvement, patriotic national devotion or indifference, or degree of religious commitment, there was a near-unanimous, semantic admission to being "sehr guter Deutscher." If German Jews were a *Volksgemeinschaft*, it was because they were a *Bodengemeinschaft*; if they were a *Bodengemeinschaft*, they were brothers in that community with the other sons of their home soil (*Ürfeld*)—the sons of Germany. German Jews and non-Jewish Germans were not "members of a civilization defined by capitalist technical materialism." They were "brothers of the same soil," "one for all and all for one in a common fate," springing from the same culture, from the womb of the Old Testament religion with all its moral idealism.[81]

In that heartbreaking and bewildering year of 1933, the CVZ pronounced again that German Jews were "fatherland-loving and freedom-loving." Their patriotism was visible in history, and it demonstrated that they had always fought for "victory for the fatherland. . . . This has always been the guiding star of the CV and German Jews. . . . [We take] great pride in our history. Also in our adherence to our religion."[82] This kind of persistent proximity of allegiance both to religion and to things German was by no means rare. German Jews believed that they had combined the two in the one, that with no tension they were simultaneously "sehr gute Deutschen" and "sehr guter Juden." History defined the former, and the ethics of Judaism defined both.

N O T E S

1. *Die Israelit*, No. 29 (July 20, 1933).
2. Ibid.
3. James Joll, *Three Intellectuals in Politics* (New York: Random House, 1960), pp. 60–61, 66.
4. *CVZ*, IV (January 23, 1925).
5. Cf. *CVZ Monthly*, I–IV; Margaret T. Edelheim-Muesham, "Die Haltung der jüdische Presse gegenüber der nationalsozialistischen Bedrohung," *Leo Baeck Yearbook* (1966).
6. Edelheim-Meusham, "Die Haltung der jüdische Presse."
7. Goldmann, *Der Jude*, p. 55.
8. Hilberg, *The Destruction*, p. 45. It should be noted that the law read "religion of his ancestors."
9. Ibid., p. 50.
10. *Völkische* and radical Nazi theorists, of course, did not subscribe to this definition of classification of Jews as a religious group. The classification "non-Aryan" was presumably not national or religious but biological, that is, racial. National Socialist legislation suffered from an inadequate definition of the Jew. It was a problem that plagued the Nazis, at least until after the Nuremberg Laws of September 1935. See Karl A. Schleunes, *The Twisted Road to Auschwitz. Nazi Policy Toward German Jews 1933–1939* (Urbana, Chicago, London: University of Illinois Press, 1970), pp. 103f.
11. Hermann Hesse, *Demian*, trans. Michael Roloff and Michael Lebeck (New York: Bantam Books, 1968), pp. 25–27; cf. Theodor Gastner, *Myth, Legend, and Custom in the Old Testament* (New York: Harper & Row, 1969), pp. 51–75, "Cain and Abel."
12. Hesse, *Demian*, p. 26.
13. Reisner, *Die Juden und das deutschen Reich*, p. 194.
14. Toury, "The Jewish Question."

[15]Rabbi Goldschmidt, "Die Sprüche der Väter," *CVZ Monthly,* I (April 1928); Rabbi Rosenthal, "Der Einfluss der Talmud," *CVZ Monthly,* I (May 1928); Goldmann, *Der Jude,* p. 19; Theilhaber, *Der Untergang,* p. 20.

[16]Goldmann, *Der Jude,* p. 88; *Wir Deutschen Juden,* pp. 27ff; Hermann Cohen, *Deutschtum und Judentum* (Giessen: Töpelmann, 1923), pp. 23ff; Caesar Seligmann, "Das Problem der jüdischen Kultur," *Jahrbuch für jüdische Geschichte und Literatur,* XXIII (1920), 88–101.

[17]Kaulla, *Der Liberalismus,* p. 5.

[18]Theilhaber, *Der Untergang,* p. 42.

[19]Hoffmann, "Gottes Volk."

[20]Wassermann, *Mein Weg,* pp. 109, 118.

[21]Albert Lewkowitz, "Judentum und Kulturidee," *CVZ Monthly,* I (March 1928); Goldmann, *Der Jude,* p. 123; Cohen, *Die Bedeutung des Judentums für den religiösen Fortschritt der Menschheit. Sonderausgabe aus dem Protokoll des 5 Weltkongresses für Freies Christentums und religiösen Fortschritt* (Berlin: Protestantischer Schriftenvertrieb, 1910), p. 4; Seligmann, "Das Problem der jüdishchen Kultur."

[22]Schleiermacher, *Speeches,* pp. 2, 9, 155, passim.

[23]*Moses and Monotheism, Works,* Vol. XXIII, pp. 112, 113.

[24]Michael Guttmann, *Das Judentum und seine Umwelt. Eine Darstellung der religiösen und rechtlichen Beziehungen zwischen Juden und Nichtjuden mit besonderer Berücksichtigung der talmudisch-rabbinischen Quellens* (Berlin: Philo-Verlag, 1928), p. 15.

[25]Goldmann, *Der Jude,* p. 69; Theilhaber, *Der Untergang,* p. 41; Guttmann, *Das Judentum,* p. 16, passim.

[26]See chap. ii.

[27]Baron, "Aspects of the Jewish Communal Crisis."

[28]Lessing became a *cause célèbre* when he denounced and criticized Hindenburg. He was released from his teaching position at the Hannover Academy in a flurry of anti-Semitic accusations. The CV reluctantly took up his cause, at all times stressing that his socialist politics were not theirs. He was killed by the Nazis in 1933. Cf. C. A. Stonehill, *The Jewish Contribution to Civilization,* p. 103.

[29]Theodore Lessing, *Deutschland und seine Juden* (Prague: Weremann & Co., 1933), p. 4.

[30]Ibid., p. 6.

[31]Ibid., p. 7.

[32]Guttmann, *Das Judentum.*

[33]Ibid., p. 98.

[34]Ibid., p. 15.

[35]Ibid., p. 103, passim. Guttmann refers to the "covenant" with Noah in Genesis 8:21, 22. The "four commandments" apparently refer to the laws and restrictions vis-à-vis murder, slaughter of animals, legal punishments ("Whosoever sheddeth man's blood, by man shall his blood be shed"), and dietary prescriptions related in Genesis 9:4–9.

[36]See, for example, the review in *Zeitschrift für die Geschichte die Juden in Deutschland*, IV (1931), 419, in which the reviewer uses Guttmann's work as a springboard for a discussion of contemporary anti-Semitism.

[37]Guttmann, *Das Judentum*, p. 210.

[38]Ibid., pp. 6, 9, 16.

[39]Ibid., p. 104.

[40]Ibid., p. 19.

[41]Ibid., pp. 43–44.

[42]G. Ksinski, "Der Fremde—die Umwelt," review of *Das Judentum und seine Umwelt* by Michael Guttmann, *CVZ Monthly*, I (January 1928).

[43]Ibid.

[44]Hermann Cohen, *Die religiösen Bewegung der Gegenwart* (Leipzig: Buchhandlung Gustav Fock, 1914), p. 9; cf. Cohen, *Deutschtum und Judentum*, p. 18.

[45]Goldmann, *Der Jude*, p. 17.

[46]*Moses and Monotheism, Works*, Vol. XXIII, pp. 86, 113.

[47]Fritz Goldschmidt, "Deutschtum und Judentum zu den Grundlagen unseres Seins," *CVZ*, XII (June 8, 1933).

[48]Pinn, "'Rechtswissenschaft," in Kaznelson; Seligmann, "Das Problem der jüdischen Kultur."

[49]Goldmann, *Der Jude*, p. 19.

[50]Guttmann, *Das Judentum*, pp. 274–275.

[51]James George Frazer, *The Golden Bough. A Study in Magic and Religion* (London: Macmillan & Co., 1970), p. 106.

[52]*Moses and Monotheism, Works*, Vol. XXIII, p. 51.

[53]Guttmann, *Das Judentum*, pp. 367–368.

[54]Cohen, *Die religiösen Bewegung*, p. 2.

[55]Cohen, *Moses Ben Maimon* (Leipzig: Buchhandlung Gustav Fock, 1908), I, 116.

[56]Cohen, *Die Bedeutung Judentums*, p. 17.

[57]Cf. Julius Guttman, *Philosophies of Judaism*, pp. 352–366; Arthur A. Cohen, *The Natural and the Supernatural Jew* (New York: Pantheon Books, 1962), pp. 73–102; M. Guttmann, *Das Judentum*, has several references and statements of indebtedness to Cohen; Goldmann, *Der Jude*, p. 12; Iggers, *The German Conception of History*, pp. 146–147, 152.

[58]Cohen, *Die religiösen Bewegung*, p. 16.

[59]Goldmann, *Der Jude*, p. 73; S. Wernberg, "Des Judentums Kulturbildene Kraft," *CVZ*, VIII (September 10, 1929).

[60]Weinberg, "Des Judentums."

[61]George L. Mosse, *Germans and Jews. The Right, the Left, and the Search for a "Third Force" in Pre-Nazi Germany* (New York: Howard Fertig, 1970).

[62]Ibid., pp. 171–225. Mosse's thesis here is that the infusion of ethical idealism into left-wing politics resulted in impotence and disastrous failure both for the left and for the Republic. This thesis seems to concur

with or borrow from an article by Gordon Craig. "Neutrality and Engagement," *Journal of Contemporary History*; and from Istvan Deak's *Left Wing Intellectuals in the Weimar Republic* (Berkeley & Los Angeles: University of California Press, 1968), although Mosse does not mention them.

[63]Mosse, *Germans and Jews*, p. 172.

[64]Ibid., p. 176.

[65]Ibid., p. 186; Iggers, *The German Conception of History*, pp. 144–147.

[66]Mosse, *Germans and Jews*, p. 186.

[67]Ibid., pp. 191–192.

[68]Ibid., pp. 204–205.

[69]Ibid., p. 205.

[70]Ibid.

[71]Cf., for example, Cohen, *Die religiösen Bewegung*, pp. 10–11.

[72]"Deutsch-jüdische Wirklichkeit," *CVZ*, XII (April 13, 1933).

[73]Mosse, *Germans and Jews*, p. 204.

[74]Ernst Toller, *Briefe aus dem Gefangnis* (1935), p. 39.

[75]Ibid., p. 11.

[76]Ibid., p. 48.

[77]Cf. Elbogen, *Die Geschichte der Juden*, pp. 274–275, for a representative example.

[78]There were bitter campaigns conducted between Zionists, National German Jews, and CV liberal German Jews. The thrust of the position held by the last group was to affirm Zionism for the *Ostjuden*. Zionists in Germany usually recognized this deep feeling of assimilation among German Jews, and the hostility toward them apparently grew from exaggerated ideas of the attempts to woo German Jews from Germany. Realistic Zionists strove largely for funds from German Jews to aid East European Jews. It would seem that they were often unsuccessful in these endeavors. Cf. Ludwig Hollander, "Klarheit und Wahrheit," *CVZ*, IV (January 16, 1925); "The Revelation of the German Character," *CVZ*, IV (January 23, 1925); interviews with the former director of the Dresden Bank of Berlin and with a former Russian Zionist who had worked in the Weimar Republic, November 1966.

[79]Mosse, *Germans and Jews*, p. 92.

[80]Naumann, "Grüne Fragen und gelbe Antworten," *Klärung*, pp. 70–89.

[81]"The Structure of Our Volksgemeinschaft," *CVZ*, IV (April 9, 1925).

[82]"Für de Aufsteig des Vaterlandes. Der Tag von Potsdam," *CVZ*, XII (March 23, 1933).

V

Lord of the Rings

If each of you has his ring from his father, then may each one surely
believe his ring to be the real one. It is possible that the father now
would no longer tolerate in his house the tyranny of the one ring.
And it is certain that he loved all three of you and loved you equally
by not wishing to oppress two in order to favor one. Let each one
of you follow zealously his uncorrupted, unprejudiced
love! ... Assist that power by gentleness, by heartfelt peaceability,
by charity, by fervent devotion to God!

GOTTHOLD EPHRAIM LESSING, Nathan the Wise

The initial, mass Jewish encounter with what was later perceived as the model German occurred in the eighteenth century.[1] Jews wandering and in flight from oppressive and openly, almost officially, hostile Eastern governments came to Germany in an age of Enlightenment and revolution. It was their first contact with the West since the medieval migrations eastward, and it came at a moment when Germany's culture seemed at its zenith.[2] Because it was the first encounter on the road west, and because it presented an apparently startling contrast to the east, the meeting was decisive.

Jews perceived the representatives of Germany to be intellectuals like Schiller and Lessing, men who spoke eloquently and wrote poetically in favor of assimilation. German Aufklärer seem to have exerted an intellectual influence on Jews that was greater in intensity and range than on any other men in Europe. Their memory was indelibly imprinted upon the minds and consciousness of

91

German Jews. It was to these enlightened philosophers and *philosophes* that German Jews in the Weimar Republic appealed. Not Treitschke, Ahlwardt, or Stöcker, but Schiller, Goethe, and Lessing were their symbols of Germany and German culture. These last were, after all, the founding fathers of German *Geist, Kultur,* and *Volk.* Many Europeans claimed that they could not understand Rathenau's murder or Hitler's growing following in 1932 among so high-minded a people—the children of these great, classical founding fathers.[3]

Weimar Jews, like nineteenth-century German Jews, theorized that from the dark ages of militarism, strife,and war of the sixteenth and seventeenth centuries came forth Leibniz and Christian Thomasius, Frederick the Great, and Immanuel Kant.[4] They compared this intellectual flowering to the white, rational beauty of Greek classicism bursting forth from the dark caverns of Mesopotamia and Egypt. The principles of religious and philosophical freedom suddenly seemed to blossom in Germany. It was the foundation of German intellectual life; Thomasius and his circle at the University of Halle were hailed as the founders of Germany's honor.[5] It was the dawning of a new age, "the magnificent decades"[6] when "dark clouds began to fade" and there was light, or enlightenment, and understanding. Here was the basis for Byron's epithet for the Germans: "The people of poets and thinkers." Here, in Germany, in the eighteenth century was Christian Wolff, praised by Hegel and Goethe as the father of the spirit of the new epoch in Germany, whose disciples were alleged to be all of Germany, "the friends of truth."[7] The eighteenth century in Germany was the age whose prevalent ideas were Reason, Truth, Freedom, Equality, and Humanity. "The great epoch of the Enlightenment" was, according to German Jews, greatest in Germany.[8] The eighteenth century achieved its peak in the founders of the German soul, in

Kant and in Leibniz,[9] "a German and yet a cosmopolitan of the range of Newton and Voltaire."[10]

All these men and those around them typified what German Jews called the *German* philosophy with its "critical spirit." The successors of Kant, Wolff, and Leibniz were Goethe, Fichte, Hegel, Schopenhauer, Nietzsche, and Meinecke—all distinguished as creators and artists in *all* cultural areas.[11] Not national but world history and world philosophy were their fortes. Not a narrow provincialism but a broad supranationalism was their concern.

To German Jews the representative of cosmopolitanism was first of all Friedrich Schiller, a symbolic figure of the brightness and splendor of his age. He was one of "the most obvious, most imposing, and most influential" of the German thinkers read by German Jews.[12] In *Kabale und Liebe* he spoke out against inequality, in *Don Carlos* for the community of man.[13] His plays and essays seemed to bear a moral of freedom and humanity. Schiller continued to be the spokesman of pure humanity for generations of German Jews, the representative of "the highest ideals of mankind," and the embodiment of "what they wanted to feel or had felt as Germans."[14]

Schiller was, in fact, the national poet of Germany, a role he maintained throughout the nineteenth century.[15] The man was real; he was not false in tone; he was popular; he was adored by the German people. And he spoke of humanity and of humanitarianism—what Jews most fervently sought. The symbol of the national German culture spoke words that were pleasingly familiar to German Jews. One can sense among many Jews in Germany who read Schiller a collective, complacent nod, accompanied by a feeling of security in common belief.

Weimar's German Jews noted that increased feeling of security that had soothed their forefathers in the second half of the eighteenth century.[16] In the brief period from

93

1924 to 1928 they expressed comparable feelings of security and optimism.[17] Few German Jewish homes from the nineteenth century on were without some or all the works of Schiller. They were shelved next to the works of Goethe, Lessing, and the Old Testament.

In retrospect the German Enlightenment seems to have signaled a mutual attraction among German and Jewish intellects. Heraclitus, Plato, and Socrates were blended with Philo, Moses Maimonides, and Spinoza; the Old Testament was blended with the New Testament. In the 1920s and 1930s German Jews, and some German non-Jews, agreed with one German Jewish author that "in no part of the Diaspora was this [mutual attraction] felt with such depth as in Germany."[18] The universal teachings of Judaism seemed to have found a sounding board, a mirror, a secular, modern expression in the humanism of Schiller, Kant, Goethe, and in the cosmopolitanism of Herder and Fichte. The *CVZ Monthly* referred to the spirit of the Bible as the outstanding quality in works like Kant's *Ethics*, Lessing's *Nathan the Wise*, and Herder's *Geist der hebraischen Poesie* and *Alteste Urkunde des Menschensgeschlechts.*[19] Hermann Cohen and several of the Neo-Kantians found in Kant the affirmation of the Old Testament objectivity in ethics and morality.[20] Otto Flake, a non-Jew, considered the "Jewish *Geist* absolutely theological, rationalistic, metaphysical-scholastic."[21] Because the "Jewish *Geist*" bore these qualities, it was ideal for coping with the most important problems of world history, which were universal. In 1921 Flake believed that the German *Geist* had lost these qualities, which it had been fortunate to possess in the eighteenth and nineteenth centuries.[22]

In short, Jews "had sympathy" with their surrounding intellectual and national environment. John Layard pointed out that to "have sympathy" in the German sense indicates the existence of a bond or relationship, a "mutual understanding."[23] German Jews believed this understanding, this sympathy, had begun in the eighteenth century with men like Friedrich Schleiermacher. Schleiermacher spoke in 1799 to his "cultured friends" of the thing they despised (religion) and called it the basis of culture and nation.[24] Felix Theilhaber in 1921 wrote that only then, in the eighteenth century, did Judaism truly become a religious and consequently a cultural community, "bound to its environment by general ethical principles."[25] From then on German Jews could speak of their German culture that they had "drunk . . . with [their] mothers' milk," which formed an historical, traditional, spiritual, and cultural tie.[26] They believed Germany was formed and defined in that era by those ideals.

Weimar Germany seemed to cry out for such definitions. Despite the unilateral view that German Jews had of the Republic, it was riddled with paradoxes from the beginning: a republic, but an empire; religiously tolerant, yet torn almost from the start with desecrations of religious places; the home of enormous intellectual creativity and talents, but with a public that rejected them.[27] German Jews in Weimar fastened upon what they considered the essence of Germany. Again and again the CVZ characterized Germany as the teacher and bearer of the Enlightenment, of morality, tolerance, and humanism. Were these values alien to Germany? The answer was self-evident. Were they alien to Judaism? Again, a rhetorical question, answered in articles and books that rang with righteousness, sincerity, and conviction. "The moral teachings of Kant and the moral teachings of the Talmud, the pathos of Schiller and the pathos of the prophets, the language of Herder and the language of the Bible" were seen in harmony, indeed in unison, in Germany.[28] German culture possessed the same feeling as Old Testament culture, and German Jews brought the two together.[29]

As early as 1891 an anonymous author claimed that "Jews and Germans have individual, specific characteristics in common with each other."[30] That conclusion was an expression of deep-seated feelings on the part of Jewish

Germans. When German Jews spoke of the German Jewish symbiosis, they spoke in terms of "common characteristics" of the spirit. H. G. Adler called the "noblest fruit of the German Jewish symbiosis a Judaism which does not deny itself."[31] There was no need here for denial. Why deny one's self?

The Enlightenment was envisioned as the first insinuation of Jewry into *Deutschtum*. Few honest surveys of German culture, especially of German literature, exclude at least a mention of the role of German Jews in the Enlightenment and in the Romantic era that followed it. Theodore Fontane, not noted for his philosemitism,[32] acknowledged that German Jews were an essential part of Berlin and German culture through friendships, salons,and professional and private relationships.[33] In the twentieth century German Jews emphasized this 150-year-old role of the German Jew as promoter of and contributor to German culture. It is probably an exaggeration to consider German Jews absolutely essential to the Enlightenment and Romantic eras in Germany. Nevertheless, their participation was significant.

Goethe! The name seemed to bear magical powers for all Germans. Even more than Schiller he was unanimously considered to be Germany's greatest poet. Although they denounced other poets and artists, it is significant that even the most racist and conservative ideologues tried to adapt Goethe to their ideas.[34] Along with Lessing and Schiller, his name is liberally sprinkled throughout German Jewish literature of the 1920s and 1930s. If Jews had always been the people of the Bible or the Torah, *German* Jews were "the children of the Torah and Goethe."[35]

German Jews in the Weimar Republic could say that Goethe "was and still is heard" as the man perhaps more concerned with human culture than any other of his time.[36] Goethe prizes were celebrated among German Jews; the societies that bore his name abounded with German Jewish members; German Jews were among the greatest Goethe critics and scholars;[37] Goethe and Heine were praised together (with Heine considered a Jewish poet).[38] Julius Bab, one of the finest Goethe scholars in the Weimar Republic, discussed the great poet's personal and professional relationships with Jews.[39] In his review of Heinrich Teweles' *Goethe und die Juden*, Arthur Eloesser indignantly rejected Teweles' contentions that Goethe had been anti-Semitic. Goethe, wrote Eloesser, expressed hostility for Germans, both Christians and Jews, but not for Jews as Jews. Quite the contrary. He praised them as strong individuals, and saw in Judaism a "bravery and strength" lacking in the Christianity of his day.[40] By the use of numerous excerpts from Goethe's letters and works, Bab "proved . . . that in no sense was Goethe anti-Semitic."[41] Bab tried to establish irrefutably that Goethe had valued Jews as courageous, poetic, virtuous, "the most noble people of the earth," because they directed their messianism to the betterment of all men.[42]

Of all the great German intellects it was Goethe who allegedly "was the spiritual leader of all [the literary] salons." His ties to German Jews, especially to those women whose homes became meeting places for the eighteenth and nineteenth century intelligentsia, become apparent through that social medium. The hub of Germany's intellectual elite social life were the salons of Rahel Levin, Henriette Herz, Dorothea Veit, Marianne Meier, and others like them.[43] They were German Jewesses, and their homes were "the centre of cultural assimilation."[44] Goethe, the soul of Germany, German in his soul, whose works, *Geist*, and language were purely German, praised those Jewesses and admitted that Jews played a major role in his work.[45]

Goethe's goal, wrote literary critic Fritz Friedlander in 1932, was the integration of Germans and Jews through German and Jewish cultural coalescence.[46] It was for that reason that the salons of Berlin brought him joy. Friedlander strained to make Goethe a philosemite, and he probably magnified and dramatized Goethe's concern for the blending of *Deutschtum* and *Judentum*. Yet his article was indicative of efforts to anchor German Jews in the soul of Germany through the soul of Goethe. When Felix Goldmann described Jewish culture in Germany, he characterized it as concerned with world culture and mankind. Without explicit reference, his words echoed those he had used in describing Goethe.[47]

Schiller and Goethe were two members of what became for German Jews a sacred, secular trinity of German philosophers. To German Jews the "great German classics" and the spirit of the Enlightenment were typified in one man, the third member, more than any other. It is significant that an historical survey article in the *CVZ Monthly* mentioned Gotthold Effraim Lessing as the most important German thinker of all time.[48] More than Goethe or Schiller, Lessing seemed to embody what German Jews saw as the German Enlightenment and subsequently as the German *Geist*. Both Schiller and Goethe acknowledged intellectual, moral, and aesthetic debts to Lessing.[49]

Thomas Mann called Lessing the founder of a mythical type, the "true son and faithful knight" of the German Enlightenment,[50] the "classic" or prototypical German *Aufklärer*.[51] *Nathan the Wise* was more than once described by critics in the Weimar Republic as the culmination of the Enlightenment. For many who disagreed that *Nathan* was of such great importance, it was Lessing's *The Education of the Human Race* that assumed that position of high honor.[52]

Arnold Zweig, among the leading novelists and literary critics in Germany, viewed Lessing in an historical and philosophical, as well as aesthetic perspective. Zweig formulated a linear development in which Lessing stood among Luther, Wolff, the German Pietists, Goethe, and Beethoven.[53] It was illustrious company. It was German company. The Lessing Museum in Berlin housed not only Lessing treasures but memorabilia of Goethe, Schiller, and others like them. It was a house of the German Enlightenment, and it was Lessing's house.[54] In 1924 Zweig castigated those who denounced Lessing as "men who ignore the fact" that Lessing was a German master and a German genius.[55] Lessing's style, he said, was "the most personally German since Luther."[56] The man was a creator of a more German literature,[57] "a soldier of intellect, truth, tolerance, mankind, the magisterial Reason of the great Enlightenment, the wonderful spokesman of humanity, *an ambassador of the German character.*"[58]

Innumerable such statements illuminate the judgments of literary critics, historians, novelists, poets, philosophers, and journalists that Lessing was the "living individual embodiment" of the Enlightenment philosophy in all its rationalism, classicism, humanitarian idealism, and attendant ideas of tolerance and egalitarian freedom; and the essence of Germanism in the modern era.

More than those of his contemporaries, Lessing's works were not only designed as vehicles for abstract and general theories, but they were also fashioned to be applied to real and specific situations. Like most of the great eighteenth-century thinkers, Lessing dealt with the concepts of Love, Equality, and Justice. He also aimed his philosophy and words at more specific and distinct targets. The basic ethic of Lessing's life was religious tolerance, and his didactic dramas carried that message. It was that eternal moral which Zweig said made Lessing's memory lasting and immortal. *Nathan* was timeless, and "time has no power over him [Lessing]."[59]

Because of that ethic of tolerance, Lessing was the acknowledged leader of the movement for freedom and equality for Jews.[60] No single man of the Enlightenment seemed to have addressed his mind and general philosophic principles so clearly and specifically to the Jews. Lessing's plays, *Die Juden* and *Nathan the Wise,* opposed religious intolerance and for the first time on the European stage, presented Jews not as comical or villainous but as human and noble characters.[61] His tolerance was unique even for the Enlightenment, which breathed a tolerance born of compassion and pragmatism; "Lessing's tolerance was one of reverence."[62] After the production of *Nathan,* this reverence was or seemed obvious, and the Jews in Germany were grateful for all that. They seemed to love Lessing from then on for his idealization of their representative on stage. Nathan appeared to German Jews as correctly espousing their own ideals. Goethe acknowledged that reverence as well by calling Lessing's *Nathan* the bearer of "divine sentiments of patience and tolerance . . . [that] ever remain sacred and precious in the nation's eyes."[63]

Nathan was written with a "conscious pedagogical goal."[64] That goal was the realization of religious tolerance. But for Lessing, "religious" had new connotations. Although he appeared to have little respect for what he considered the stagnant, hollow, formal, organized religions, he was not Voltaire: he was neither atheist nor agnostic nor Deist. Over the door of the Lessing Museum was the inscription: "Enter and find here God."[65] He had, after all, been influenced by the Pietists at Halle. His father was a Protestant pastor, and he had been thoroughly schooled in theology. It was true that he had rejected the religion of his father along with all formalized religion. But Lessing separated religion from dogma. What remained after that severance was "religiosity," and "religiosity" was religion's saving grace. The truth revealed in religion had existed long before the Bible; thus his and the Enlightenment's mistrust of holy writ.[66] The religion of Reason was Lessing's confession. Reason was truth, and truth was eternal.

Lessing was a seeker not only of truth and reason but of religious certainty. In *The Education of the Human Race,* he expressed his belief in a revealed truth that had but to unfold in time—history—and through ideas—religions.[67] Perhaps nowhere is his belief in the existence of the eternal truth hidden and then revealed in religion better expressed than in *Nathan the Wise*. In the character of Nathan, Lessing resolved the tension and dualism between pure, absolute, rational truth and factual truth; between eternal and historical truth; between theory and practice. He found absolute logic and ethics to be eternal. Absolute Reason, he believed, was everywhere and was always the same—like God.[68]

Nathan showed Reason in action; he bridged the gap between theory and practice. It was through Nathan that Lessing voiced his ethical ideal of religion. Nathan was simultaneously a flesh-and-blood creation and a philosophic ideal. He spoke of the unity of mankind, individual membership in the human community, and universal tolerance for all religions and nationalities—for outsiders as well as insiders.

In the famous parable of the three rings, Nathan mirrored Lessing's own view that it is religious content and not form that is important.[69] The value of the rings (the three great religions) rests on the possessor's decision to live a life that finds favor in the eyes of God and man. The choice of confession, of form, of ring, is irrelevant. The external form may be different, but each of the three religions contains the same eternal lessons of morality, love, wisdom, freedom, and tolerance. They are all round. No religion conveys these lessons in its ceremonial form, explained Nathan, but all do to some degree in their original teachings, in their content.

The value of religion, then, was in its theoretical content and in its historical form. The form became significant because it controlled or influenced action in life.[70] The historical form was the concrete form of life and deed; applications of religious content to an historical present.

There is little need to belabor the analogies between Lessing's ethical ideals and those ideas in theoretical Judaism as described by authors such as Michael Guttmann, Hermann Cohen, and Ismar Elbogen. Those men logically and easily adapted Lessing's principles on religion and adopted them and him as their own. Because of his ideas expressed in *Nathan*, Lessing was later lauded by a CVZ author for dedication to the sanctity of the individual.[71] Lessing had seen the importance of history, tradition, language, common fate, and common beliefs and ideals in the composition of a *Volk*. Never had those feelings of tolerance, "individualism and *Volk* been so deeply and heartfelt than in Lessing."[72]

Nathan's ethics and wisdom were Lessing's. Nathan the man was at least partly Lessing. Nathan the Wise was a composite of individuals and an embodiment of a philosophy. But perhaps more than anything or anyone else, Nathan was a harmonious blend of Lessing and Moses Mendelssohn. Beyond Lessing's ethics there was a strong, explicit, personal, human link between him and the Old Testament. Ernst Cassirer, for example saw the Judaism in Lessing's philosophy, ethics, and religion as a meeting of the minds between Lessing and Mendelssohn, another great culture hero of the German Jews in the Weimar Republic.

Mendelssohn was the link, or so it seemed, between Lessing and German Jews. Any discussion of Lessing's thoughts on religion is incomplete without Mendelssohn. The two were close friends and spiritually attuned to each other. Mendelssohn received praise not only from Lessing but from other contemporaries. Kant wrote to him that, despite philosophical differences, "your genius marks the start of a new epoch in philosophy."[73] Christian Dohm's famous work[74] had allegedly been influenced by his contact with Mendelssohn. Dohm saw Mendelssohn as the symbol of the potential resources in all German Jews, which he believed might be tapped, used, by Germans.

Mendelssohn, then, was to be considered responsible for the beginning of Christian German liberalism in the eighteenth century.[75] Lessing referred to him as "really a Jew . . . a man who has great strength in all languages, mathematics, world knowledge, and poetry. I see him as a credit to his nation [?]"[76] Lessing apparently patterned Nathan after Mendelssohn: he saw him as the personification of the Enlightenment in his "world philosophy," his human reason, and his understanding.

The contrast in early education between Lessing and Mendelssohn is worth noting. They came from radically divergent backgrounds; the one raised in the atmosphere of Protestant theology, the other among the works of Moses Maimonides and the Talmudic commentators. Yet they represented the same type of religion—Vernunftsreligion, religion of reason. There was a recognition of identical striving and attitude.[77] Cassirer called it "amazing" that this should be the case and explained it as a product of "mutual education."[78] Lessing possessed and conveyed to Mendelssohn his sense of history and knowledge of philology. In return, Mendelssohn showed his friend and spiritual compatriot the heart of the Old Testament logic, philosophy, and metaphysics.[79] Together they were Nathan.

Judaism to Mendelssohn and to Nathan was above custom and ritual. It was Mendelssohn's idea of revealed law, the unity of morality (Sittlichkeit), not the uniqueness of custom (Sitten), that sparked a sympathetic flame in Lessing. Mendelssohn honored the memory of Christian Wolff, but saw the source of philosophical rationalism not in Wolff or Plato but in Maimonides and earlier in the Old Testament. The Bible was revelation of Reason, "the eternal truth." There were no conflicts between Reason and this religion.[80] It was the end of Lessing's quest: Vernunftsreligion. Judaism brought history and reason together and eliminated the chains of dogma.[81] Hermann Cohen would later recognize the same ideas, the same harmony between the idealism of Judaism and the idealism of Kant; Ernst

Cassirer would extol the similarities between the messianism of the Old Testament and the messianic optimism of Lessing in *The Education of the Human Race*.[82]

Mendelssohn was a member of the Enlightenment elite. German Jews in the twentieth century tried to establish without doubt that he was one of the unequivocally *German* Enlightenment greats. Ernst Cassirer placed him as a bridge between Lessing and Goethe on the one hand, and Herder, Schleiermacher, and Hegel on the other.[83] Arthur Eloesser compared him to Kant and Herder in the depth of his Germanness.[84] By such associations, he embodied the synthesis of Protestant and philosophical ideals of freedom and universal reason with the universal moral truth of the Old Testament. Perhaps no other man of their collective past received such massive attention from German Jews in the Weimar Republic.

In the first issue of the *Zeitschrift für die Geschichte der Juden in Deutschland* (1929), there were no fewer than eight articles on Mendelssohn.[85] Each subsequent issue had at least one article about him or a review of a book on him.[86] On his two-hundredth birthday there were celebrations in German Jewish synagogues, speeches at public gatherings, sermons in churches, *Festschriften* and lectures by both Jews and non-Jews in his honor. A *CVZ* special issue bore an ornate front page with a picture of the philosopher gazing benignly and wisely at German Jewish readers; beneath the portrait stood the inscription: "Moses Mendelssohn, the First German Jew, the Spiritual Father of Our Equality, the Strong Forger of German Intellectual Life," written in bold lettering.[87] One article in that issue, "Legende und Charakter," began: "The father was a Hebrew writer. The son was a German author."[88] The rest seems to have been commentary.

To his German Jewish admirers, Mendelssohn exemplified the "cultural Germanification" of Germany's Jews.[89] That he was Lessing's friend was, of course, crucial. The title of "First German Jew" was based partly on the idea that Mendelssohn, "the best of the Jews," joined in lasting friendship with Lessing, "the best of the Germans."[90] But that friendship was not the only bridge to his Germanness. Before the eighteenth century—before Mendelssohn—German Jewry was dominated by "Jewish" culture. The Enlightenment changed all that, and Mendelssohn was considered the man most responsible for dragging Jews out of their self-imposed cultural isolation as he fought for emancipation on other fronts. One journalist in 1930 referred to him as "the Luther of the German Jews."[91]

His goal was incorporation of Jews into the German-European cultural community, and the first step was language. Lessing allegedly brought Mendelssohn to the German language.[92] Language was the first key to the multiple lock that opened the door to Germanism. Mendelssohn the educator taught the universal values of Truth, Beauty, and Goodness: he taught them not in Hebrew or Yiddish but in German. When Lessing called Mendelssohn "a credit to his nation," when Heinrich Stern wrote that Mendelssohn "brought to his nation the conviction of the Bible," when Mendelssohn himself commented on unjust criticism of Lessing's *Die Juden* that he felt "humiliation for our harassed nation,"[93] one cannot be certain to which "nation" they referred.

The CVZ viewed Mendelssohn in a specific context of what it meant to be German. It perceived the German spirit of the eighteenth century as supremely cosmopolitan. Mendelssohn was German in his fulfillment of the knowledgeable, classical, cosmopolitan Enlightenment stereotype. In that cosmopolitan spirit bred of the Enlightenment, he undertook the Germanizing of German Jews by renewing and modernizing their religious values and making them "ripe for emancipation,"[94] Achievement of emancipation became a product of the synthesis of Jewish ideals and the "consciousness of the times."[95]

Mendelssohn was labeled a *philosophe*: he was mentioned with all the German *philosophes* from Wolff and

Leibniz to Kant and Lessing. But he was identified through association with others who were not German nationals or German greats. Like Lessing, Mendelssohn was allegedly "Socratic." The memorial issue of the CVZ depicts Mendelssohn's silhouette with his friend Lavater's comment as caption: "Socratic—like Plato, Abraham, and Moses."[96] A painting in the same issue portrays Mendelssohn's cameo facing Socrates; behind a skull that symbolizes eternal values and truths. Hermann Cohen discussed Mendelssohn in the context of philosophical similarities to Plato, Socrates, Maimonides, Lessing, Kant, and the biblical patriarchs.

How does identification with Greek philosophers grant a German pedigree? Peter Gay has described the men of the Enlightenment as emulators of the Greeks.[97] Classical scholars and philologists have shown fundamental affinities between Greek and Hebrew thought, epistemology, language, and general *Weltanschauung*.[98] It was in this vein that German Jews identified with the German Enlightenment *philosophes*. In this interpretation Lessing converged with Maimonides in their common bond with Plato. Through the German Enlightenment, German Jews wound their way to the Greeks, and from them to the Hebrews and the Old Testament. Herder, to whom German Jews would turn to express their nationalism,[99] seemed to confirm the assertion of Greek and Hebrew similarities in his works, comparing Hebrew and Greek myths, legends, poetry, and language.[100]

The comparisons to the Greeks are therefore significant as another identification of German Jews with the German Enlightenment masters. To twentieth-century German Jews, Socrates, with Mendelssohn and other *philosophes*, represented the "philosophy of a healthy human understanding,"[101] the philosophy of the world, the philosophy of Greece *and* Israel.

None of these philosophies was rare in the eighteenth

century. None was superficial. They were united by their ideals. It was Germany's honor, dignity, and pride that she had renewed the ancient wisdom of Socrates, Plato, and, through Mendelssohn, of Abraham and Moses.[102] It was, in the eyes of Weimar's Jews, an equation of the essence of German with the essence of Jewish. Those who proclaimed that equation were Weimar's German Jewish patriots.

The worship of the age of the German Enlightenment and its leaders critically affected the actions of German Jews in the nineteenth and twentieth centuries. In 1932 Ernst Johannsen, a non-Jew, wrote that the Jews of Germany for years had used a 'naïve method of defense" against anti-Semitism, based on misconceptions of Germany and Germans.[103] The nature of that defense, he said, had been and continued to be apologetic: German Jews found excuses for the anti-Semites.[104] Eternal waiting for the "good time" when anti-Semitism would be no more was frustrating to Johannsen, but, he said, apparently not to the victims themselves.[105]

Anti-Semitism had, of course, frustrated its victims. But Johannsen's barbs against the Jewish community's methods of defense were justified. The defense was naïve and revealed again a view that German Jews held of non-Jewish Germans. It assumed that the Enlightenment values of scientific, rational understanding were equally respected and acknowledged by all Germans. It assumed that the power of empirical knowledge and the consequent solution to a problem or "question" was as readily discernible by non-Jewish Germans as by Jewish Germans. It assumed that education—if not of the human race, at least of Germans—was the key to all problems. It assumed, finally, that the nation of the Enlightenment would accept an enlightened study of the Jewish Question and would cease the nonsense or irrational criticism of fellow men—of fellow Germans. In short, German Jews involved in the fight against anti-Semitism projected their own intellectual values onto *all* Germans.

Liberal Germans perceived the age of the Enlightenment as the foundation of the liberal ethic for all German citizens and as the turning point for Jewry in Germany. To German Jews and German liberals, its standard-makers were men like Lessing and Medelssohn. They believed that it established the human right to freedom and that its leaders possessed an ethical verisimilitude with Old Testament archetypes. It was the Jewish dream come true: the harmonious synthesis of German and Jewish cultures. That identity of values fostered the lasting belief that "the *ideal of humanity* [is] equally German and Jewish."[106] A non-Jew writing in 1918 for *Im Deutschen Reich* (the forerunner of the CVZ) agreed with his Jewish contemporaries that German idealism was the modern form of Old Testament prophecy. The value of the national ideal was not a new element, but had been observed by Herder as it progressed toward the "general-human." Germanness in 1918—as it had been earlier—was rooted not only in Greece but in the Bible, which had demanded love of fatherland as a concomitant to love of mankind.[107]

To their panoply of Hebraic spiritual fathers—Abraham, Jacob, Joseph, Moses, Moses Maimonides—German Jews could now add German spiritual fathers—Goethe, Schiller, Lessing, and Moses Mendelssohn (the third Moses).[108] Here, then, were the identical twins: Jew and German identical in morality, ethics, philosophy of history, and cultural values. It was a cultural identification.

NOTES

[1]Salo W. Baron, *A Social and Religious History of the Jews*, 3 vols. (New York: Columbia University Press, 1937), II, 163–164ff.; Rosenthal, "Trends in the Jewish Population"; Scholem, "Germans and Jews"; Scholem, *Deutsche und Juden*, pp. 22–34.

[2]Scholem, "Germans and Jews"; Baron, *A Social and Religious History*, II, 212–217.

[3]Rosenberg, "Jedoch als Deutscher schäm ich mich."

[4]Josef Feiner, "Christian Thomasius, der erste Verkünder religiöser Duldung in Deutschland," *CVZ Monthly* I (December 1928).

[5]Ibid.; J. G. Robertson, *A History of German Literature*, ed. Edna Pardie, 3rd ed. (London, Edinburgh: William Blackwood & Son, Ltd., 1959), pp. 204–205.

[6]Paul Wiegler, "Deutsche Aufklärung," *CVZ*, VIII (August 30, 1929).

[7]Ibid.

[8]"Before the Decision," *CVZ*, IV (January 29, 1925).

[9]Goldmann, *Der Jude*, p. 46.

[10]Wiegler, "Deutsche Aufklärung."

[11]Goldmann, *Der Jude*, p. 48.

[12]Ludwig Geiger, *Die deutsche Literatur und die Juden* (Berlin: Reimer, 1910), pp. 125–160; Scholem, *Deutsche und Juden*.

[13]Friedrich Schiller, *Kabale und Liebe*, ed. Elizabeth M. Wilkinson and L. A. Willoughby (Oxford: Basil Blackwell, 1968), p. xviii; Schiller, *Don Carlos*, in *The Classic Theatre*, II, ed. Eric Bentley (Garden City: Anchor Books, 1959); cf. also Arthur Eloesser, *Das bürgerliche Drama* (Berlin: 1898), p. 80.

[14]Samuel Meisels, *Deutsche Klassiker im Ghetto* (Wien: Verlag Die Neuzeit, 1922), pp. 9ff.; Scholem, *Deutsche und Juden*. Evidence of this is further substantiated by Siegmund Kaznelson, "Verlag und Buchhandel," in Kaznelson, pp. 131–146.

[15]Eloesser, *Das bürgerliche Drama*, p. 19; Koppell Pinson, *Modern Germany, Its History and Civilization*, 2nd ed. (New York & London: Macmillan Co., 1966), pp. 13–22; Hajo Holborn, *A History of Germany*, 3 vols. (New York: Alfred A. Knopf, 1967), II, 333.

[16]"Unsere deutscher Heimat: Alte jüdische Kunst in Bayern," *CVZ Monthly*, I (February 1928).

[17]Paucker, "Der jüdische Abwehrkampf."

[18]*Juden und Judentum in deutschen Briefen aus drei Jahrhunderten*, ed. Franz Kobler (Vienna: Saturn Verlag, 1935), p. 52.

[19]Albert Lewkowitz, "Judentum und Kulturidee," *CVZ Monthly*, I (March 1928); cf. Cohen, *Moses Ben Maimon*, pp. 90–93.

[20]G. Mosse, *Germans and Jews*, pp. 171–225; Cohen, *Deutschtum und Judentum*, p. 10.

[21]Otto Flake, "Zum jüdischen Problem," *Der Neue Merkur*, V, No. 5 (August 1921) 297–317.

[22]Ibid.

[23]John Layard, "Identification with the Sacrificial Animal," *Eranos Jahrbuch*, XXIV (1955), 341–406.

[24]Schleiermacher, *Speeches*, p. 92, passim.

[25]Theilhaber, *Der Untergang*, p. 41.

[26]Hans Baer, "Für Deutschtum und Judentum. Stolz sein!" *CVZ*, XII (June 22, 1933).

109

[27]Peter Gay, *Weimar Culture. The Outsider as Insider* (New York: Harper & Row, 1968).

[28]Selma Stern-Täubler, "Zeitbild vom Judentum," *CVZ*, VII (August 30, 1929).

[29]Ernst Lissauer, "Der deutsche Jude und das deutsche Schriftum," *CVZ*, XII (June 22, 1933).

[30]*Civis Germanus Sum*, p. 22.

[31]Adler, *Die Juden in Deutschland*, pp. 159–160.

[32]Roy Pascal, *The German Novel* (London: Methuen & Co., 1956), pp. 178ff.; Ernest K. Bramsted, *Aristocracy and the Middle-Class in Germany. Social Types in German Literature 1830–1900* (Chicago: University of Chicago Press, 1964), pp. 262–268; G. Mosse, *The Crisis of German Ideology*, pp. 18–19, 135.

[33]Bramsted, *Aristocracy and the Middle-Classes*, p. 263; Eloesser, "Literature," in Kaznelson, pp. 1–67.

[34]See, for example, Franz Koch, "Goethe and die Juden," *Schriften des Reichsinstitutus für Geschichte des neuen Deutschlands*, Band II, *Forschungen zur Judenfrage*, 8 vols. (Hamburg: Hanseatische Verlag-anstalt, 1937), 116–143; Roland V. Layton, Jr., "The *Völkischer Beobachter*, 1920–1933: The Nazi Party Newspaper in the Weimar Era," *Central European History*, III, No. 4 (December 1970), 353–a1382.

[35]Gruenwald, "*Der Anfang der Reichsvertretung*," *Deutsches Judentum: Aufsteig und Krise*, pp. 315–325.

[36]Goldschmidt, "Deutschtum und Judentum. Zu den Grundlage unseres Seins."

[37]Samuel Meisels, *Goethe im Ghetto* (Wein: Verlag Die Neuzeit, 1932); "Goethe Jahrbuch," *CVZ*, IV (September 18, 1925); "Ein offenes Wort," speech delivered by Heinrich Hirsnh on receiving the Goethe Plaque, *CVZ Monthly*, IV (October 1932).

[38]William Rose, *Men, Myths, and Movements in German Literature* (London: George Allen & Unwin, 1931), pp. 157–180; Julius Bab, *Goethe und die Juden* (Berlin: Philo Verlag, 1926), p. 22; Eloesser, "Literatur"; Bab, "War Goethe Antisemit?" *CVZ*, XI (March 18, 1932); cf. Koch, "Goethe und die Juden" for anti-Semitic denials of Goethe's and Heine's friendship or similarities.

[39]Bab, *Goethe und die Juden*, pp. 2, 8, passim.

[40]Arthur Eloesser, "Der geschundene Goethe," review of Heinrich Teweles, *Goethe und die Juden*, *CVZ*, IV (June 19, 1925).

[41]Bab, *Goethe und die Juden*, p. 35; Bab, "War Goethe Antisemit?"; Bab, *Leben und Tod des deutschen Judentums*, p. 15.

[42]Bab, *Lieben und Tod des deutschen Judentums*, p. 14.

[43]Abraham Myerson and Isaac Goldberg, *The German Jew: His Share in Modern Culture* (New York: Alfred A. Knopf, 1933), pp. 122f. Selma Stern-Täubler, "The First Generation of Emancipated Jews," *Leo Baeck Yearbook*, XV (London, New York, Jerusalem: East and West Library, 1970), 3–40; Osborne, *Germany and Her Jews*, pp. 65–68; Stonehill, *The Jewish Contribution*, pp. 36, 89.

[44]Fritz Friedlander, Fritz Engel, Käte Hamburger, "Verkünder des Goe-

theschen Geistes ... in der Literatur, auf dem Theatre, und in dem Salons," *CVZ*, XI (March 18, 1932); Friedlander, "Ein Charakterbild in der Geschichte. Zu Wilhelm Grau: Wilhelm von Humboldt," *CVZ*, XIV (July 11, 1935); Eloesser, "Literatur."

⁵Meisels, *Goethe im Ghetto*, pp. 2, 9, passim; Paul Wiegler, "Die Rahel," *CVZ*, IX (April 25, 1930); "Rahel Levin," *CVZ*, XII (March 2, 1933); Bab, *Goethe und die Juden*, p. 29; Myerson and Goldberg, p. 122.

[46]Friedlander, "Verkünder des Goetheschen Geistes."

[47]Goldmann, *Der Jude*, pp. 54, 49.

[48]Zielensiger, "German Jews in the German Economy."

[49]E. L. Stahl, *Friedrich Schiller's Drama: Theory and Practice* (Oxford: Clarendon Press, 1954), p. 49; Paul Bockmann, "Die innere Form in Schillers Jugenddramen," *Dichtung und Volkstum*, XXXV 1934); Schiller, *Kabale und Liebe*, p. xiv; Robertson, *A History of German Literature*, p. 287.

[50]Thomas Mann, "Lessing," *Essays of Three Decades*, trans. H. T. Lowe-Porter (New York: Alfred A. Knopf, 1948), pp. 189–201.

[51]Ibid.

[52]Pinson, *Modern Germany*, p. 13; Wiegler, "Deutsche Aufklärung"; Peter Gay, *The Enlightenment, An Interpretation. The Rise of Modern Paganism* (New York: Alfred A. Knopf, 1967), pp. 38, 197; Meisels, *Deutsche Klassiker*.

[53]Arnold Zweig, "Versuch über Lessing" (1922), *Essays. Erster Band, Literatur und Theater* (Berlin: Aufbau-Verlag, 1959), pp. 41–57.

[54]Ernst Lissauer, "Für das Lessing Museum," *CVZ*, XII (January 3, 1933).

[55]Zweig, "Das Dauernde" (1924), *Essays*, pp. 62–79.

[56]Ibid.; cf. Gay, *The Enlightenment*, p. 14. Gay, not unlike Zweig, attributes the structuring and perfecting of a purely German linguistic form and style to Lessing.

[57]Zweig, "Das Dauernde," Gay, *The Enlightenment*, p. 14; H. B. Garland, *Lessing, the Founder of Modern German Literature* (London: Macmillan & Co., 1962), Introduction.

[58]Zweig, "Versuch über Lessing" (italics added). In the same essay, Zweig refers to Lessing as the representative of the "captivating possibilities of the German nature."

[59]Zweig, "Das Vergangliche" (1922), *Essays*, pp. 58–62.

[60]Stern, *Warum sind wir Deutsche?*, p. 5.

[61]Pinson, *Modern Germany*, pp. 13ff.; Zweig, "Das Dauernde"; it should be noted that some recent interpretations of the Enlightenment consider it as the beginning of modern anti-Semitism and racism. This is a dubious thesis at best, but especially so for the German Enlightenment, which is often distinguished from the French and British for its unequivocal denunciation of intolerance like that of, say, Voltaire.

[62]Ernst Cassirer, "Die Idee der Religion bei Lessing und Mendelssohn," *Festgabe zum Zehnjahrigen Bestehen der Akademie für die Wissenschaft des Judentums, 1919–1929* (Berlin: Akademie Verlag, 1929), pp. 22–41.

[63]Mann, "Lessing"; Bab, *Lieben und Tod.*, p. 25.

[64]Mann, "Lessing."

[65]Lissauer, "Für das Lessing Museum."

[66]Hannah Arendt-Stern, "Aufklärung und Judenfrage," Zeitschrift für Geschichte der Juden in Deutschland, IV (1932), 65–77.

[67]Gotthold Effraim Lessing, Die Erziehung des Menschengeschlechts, Gesammelte Werke, ed. Paul Rilla, 10 vols. (Berlin: Aufbau Verlag, 1956), VIII, 590–615; Eliade, Myth and Reality, pp. 180–181.

[68]Cassirer, "Die Idee der Religion."

[69]Garland, Lessing, p. 167; Lessing, Nathan the Wise, trans. W. Steel (London: M. M. Dent & Sons, 1930), Act III, Scene viii. The parable is Nathan's response to Saladin's threatening question of what is the greatest of the three major religions. The story of the three sons, each of whom was given one ring by their father, signifies the essential sameness of the three religions (Judaism, Christianity, and Mohammedanism) and the common bond (one father). Cf. Gay, The Enlightenment, pp. 62, 172–173.

[70]Lessing, Nathan III. viii; Cassirer, "Die Idee der Religion"; Lessing, Die Erziehung des Menschengeschlechts, esp. §3.

[71]Ernst von Aster, "Über allem der Mensch," CVZ, IX (February 21, 1930).

[72]Ibid.

[73]Heinrich Levy, "Der Philosoph," CVZ, VIII (August 30, 1929).

[74]See Appendix A: Dramatis Personae.

[75]Bab, Leben und Tod, p. 24; Stern-Täubler, "The First Generation"; Baron, Social and Religious History of the Jews, II, 210, 213–214, passim.

[76]Hugo Lachmanski, "Freund Lessing," CVZ, VIII (August 30, 1929); Eloesser, "Literatur."

[77]Cassirer, "Die Idee der Religion."

[78]Ibid.

[79]Ibid.

[80]Guttmann, Philosophies of Judaism, pp. 291–303.

[81]Arendt-Stern, "Aufklärung und Judenfrage."

[82]Cassirer, "Die Idee der Religion"; Cohen, Die religiösen Bewegung, pp. 9–10; Cohen, Moses Ben Maimon, p. 104; Lessing, Die Erziehung des Menschengeschlechts.

[83]Cassirer, "Die Idee der Religion."

[84]Eloesser, "Literatur."

[85]Zeitschrift für die Geschichte der Juden in Deutschland, I (1929).

[86]Ibid., Vols. I–IX.

[87]CVZ, VIII (August 30, 1929).

[88]Leo Hirsch, "Legende und Charakter," CVZ, VIII (August 30, 1929).

[89]Stern, Warum sind wir Deutsche? p. 6.

[90]Benno Jakob, "Der erste deutsche Jude," CVZ, VIII (August 30, 1929).

[91]Stern-Täubler, "The First Generation"; Stefan Behr, Der Bevölkerungsrückgang der deutschen Juden (Frankfurt am Main: J. Kauffmann Verlag, 1932), p. 30.

112

[92]Cassirer, "Die Idee der Religion"; Lachmanski, "Freund Lessing"; H. Stern, "Der Erzieher," *CVZ*, VIII (August 30, 1929).

[93]Moses Mendelssohn to Aron Emmerich Gumpertz, Berlin, June, 1754, in *Juden und Judentum in deutschen Briefen aus drei Jahrhunderten*, p. 56.

[94]Fritz Friedlander, "Der Reformator," *CVZ*, VIII (August 30, 1929).

[95]Max Wiener, "Moses Mendelssohn und die religiösen Gestaltung des Judentums in 19 Jahrhundert," *Zeitschrift für die Geschichte der Juden in Deutschland*, I (1929), 201–212.

[96]*CVZ*, VIII (August 30, 1929).

[97]Gay, *The Enlightenment*; see also E. M. Butler, *The Tyranny of Greece Over Germany* (Boston: Beacon Press, 1958).

[98]See, for example, Thorlief Boman, *Hebrew Thought Compared with Greek* (New York: W. W. Norton, 1970); Cyrus H. Gordon, *The Common Background of Greek and Hebrew Civilizations* (New York: W. W. Norton, 1965); and the most interesting, David Diringer, *The Alphabet. A Key to the History of Mankind*, rev. with the collaboration of Reinhold Regensburger, 2 vols. 3rd ed. (Great Britain: Alden & Mowbray, 1968), I.

[99]See Chap. vi.

[100]Herder, "Jüdischen Parabeln," *Werke*, II, 187–228.

[101]Heinrich Levy, "Der Philosoph."

[102]Ibid.; F. Wachsner, "Auch wir müssen von den anderen lernen!" *CVZ*, VIII (September 27, 1929).

[103]Ernst Johannsen, "Über den Antisemitismus als gegebene Tatsache," *Klärung*, pp. 11–30.

[104]Ibid.

[105]Ibid.

[106]W. Kinkel, "Humanität!" (Memorial to Hermann Cohen), *CVZ Monthly*, I (May 1928).

[107]Dr. Beerman-Heilbronn, "Unsere Propheten und der Völkerbund," *Im Deutschen Reich*, XXIV, No. 12 (December 1918), 449–451.

[108]Theodore Lessing, *Deutschland und seine Juden*, p. 30.

113

VI

In Search of a Hero

The mighty properties which he ascribed to Him were probably
God's original possession, Abraham was not their creator. But was
he not so after all, in a certain sense, when he recognized them,
preached them, and by thinking made them real? The mighty
properties of God were indeed something objective, existing out-
side of Abraham; but at the same time they were also in him and
of him.

THOMAS MANN, *Joseph and His Brothers*

Thomas Mann called Lessing a "mythical type."[1] The
ramifications of that statement are almost infinite. Mann
treated mythology not as legend and fairy tale, but as the
serious culture creator and supporter that it had been for
archaic man.[2] Mythopoeic thought of the sort Mann described can afford a framework within which the "how"
and the "why" of German Jewish defensive action against
anti-Semitism can be explained.[3] The force of German
Jews' faith, their conviction in their Germanness, was not
simply a rebirth of religion in the form of secular ethics. It
was a response to a psychological urge. Their attitudes,
postures, and actions conform to the principles of my-
thology-based life. The specifics or forms are their own, but
the principles of mythology provide a theoretical system
for explanation of both their ideas and their deeds.

Myth, with its history and religion, its mental and physical powers, its illusion and reality, immures the critical
elements of cultural life. Malinowski as well as Freud

114

recognized the great importance of mythopoesis for culture (or civilization).[4] Neither of them was so naive as to believe that the mythical mind and the viability of myth were confined to "primitive" or tribal societies. Mythology has contemporary relevance. Carl G. Jung claimed to have discovered that archaic psychic processes were active not only in primitive man, but in "every civilized human being ... at the deeper levels of his psyche."[5] Freud, in different terms, seemed to concur with this judgment in his essays dealing with art, religion, love, and culture, and especially in his final work, *Moses and Monotheism*.[6]

Independent of the study of mythology, some psychoanalytic theorists have described a process of identification that is identical in most respects to mythopoeic identification with archetypes. Identity in archaic societies came through a process of identification with archetypes or heroes who served as models for behavior.[7] Freud formulated the process of identification as "the assimilation of one ego to another," clarifying in a footnote that he meant "one ego coming to resemble another."[8] The consequence, Freud wrote, was that the first ego "takes up into itself" the second, the "superego" or "ego-ideals."[9]

This identification with an ego-ideal is analogous to archaic identification with an archetype. Both archetype and ego-ideal are models, heroes, or exemplary moral figures. Without ego-ideals societies cannot exist, said Freud, and the dictum holds true for archetypes in archaic societies.

To maintain the survival of a culture or community, therefore, archetypal acts require emulation. Because he repeats the acts of the archetype, an individual can identify with that archetype and gain an identity. Freud conceived of the ego-ideal as irresistible, with a power that forced imitation. Similarly, myth in archaic societies provided models for human behavior which had to be believed and emulated because they legitimized life, gave it meaning, purpose, and value.[10]

115

Identity in myth-believing cultures was achieved by more than imitation, however. Even Freud acknowledged that identification was more than "mere imitation." The wearer of the mask, by identifying with the hero, became (at least in his own mind) the original.[11] The life of a "collective image" or archetype is not simply reflected upon, but is lived as men are unconsciously animated by it.[12] Belief in a mythology involved more than commemoration of archetypal lives; it demanded participation in those lives by identifying with them completely and becoming contemporary with the archetypes.[13]

Wilhelm Reich seemed to grasp implicitly the potential similarities between psychoanalytic and mythological identification when he redefined psychoanalytic identification as a "process by which a person begins to *feel at one* with another person . . . and in his fantasy puts himself in the other's place."[14] In other words, the first becomes one with the second. Reich agreed with Freud that the process involved erection of a psychic reality and that it begins as one "being like" the other. But gradually, he continued, *true* identification occurs when an individual—not unlike archaic man and his archetype—believes he actually is the ego-ideal.[15]

This is a crucial concept, and one that Thomas Mann recognized as essential for an understanding of myth and mythical consciousness. Mann spoke of the phenomenon of mythological identification as "the lived life." The key idea of the "lived life" is "life as moving in others' steps as identification,"[16] as a lived myth or archetypal life that relies upon a "making present of the past."[17] Thus, life in the myth is not simply a simulation of a similar situation, but is also an actual reliving of a paradigmatic life.[18]

Mann, like Freud and Reich, believed that within civilization or culture, individuals live their lives through the impact of exemplary individuals with whom they identify and who symbolize achievements to be emulated.[19] But it

116

was Geza Roheim who most clearly and simply defined and applied psychoanalytic theories of identification to cultural, group analysis. He went beyond Freud and even Mann as he more directly addressed the question of the unconscious motivations and reasons for the process of social or group identification. Following his thesis that "human groups are actuated by 'group ideals,'" Roheim determined that by identifying with "good" ideals, men gain a deeply desired sense of security.[20] Insecurity is therefore the motivating force behind the process, and security is its end product.

Erik Erikson corroborated Roheim's thesis in his studies of identity crises. He traced insecurity feelings to a lack of identity, and lack of identity to lack of identifications.[21] Malinowski, like Freud and Roheim, considered the repetition or emulation of paradigmatic acts and lives to be of prime importance to culture. "There is no doubt," he wrote, "that the main cultural function of mythology is the establishment of precedent," which comes from a "true past" and "which holds promise of a better future."[22] Myth is evocative, recalling and calling up a golden era to be reborn through its heroes. That is the "better future" it promises. Among the functions that Joseph Campbell attributed to myth in his massive four-volume work, The Masks of God, was enforcement of a moral order.[23] That enforcement provided protection of an individual's integrity by granting him both individual and social identity.[24] It also provided security for the individual within a cultural environment.

Despite their differences, all these men concerned with the study and dynamics of culture agreed that membership in a group gives identity through identifications. In light of the thesis that identification brings security, it is significant that a CVZ editorial of January 1932 used the term "inner security" when identifying the German consciousness

117

of German Jews with that of the *Deutsche Adelsgenos-senschaft*, the German Society of Nobles, and basing the identification on common intellectual and national ancestors.[25]

If archetypes embody the essence of German culture, German Jews could identify exactly their position in that culture by knowing exactly the nature of German archetypes. If they could share the fixed point, they could share the entire cultural identity. Arnold Zweig spoke of Lessing as eternal and "a man of today and of the future."[26] What the "real" Lessing was like was irrelevant in this context. In popular memory the distinction between self and image is often blurred. It was not the self of Lessing but the image of Lessing that was the directing force, the conviction that was psychically real and that influenced life. Perception determined identification, identification determined identity and activity. Reification, the mental materializing of Lessing, and the repetition of his life-style conformed to primitive peoples' reification and repetition of the paradigmatic gestures of their archetypes. German Jews and some German non-Jews like Thomas Mann thought of Lessing in a soothing light and, in Mann's words, "by thinking made [him] real."[27]

Just as they did Lessing, German Jews molded Schiller, Mendelssohn, Goethe, and others into concepts and made them intellectual institutions. They were accepted as the exemplary models of German culture by the majority of German Jews as a group. This is crucial to their importance. The "primary image" (*urtumliche Bild*) or archetype (*Urbild*) is always collective, common to a people or to a period of history.[28] Again, the "real" men were of secondary importance to the vague, misty, and mysterious popular recollection. Collective memory is "anhistorical" because it concerns "categories instead of historical events, archetypes instead of historical personages," institutions instead of individuals.[29] As a group, then, German Jews partook of "cultural" Germany by agreeing upon German archetypes.

118

Instead of the collective acceptance of institutions,[30] culture now converts to the collective acceptance and propagation of certain archetypes or ideals and their attendant myths. Those myths provided axiomatic values. And German Jews believed that a marriage of cultures, a blending together, like a merging, had occurred between Germans and Jews in Germany because *all* their lives were circumscribed by an order ordained by a *German* system of axiomatic values that had been originated by German archetypes, which reaffirmed an ancient system originated by Old Testament archetypes.

Because they are sunk in the depths of collective memory, buried deep in the minds and nature of "collective representations," origins of the social order as defined by myth are at best hazy. Origins are an historical problem, a problem of the bottomless well of the past. That problem plagued, among others, Thomas Mann. He sought origins by venturing into the well and found himself engaged in a "deluded pilgrimage ... an onward-luring hoax,"[31] a descent into hell, a protean task whose end was to remain an insoluble mystery forever buried in the unfathomable collective memory.

In *fact* (reality), it was a pointless quest, Mann conceded, for what mattered was existence, not origins. Men needed local myth, however, be it Abraham or Atlantis, to assuage *Angst* about their origins and their place in the universe.[32] Because the myth believer learned about origins, he knew who he was, why he was, where he was from.[33] His experience was organized by a convincing world image and system that fulfilled a fundamental psychological urge.[34] The quest may have been pointless, unfathomable, deluded, insoluble, but it was humanly necessary. What matters is some fixed point in the mind—the collective mind. Such a point was "the beginning of all things—that is, of all that mattered" to a particular individual (for example, Joseph) or to a group (for example, the Hebrews).[35]

The temporal (or atemporal) fixed point in primitive or

archaic mythology is the mythical era, the *Urzeit*.[36] It was the original time—the time of origin; the beginning of morality, values, society, and culture. Archetypal men, fixed points of another sort, lived in that Creative Time, molded the particular culture, and gave it its system of morality. The time of creation continues to live through its rules, as its precepts, values, and codes are (for believers, must be) continually revived. Absolute and normative *Urzeit* then becomes perpetual present (*gegenwartige Zeit*) and *Endzeit* as well, since it is to be perpetually relived.[37]

An *Urzeit* exists in the mind of archaic man and it is necessarily a remote time. Freud wrote that "remote times have a great attraction . . . for the imagination."[38] Folk epics, he said, originate with a period in history which is afterwards regarded as "eventful, significant, grandiose, and perhaps . . . heroic"[39]—the Golden Age. In an earlier work, although not referring to myth or mythical consciousness, Freud had posited the goal of life as the return to "an old state of things, an initial state . . . to which [the living entity] is striving to return."[40] That work was pregnant with significant contributions to a psychological theory of myth that could explain the yearning to return to a golden age, a lost paradise.

The idea of *Urzeit* is easily transposed to the German Enlightenment if one considers nineteenth- and twentieth-century German Jews the counterpart or analogue to myth-believing, archaic people, and the Enlightenment myth the counterpart of primitive myth. Ernst Cassirer spoke of Lessing and Mendelssohn as representatives of a type of religion and of a specific milieu which he deemed "wonderful" or "miraculous."[41] The eighteenth century was "a miracle as no other epoch in history . . . the century of the Enlightenment" in Germany.[42] Mann described Lessing and his era as the beginning of the history of the German *Volk*. The Enlightenment worked a spell upon German

Jews (and some non-Jews like Mann), virtually the same spell that a mythical *Urzeit* worked upon archaic peoples.

The return to the *"goldene Zeit"* was a recurrent if unconscious theme in works of many German Jews in the twentieth century. A shining halo was placed upon the Enlightenment and the nineteenth-century "liberal era." It was blinding. Weimar's Jews could see nothing else of German history. Such an extreme limitation of experience of the mind "focusing of all forces on a single point is the prerequisite for all mythical thinking and mythical formulation."[43]

The goal of life in archaic cultures was to reinstate the same milieu of the Creative Time. So, too, did German Jews seem to want to reinstate the intellectual and ethical milieu of eighteenth-century Germany. It assumed an almost sacred aura. The German Enlightenment was seen as the "first manifestation of a thing that is significant and valid,"[44] in this case, tolerance and Reason. It bore the perfection of a mythical beginning; it was a lost paradise. Its commandments were life devoted to Reason and rationality; its virtues were dispassionate study of history and ethics; its sins were intolerance and dogmatism; its covenant was repetition. Most important, its heroes were virtuous men who were wise and truth-seeking. Men who were the keepers of universal values that were timeless.

And they were German men: Lessing, Goethe, Schiller. They were analogous to gods and heroes of mythological cultures. Their lives were lived in an age that was seen as the Beginning. They were celestial and had created the culture. They replaced in the new, secular era the religious archetypes of Abraham, Joseph, and Moses—the men who had created and identified Jewish culture, *all* Western culture.

The response to "What is German?" became "One who

assumes the life of those model Germans,"[45] one who identifies with the German ego-ideals or archetypes. Goethe, Lessing, Schiller were the models; and emulation of their lives by German Jews, the living *as if*, would certainly make German Jews unquestionably German. Gaining an identity—assuming a persona—occurs in archaic cultures, where "each individual grows up by wearing a mask," by imitating an elder or ancestor.[46] In a similar fashion, German Jews, through countless statements, identified strongly with this German archetype—the Enlightenment man of tolerance, wisdom, and compassion—and assumed that persona. It mattered not if it were Lessing or Nathan, the German or the Hebrew archetype, since in Lessing's own words they were the same. In *Nathan*, Lessing's Friar exclaims: "Nathan! Nathan! You ae a Christian. . . . No truer ever was!" to which Nathan replies: ". . . what to you makes me a Christian [read "German"], so makes you to me a Jew."[47] The archetypes were equated.

The appeal to German *Aufklärer* and the Enlightenment provided an "interpretive total image" of Germany, whose most vital product was a sense of "contemporary consciousness."[48] Nathan's "what makes me" and "makes you" defined his own and Lessing's "true Christian" identity. German Jews could find peace by creating their own world, their own myth, which cured their insecurity and isolation because it gave them a sense of identity.[49]

There is no paradox in this total identification because it is mental, imaginative, and poetic. Mythological thought unifies people and time, past and present, *mentally* not literally.[50] Concepts, convictions, myths arise "from the autonomous activity of the mind,"[51] an autonomy that is freedom from history or profane change. In mythology the mental configurations remain the same, and their physical, historical projections change.[52]

Imagination, then, is the realm of mythology, and myth therefore bears a remarkable likeness to poetry. Myth has

122

been described as "a form of poetry . . .in that it proclaims a truth."[53] Lucien Levy-Bruhl called myths "*poetic* expressions of the most sacred collective representations."[54] C. Kerenyi began his discussions of mythology by comparing it to poetry and music.[55]

Poetry, literature, and myth are products of the imagination. But because it is imaginary, myth is not unreal. Myth does not move in a "purely invented or made-up world but has its own mode of necessity and therefore . . . its own reality."[56] It may not mirror material or external reality, but it is nevertheless an expression of a psychic reality. Myth as much as poetry is the "unacknowledged legislator" of the world despite, or because of, its mental, psychological origin, form, and content. Poetry and imagination are forms of truth that arise from the structure of men's minds, wrote Wordsworth.[57] Poetry, in Coleridge's interpretation, seeks to "*harmonize existence and perceptions.*"[58] William Blake, the poet perhaps more openly involved with myth than any other, wrote that "The Eternal Body of Man is the Imagination."[59] In all his mythical mindedness Blake refused to concede any split between the real and the ideal (or mental).[60]

Myth and poetry are personal formations of mind, imagination, and perception and need not relate to external or profane things. Blake's, Shelley's, and Coleridge's fusions were derived from their own perceptions as poets. Like that of poetry, the force of mythology is not so much sociological as epistemological; it is more a matter of psychological and perceptual experience than of economic and revolutionary consciousness. It is mental and intellectual. Mentally, intellectually, myth creates a world of its own for believers.

For German Jews the real world of Germany was the way they perceived and mythicized it: enlightened. Just as the man of archaic society became his society's archetype,

German Jews became Lessing by assuming his values, ideals and morals, and by believing. Furthermore, just as archaic man identified all others in his society by means of his archetypes, German Jews identified other Germans by means of their archetypes.

Convictions and beliefs in the reality (past and present) of the German Enlightenment archetypes governed major aspects of individual and collective German Jewish life. Consideration of Germans as being the Lessing-type involved a mechanism of transference and reification from the particular hero (Lessing) to the group (all Germans). Such considerations suggest the primary characteristic of mythical thinking, the undifferentiated unity of mythical consciousness.[61]

The symbols of Enlightenment ethics were individuals, specific "organs of reality,"[62] but to the German Jewish consciousness they represented the "totality" of Germans.[63] The consequence of this generalizing or conceptualizing of Lessing was the equation of all Germans with the German *Aufklärer*.[64] By means of this generalizaiton, the individual symbol became objective, the part became the whole. An obvious problem in such an equation is time. How could Lessing the particular be identified with all Germans of the twentieth century?

The answer again lies in the nature of mythical thought. In mythical consciousness, wrote Ernst Cassirer in his classic *Philosophy of Symbolic Forms*, "all things crowd together into a single plane of reality."[65] Just as no distinction is made between the parts and the whole, so too is there no differentiation between past and present. Mythology homogenizes times, beings, and objects that are "intimately interchangeable," in the words of Levy-Bruhl, because they participate in the same "ensemble of qualities."[66] The dead survive because they are believed to live with the members of the groups and create a "mystic-concrete symbiosis"; and the *Urzeit* is everpresent in its revived archetypes.[67]

124

Lessing, then, still "lived with" twentieth-century Germans, his soul was "reincarnated" in theirs.[68] Lessing, the ancestor, was the "mythical being ... whence others [twentieth-century Germans] derive their reality," their identity.[69] He and other figures like Goethe, Herder, and Schiller were kept alive by the passing down or passing on of their memory from generation to generation, creating what John Layard called a "participation mystique" and a resultant "sense of oneness or identification."[70] Participation in their identity, "soul," and values were imagined or felt as strongly by German Jews in the 1920s, the myth-believers, as by those who may have known or known of the first Lessing or Herder in the eighteenth century.

This phenomenon of blurring times and people is clarified and supplemented by a concept of R. D. Laing's, another psychoanalytic theory that is easily applicable to mythology. Laing theorized that the initial perception of a figure often colors subsequent relationships with it.[71] Laing's theory is in accord with Freud's statement that "the effects of ... first identifications ... will be general and lasting."[72] Freud was here examining the origin of the ego-ideal and, like Laing, was hypothesizing about individuals. But the theory is easily transplanted to a group, and Freud, in fact, did it when he defined a group by common identification with the same ego-ideal.[73] What was achieved by such identification, he said, was identity with each other through the same ideal.[74]

In mythology, since myths concern *collective* representations, Laing's and Freud's ideas translate to mean that the impact of initial group perception remains as strong and forceful in subsequent generations as it was in the first.

Thus, German Jews in the 1920s stood possessed by the same spell as had their forefathers of the eighteenth century, felt the same devotion to Lessing and Herder as had their great-grandfathers and grandfathers.

At the start of *Stadt ohne Juden* the leading advocate of the expulsion of Jews from Austria, Schwertiger, delivers a long discourse on Jews and Germans. He knows Jews. Some are even friends of his—more or less. They are an honorable "race," with great intelligence, ability, and ambition. Germans, on the other hand, are quiet, playful, naïve, natural, musical, religious, and reverent.[75] Schwertiger continues, growing emotional and more overtly irrational. He defines Jews as intelligent in a cunning sense, able because they are demonically strong, ambitious so that they are dangerous, and unable to be German "in their hearts and blood" because they undercut all the virtues upon which *das ewige Deutschtum*, true Germanism, is based.[76]

German Jews passionately disagreed with this sort of characterization not only of Jews but of *ewiges Deutschtum*. They argued that the voices of "true Germanism" had to combat the insidious degradation of Jews by so-called *völkische* theorists. Mendacious attempts of men like Schwertiger to make Goethe and the German Enlightenment archetypes anti-Semites abused true Germanism while they abused Judaism, degraded true Germans while they degraded Jews. A distinction had to be drawn between the "deutsche Völksidee" and the "deutschvölkische Idee,"[77] between "Germanen" (Teutons) and "Deutscher" (Germans).[78]

Differences between Teuton and German were first sounded by Fichte, claimed Ludwig Hollander, and the use of Fichte by Hollander and others resembled an appeal to another sacred ancestor.[79] Invocation of Fichte's name and principles seemed to be all that was needed to refute the subversive attempts of anti-Semites. It was Lessing, Nathan, and Fichte, not the *völkische* theorists, who were the symbols of *ewiges Deutschtum*.[80]

Such invocation by German Jews and the instruction of German non-Jews were to be the swords of truth that would slay the evil and ignorant anti-Semitic dragon. The function of the archetype in mythology is to point the way to reestablishment of a favorable situation by knowing what the original situation was. Knowing was the first prerequisite of mythological life, telling was the second.[81] In their deep penchant for education (knowing), German Jews were the mythological people *par excellence*. Freud, anti-Semites, and German Jews all saw in Jews a mysterious, age-old affinity for education.[82]

Education, instruction in the lives and principles or ego-ideals like Lessing, became the prerequisites of Jewish life lived as Germans in Germany. With rigorous exegesis German Jews set out to prove that education was the subliminal commandment in the Old Testament. Education was alleged to be almost instinctual in the Jews, whose souls purportedly bore a legendary, burning desire to know, a desire handed down from the patriarchs—even if knowledge meant plumbing the very depths of hell, like Faust.[83] Sociologists and historians either marveled at or derogated the high educational level of German Jews.[84] Yet there it was, statistically proven, and historically demonstrable— education and German Jews went hand in glove.

Small wonder that the defense against anti-Semitism was to be an educative process undertaken, somewhat naïvely, by German Jews. The goal was to explain that Jews in Germany were German. Along with the now familiar enumerations of national contributions, patriotism, and loyalty,[85] this involved educating Germany in the finer points of Germanness and the German Enlightenment.[86]

The aim of this educative process, like that of education in archaic societies, was to unify the community.[87] But it would unify by demonstrating that the community was in fact already unified. German Jews determined to educate Germans to what they considered was the fact of their common ideological and physical experience and thus reveal a community of experience.[88] By means of that revelation they hoped to resurrect a feeling of togetherness, or what Erik Erikson has called a "sense of sameness."[89]

From unity of the past comes unity in the present and

127

future. Roland Barthes described myth as a *semiologie* or system of communication.[90] Ultimately, education in archaic societies is a system of communication that conveys or communicates the morals and ethics of ancestors, of the past; that binds in the present; and anchors identity with "real security." Again, the morals and ethics, the identity and security, are all conveyed through knowing and telling about certain archetypal figures, the culture heroes who give a culture its identity and its essence.

The German Jewish defense effort against *völkisch* anti-Semitism was named *Erziehung* or *Aufklärung*—education or enlightenment. A blueprint was prescribed in which it was asserted that "the CV must eduate the great number of Christian fellow citizens who have the mistaken prejudice that Jewish Germans are a foreign type."[91] At the foundation of the campaign was the innocent, blind faith in the power of reason and facts; faith in the omnipotent strength of truth in exposing and defeating untruth; the unshakable, nineteenth-century, positivistic belief in education bringing inevitable progress. Almost every issue of the *CVZ* after September 1928 carried "Aufklärung" articles which reported educational meetings all over Germany. Public discussions bore titles like "What is National?"[92] or "Jews in German Politics"[93] to illustrate their didactic nature.

Each of these discussions and articles abounded in references to Goethe, Herder, Lessing, Humboldt, or Fichte, as well as to earlier German "liberals" like Christian Wolff. Weimar's educational curriculum was attacked by the CV for its neglect of German Jews in German history and of the universal teachings of Herder, Kant, and Goethe. CV editorialists complained that German high schools were allowed to teach the *Protocols of the Elders of Zion*[94] as fact, but neglected the "facts" about Spinoza's "Jewish" influence on Kant and neglected Mendelssohn as a German worth teaching. Racist lies were to be exposed, wrote a *CVZ* editor, and the truth of Germany's moral, philosophic, ethical, and cultural foundation reborn.[95]

In a lengthy editorial, the CVZ derided the Nazi journal, *German Education*, for ascribing racism to the great German masters like Goethe and Fichte. German schools needed to teach the principles and lives of these men, the editorial declared, not, as the Nazi editor Karl Berger contended, so German youth would learn anti-Semitism, but so they would receive a "true German education."[96] This meant the abandonment of racism and, most important, that "the goal of education is and can only be nothing other than the developing of harmonious strength and unity of human nature, and summoning humanity into life."[97]

In July 1935, the lead article in the CVZ was a two-page review of a Nazi biography of Wilhelm von Humboldt. In muted but critical tones Fritz Friedlander pleaded for proper education and for truth in biography and scholarly endeavors. To him, Humboldt had been a fighter for education of all Germans, including German Jews. He was not, said Friedlander, to be faulted for that. That activity made him not inadequate as a member of the true German *Volk*, as his Nazi biographer had claimed, but more deeply a part of that *Volk*. More than ever, in 1935, German Jews and non-Jews, concluded Friedlander, had to be aware of the power of truth in education, of the need for models and their duplication.[98]

NOTES

[1]Mann, "Lessing."
[2]Ibid.
[3]Eliade, *The Sacred and the Profane*, is only one of many studies relating mythology and religion to the secular or profane world; cf. also Eliade, *Myth and Reality*, pp. 162–193; C. G. Jung, *Aion*, in *Collected Works*, ed. William McGuire, Sir Herbert Read, Michael Fordham, Gerhard Alder, 14 vols. (Princeton: Princeton University Press, 1956), IX, Part 2, 30, 34.

[4]See Chap. v.

[5]C. G. Jung, Modern Man in Search of a Soul, trans. W. S. Dell and Cary F. Baynes (London: Kegan Paul, Trench & Trubner, 1933), p. 144.

[6]Totem and Taboo, Works, Vol. XIII. C.P., Vol. IV; "Papers on Applied Analysis," pp. 173–472.

[7]This type of archetype should be distinguished from Jung's idea of archetype which includes the construct of a model but goes beyond it to a semi-mystical concept of psychic, genetic urges or predispositions.

[8]New Introductory Lectures, Works, Vol. XXII, p. 63.

[9]Ibid.

[10]Eliade, Myth and Reality, pp. 19, 31.

[11]Cf. Erik Erikson, Childhood and Society, 2nd ed. (New York: W. W. Norton, 1963), p. 158; Lucien Levy-Bruhl, The "Soul" of the Primitive, trans. Lilian A. Claire (London: George Allen & Unwin, 1965), pp. 19ff., 232–260.

[12]Jung, Man and His Symbols (Garden City: Doubleday & Co., 1964), pp. 79, 96–99; "The Psychology of the Child Archetype," Collected Works, IX, Part 2, The Archetypes and the Collective Unconscious, 151–181.

[13]John Layard, "Identification with the Sacrificial Animal," Eranos Jahrbuch, XXIV (1955), 341–406; G. Van der Leeuw, "Urzeit und Endzeit," Eranos Jahrbuch, XVII (1949), 11–51.

[14]Wilhelm Reich, The Mass Psychology of Fascism, trans. Vincent R. Carfagno (New York: Farrar, Straus & Giroux, 1971), p. 46.

[15]Ibid., p. 47.

[16]Mann, "Freud and the Future," Essays of Three Decades, pp. 420–428, italics added.

[17]Ibid.

[18]Ibid. Mann claimed in his introduction to Joseph that his speeches in honor of Freud and Lessing were part of the novel. Cf. Carl Kerenyi, "Prolegomena," C. Kerenyi and C. G. Jung, Essays on a Science of Mythology, trans. R. F. C. Hull (Princeton: Princeton University Press, 1959). pp. 1–24, for a discussion of this paradox; see also Chap. vii.

[19]Future of an Illusion, Works, Vol. XXI, p. 8.

[20]Geza Roheim, The Origin and Function of Culture (Garden City: Doubleday & Co., 1971), p. 39; see also Roheim, Psychoanalysis and Anthropology: Culture, Personality and the Unconscious (New York: International Universities Press, 1950), pp. 10–12.

[21]Erikson, Childhood and Society, pp. 132, 241.

[22]Malinowski, Sex, Culture, and Myth, p. 292.

[23]Joseph Campbell, The Masks of God, 4 vols. (New York: Viking Press, 1968), I, Primitive Mythology, 4, 466.

[24]Ibid., p. 466. See also Mircea Eliade, Myths, Dreams and Mysteries. The Encounter Between Contemporary Faiths and Archaic Realities, trans. Philip Mairet (New York: Harper & Row, 1960), p. 25; Eliade, Myth and Reality, p. 31; Jung, Aion, pp. 25, 27; Jung, Man and His Symbols, p. 25; and Harry Slochower, Mythopoesis. Mythic Patterns in the Literary Classics (Detroit: Wayne State University Press, 1970), pp. 14–15ff.

[25]"Die Deutsche Adelsgenossenschaft und Wir," CVZ, XI (January 22, 1932).

[26]Zweig, "Lessings Totenmaske" (1925), *Essays*, pp. 80–83.

[27]Thomas Mann, *Joseph and His Brothers*, trans. H. T. Lowe-Porter, 4 vols. (London: Sphere Books, 1968), II, The Young Joseph, 50.

[28]Levy-Bruhl, The *"Soul"* of the Primitive, pp. 15ff.; Jung, *Man and His Symbols*, pp. 67, 81; Jung, "The Psychology of the Child Archetype."

[29]Mircea Eliade, *Cosmos and History. The Myth of the Eternal Return*, trans. Willard R. Trask (New York: Harper & Row, 1959), pp. 43, 75.

[30]See pp. 62–63.

[31]Mann, *Joseph*, I, Tales of Jacob, 44.

[32]Ibid., pp. 38–44, passim.

[33]G. van der Leeuw, "Urzeit und Endzeit," *Eranos Jahrbuch*, XVII (1949), 11–51.

[34]Erikson, *Identity: Youth and Crisis*, p. 24.

[35]Mann, *Tales of Jacob*, p. 22.

[36]Henri Frankfort, "Myth and Reality," in *Before Philosophy: The Intellectual Adventure of Ancient Man*, ed. Henri Frankfort and Mrs. H. Frankfort (Baltimore: Penguin Books, 1949), pp. 11–36; G. van der Leeuw, "Urzeit und Endzeit"; Eliade, *Myths, Dreams*, p. 14; Eliade, "The Yearning for Paradise in Primitive Tradition," *Myth and Mythmaking*; Eliade, *Cosmos and History*, pp. 35–39.

[37]Van der Leeuw, "Urzeit und Endzeit."

[38]Future of an Illusion, *Works*, Vol. XXI, p. 54.

[39]*Moses and Monotheism*, Works, Vol. XXIII, p. 71.

[40]*Beyond the Pleasure Principle*, Works, Vol. XVIII, p. 38.

[41]Cassirer, "Die Idee der Religion bei Lessing."

[42]Ibid.

[43]Ernst Cassirer, *Language and Myth*, trans. Susanne K. Langer (New York: Dover Publications, 1946), p. 33.

[44]Clyde Kluckhohn, "Recurrent Themes in Myth and Mythmaking," *Myth and Mythmaking*, pp. 46–60.

[45]Cf. Erikson, *Childhod and Society*, pp. 36, 73, 131.

[46]Roheim, *Psychoanalysis and Anthropology*, p. 12; Kerenyi, "Prolegomen", Jung, "The Psychology of the Child Archetype."

[47]Lessing, *Nathan* IV. viii.

[48]Campbell, *Primitive Mythology*, p. 4, passim; Erikson, *Childhood and Society*, p. 42.

[49]Alfred Kazin, "Introduction" to *The Portable Blake* (New York: Viking Press, 1968), pp. 1–58. Kazin's description of how myth affected Blake's life is a good analogue to the way myths of Germany and Germans affected German Jews.

[50]Campbell, *Primitive Mythology*, p. 23; Jung, *Modern Man in Search of a Soul*, p. 70; Cohen, *Die religiösen Bewegung*, pp. 2–5.

[51]Cassirer, *Language and Myth*, p. 31; Jung, *Modern Man in Search of a Soul*, p. 163; Jung, *Aion*, p. 18; Jung, "Phenomenology of the Spirit in Fairy Tales," *Collected Works, The Archetypes and the Collective Unconscious*, IX, Part 1, 207–254.

[52]Cf. Campbell, *Primitive Mythology*, pp. 14ff., his disucssion of Adolf Bastian's categories of *Völkergedanke* and *Elementärgedanke*.

[53]Frankfort, "Myth and Reality."

[54]Levy-Bruhl, The "Soul" of the Primitive, p. 55, italics added.

[55]Kerenyi, "Prolegomena."

[56]Ernst Cassirer, The Philosophy of Symbolic Forms, trans. Ralph Man heim, 3 vols. (New Haven & London: Yale University Press, 1955), II Mythical Thought, 4.

[57]William Wordsworth, "Preface to the Lyrical Ballads," William Words worth, Selected Poetry, ed. Mark van Doren (New York: Modern Library, 1950), pp. 675–698.

[58]Samuel Taylor Coleridge, Biographia Literaria, in Coleridge: Selected Poetry and Prose, ed. Elisabeth Schneider (New York: Holt, Rinehart & Winston, 1951), pp. 186–372.

[59]William Blake, "The Laocoon Group," The Portable Blake, p. 497.

[60]Kazin, "Introduction."

[61]Cassirer, The Philosophy of Symbolic Forms, pp. xiv–xv.

[62]Cassirer, Language and Myth, p. 8.

[63]Ibid., p. 19.

[64]Cf. Levy-Bruhl, The "Soul," p. 59.

[65]Cassirer, Mythical Thought, p. 42.

[66]Levy-Bruhl, The "Soul," pp. 19, 49. In his essay in Myth and Mythmaking, Clyde Kluckhohn discusses myths as "holophrastic" systems; that is, systems in which the part stands for the whole. Cf. Kluckhohn, "Recurrent Themes in Myth and Mythmaking."

[67]Van der Leeuw, "Urzeit und Endzeit"; Levy-Bruhl, The "Soul," pp. 340–341; Mann, Joseph, III, Joseph in Egypt, 24, passim.

[68]Mann, Tales of Jacob, p. 34; Levy-Bruhl, The "Soul," p. 260.

[69]Mann, Joseph in Egypt, p. 97; Levy-Bruhl, The "Soul," p. 128.

[70]Layard, "Identification with the Sacrificial Animal."

[71]R. D. Laing, The Divided Self. An Existential Study of Sanity and Madness (Baltimore: Penguin Books, 1965), p. 20.

[72]Freud, The Ego and the Id, trans. Joan Riviere (New York: W. W. Norton 1962), p. 21.

[73]Ibid., p. 27.

[74]Freud, Group Psychology and the Analysis of the Ego, pp. 59, 61.

[75]Bettauer, Stadt ohne Juden, pp. 9–10.

[76]Ibid.

[77]Moritz Goldstein, Deutsche Volksidee oder deutschvölkische Idee (Berlin, 1927); "Die Juden in Geschichtsunterricht," CVZ Monthly, IV (October 1932); "Deutsche oder völkische Erziehung," ibid.

[78]Stern, Warum sind wir Deutsche? p. 23.

[79]See, for example, Ludwig Hollander, Deutsche-Jüdische Probleme der Gegenwart. Eine Auseinanderung über die Grundfragen des Central-Vereins deutscher Staatsbürger jüdischen Glaubens (Berlin, Philo-Verlag, 1929), p. 11.

[80]Fritz Friedlander, "Irrwege und Wege ins neue Deutschland," CVZ, X (July 24, 1931).

[81]Claude Lévi-Strauss, Structural Anthropology, "The Structural Study of Myth," trans. Claire Jacobson and Brooke Grundfest Schoepf (Garden City: Doubleday & Co., 1967), pp. 202–228.

[82]Freud, *Moses and Monotheism*, pp. 109, 158; see also Werner Sombart, *Die Zukunft der Juden* (Leipzig: Dunker & Humblot, 1912), pp. 14ff.; Ruppin, *The Jews in the Modern World*.

[83]See Chap. i of Mann's *Tales of Jacob*; also Erich Heller, *The Ironic German. A Study of Thomas Mann* (London: Seecker & Warburg, 1958), p. 188.

[84]Cf. Ruppin, *The Jews*, pp. 16–17; Osborne, *Germany and Her Jews*, p. 8.

[85]See Chap. ii.

[86]Flake, "Zum jüdischen Problem"; Hollander, *Deutsche-Jüdische Probleme*, p. 31.

[87]Eliade, *Cosmos and History*, p. 75; Eliade, *Myth and Reality*, p. 139; Roland Barthes, Mythologies (Paris: Editions du Seuil, 1957), p. 224; Levi-Strauss, "The Structural Study of Myth."

[88]Cf. Levy-Bruhl, *The "Soul,"* pp. 16–19, passim.

[89]Erikson, *Identity: Youth and Crisis*, p. 19.

[90]Barthes, *Mythologies*, pp. 217ff.

[91]Hollander, *Deutsche-Jüdische Probleme*, p. 32.

[92]"Was ist national?" *CVZ*, XII (March 3, 1933).

[93]"Aufklärung auf dem Lande," article reporting a public meeting in Fischbach at which the topic of discussion was "Jews in German Politics," *CVZ*, XII (March 3, 1933).

[94]The CV demanded disciplinary action against anti-Semitic practices among students and teachers in provincial schools that taught anti-Jewish and anti-Republican lessons. See Paucker, *Die jüdische Abwehrkampf*, p. 75.

[95]" 'Auf Deutschlands hohen Schulen,' " *CVZ*, I (November 30, 1922), 341 –342; "Der Antisemitismus in der hohëren Schule," *CVZ*, I (October 5, 1922), 273; Karl Aner (non-Jewish Berlin clergyman), "Herders Stellung zur Judenfrage," *CVZ*, I (June 8, 1922), 79–81.

[96]"Die Juden im Geschichtsunterricht," and "Deutsche oder völkische Erziehung."

[97]"Die Juden im Geschichtsunterricht."

[98]Fritz Friedlander, "Ein Charakterbild in der Geschichte. Zu Wilhelm Grau: *Wilhelm von Humboldt*," *CVZ*, XIV (July 11, 1935).

VII

The Well

Das Rätsel der Zeit ist das Rätsel des Anfangs.
HERMANN HESSE

They were told that the King was alive, and as no one wanted to believe the contrary, this body was for a while the King.
HEINRICH MANN, *Henry, King of France*

In a paradoxical way, history and myth coexist. Commentators and scholars as antagonistic to each other as Malinowski and Freud, Freud and Jung, or Malinowski and Claude Lévi-Strauss have some common ground in their considerations of myth and certain aspects of culture. They have shown, then, that myth, a timeless phenomenon, is considered the chronicle of an historical, "kairotic" (an originary, generative, and formative), event.[1] Mythological education instructs a people in a tradition that is historical. The myth therefore serves to keep a tradition and a culture alive as it instructs the living in the ways of their original, historical forefathers, in how to play their roles in the game by walking in others' footsteps.[2] A member of a society or culture then participates in the myth and gains an identity from that participation. History gives myth its authority, and it is the history that needs examination, which adds to the understanding of German-Jewish actions within a mythological framework.

134

Knowing the myth and its elements and knowing with what one had to identify had to come first. And since it was the knowing of events and lives of a distant past, this paradoxical history that was atemporal was stressed in archaic cultures as the essential study for identity. History of a mythological type preserves the memory of archetypes (distorted or not). Men of the Renaissance had sought to discover, through studying history, "models for behavior of the perfect man,"[3] just as Livy had urged the study of history to find "models for ourselves and our country."[4] History was to provide an identity by a re-cognition of self in the past. It revealed a tradition that encompassed "true ideas" that were self-evident and created a community and a communal identity.[5]

Models, memories, history, and traditions carried German identity. But which history and tradition? Which archetypes and myths were to be known? Which ego-ideals were to be emulated? On the brink of catastrophe, with an ominously presaging tone, Werner Cahnmann, a prominent and frequent contributor to the CVZ, tried to define deutsche Tradition in the CVZ Monthly.[6] Cahnmann identified the tradition with Reich, which had always meant, he said, "freedom" for Germany. In the Middle Ages, with the emperor defending Christendom and "holy Christian freedom," and in the Great Enlightenment and the Romantic eras, Reich was synonymous with "German" and German was therefore synonymous with freedom.

Cahnmann's purpose was first to warn against Nazism and second to expose the true German tradition of real freedom, the real freedom of the German Enlightenment, and to juxtapose it to the false one of racism and intolerance.[7] Arguing from their liberal and enlightened notions of "nation" and deutsche Nationalität, most German Jews dismissed the barest possibility of contradiction between Judentum and Deutschtum.[8] Ludwig Hollander, then president of the CV, again spoke for that organization and through it for the majority of German Jews when he equated the German *Geist* and the German Jewish *Geist*. Both had what he termed the same "water as source"—liberalism— from which the fathers and grandfathers of contemporary German Jews and German non-Jews had drunk in the nineteenth century and for which their sons had bled and died in two wars.[9]

German Jewish notions of *Deutschtum* implied freedom, humanity, morality, and "all the characteristics which were hallmarks of Judaism."[10] German Jews asserted that the Enlightenment and the nineteenth century provided the sources of *ewiges Deutschtum*, and that the source of the Enlightenment was the Old Testament. Consequently the "new Noah," the moral, pious, enlightened, and humanitarian chosen of the Enlightenment was the German, and especially the German Jew.[11]

When German Jews physically and intellectually defended Germany in World War I they defended that free Germany, that "holy Germany," and its *Geist* with which they identified.[12] Having fixed upon the Enlightenment as the formative age, German Jews perpetuated the archetypes into the present by projecting their characteristics onto twentieth-century Germans. German Jewish feelings and thoughts were German feelings and thoughts because they were based on a German *Humanitätsbewustssein*, or consciousness of humanity.[13]

The thrust of German Jewish assimilationist perorations was spiritual sameness: Germans and Jews were kindred spirits in the twentieth century just as they had been in the eighteenth century. Articles in memory of Hermann Cohen praised his idea of one morality for one mankind because he recalled Kant—because he was "in the spirit of *das ewiges Deutschtum*."[14] Accordingly, his German Jewish interpreters judged that Cohen had received the torch from an illustrious line of Germans: Kant, Lessing, Mendelssohn, Herder, and Fichte. Proof of his Germanness was therefore in his will to be German, in his care for humanity. The final

136

article in the CVZ memorial issue for Cohen brings together the several themes that German Jews incessantly repeated in the Weimar years: "The *ideal of humanity* [is] equally German and Jewish"; Jews have added valuable contributions to German culture (of which Cohen is a notable example); German Jewish names—Kant and Cohen, Fichte and Mendelssohn, Lessing, Lessing again; and, finally, Germany must be reeducated in schools to these facts of history.[15]

Leaders of the German Jewish community proclaimed that it was German Jewry's duty to defend German culture and *the* German tradition. The ideal of humanity, which was so thoroughly a part of the German Enlightenment, was also Gabriel Riesser's and Hermann Cohen's. Since they had the same source, namely, the Old Testament; the German Enlightenment pantheon, and by projection all Germans, were seen by German Jews as irrevocably bound to men like Cohen, who represented all German Jews.[16] Two peoples had never been so alike: similar in "holiness," in "chosenness,"[17] and in *Weltlichkeit.*[18] Jakob Wassermann had dreamed that Germans and Jews were mirror images.[19] In a similar vein, Ferdinand Lion wrote that they reflected each other, and that the "Jew stands to the German as a mirror in which his own past and fate are reflected."[20]

Such metaphors seek to define German Jewish identity. Identity is sunk in origins, archetypes, and "far-away time,"[21] and Weimar Jews increasingly became preoccupied with the question of history and origins. With greater frequency they posed the question: "What is German?" Ludwig Hollander, in a bold-type inset on the front page of the CVZ, announced that *"Origins must be examined."* Only an historical answer could supply a solution to that "muddled question."[22] Addressing the same question, another CV editorialist wrote that "history is what makes a rich culture like the German so important," because it, history, and not race, creates *Volkstum* "based on centuries —thousands of years of development."[23] In seeking the origins of Germany, German Jews once more turned to those they deemed the originators of the search, the nationalists who could stand beside the internationalists like Lessing and Goethe.

"In the name of Herder and Goethe" (italics his), Fritz Friedlander appealed for examination of the true origins of Germanness.[24] Through them would be discovered the natural, correct consequence of Germany's development, history, and destiny.[25] With deep reverence that betrayed a melancholy revery, the CVZ summoned up the memory of the *Humanitätsidee* expounded by Herder, Goethe, and Fichte. This conception of Germany's past and tradition was proffered as the real one. To German Jews the Nazis were the idealizers, the dreamers, seeking or creating a past that had never existed—a past out of touch with reality. Herder had proclaimed the unity of mankind in an internationalism that was born of the Enlightenment. But he had not allowed humanity to be a pretext for denying the necessity of a *Volk* or nation.[26] German Jews viewed Herder, like Lessing, as speaking to the 1920s as well as to his own age. The identification of individuals and values transcended time and created a temporal identification. And like Lessing, Schiller, and all the others, and unlike many of the Nazi medieval and ancient heroes, Herder had lived and was real. His synthesis, his simultaneous devotion to *Volk* and humanity, his blending of nationalism and internationalism, made him a "good neighbor" to German Jews. Fichte had accomplished the same synthesis when he said that "love of fatherland governs my acts, *Weltbürgertum* is my idea."[27]

The Enlightenment had furnished Germany with its ideals, the humanitarian cosmopolitanism of Lessing and Schiller. The Romantic era, the age that Arthur Eloesser

138

called the second great period of assimilation for German Jews,[28] seemed to reconcile the idealism—the beautiful mirage—of the Enlightenment with the reality of rising nationalism.[29] As they had turned to Lessing and Schiller to examine their enlightened attitudes, German Jews anxious to display their nationalism and national allegiance turned to identification with Herder, Humboldt, Fichte, and again Goethe.

Hermann Cohen sounded the cry of synthesizing the ideas of the Enlightenment and Romantic eras when he wrote that the concept of man *(Menschen)* fulfills itself in mankind *(Menschheit)* first through states and nations *(Völker)* in which and by means of which the goal—uniformity—is upwardly developed. It was Fichte, said Cohen, who first recognized the Old Testament origin of the idea of a nation in the service of universal freedom.[30] The theory proclaimed a messianic future of mankind, and Cohen's many references to Herder and Fichte emphasize the similarities with them regarding ideas of that kind. Salo Baron recalled that the originally leading authors of German nationalism, Herder and Fichte, were also the preachers of true *Menschheitsnation*—a nation in the service of mankind.[31]

Descriptions of nationalism that "must go hand in hand with supranationalism *(Übernationalizmus)*"[32] multiplied. The words that described Goethe and Herder were the same as those that described the Old Testament and Old Testament prophets.[33] Hannah Arendt called Herder and the Romantics the "creators of the German tradition."[34] The Enlightenment had ignored the history of men because of its obsession with the history of man. Arendt credited Herder with freeing German thought from that error. In words that anticipated historicism, Herder had differentiated men on the basis of history and nationality, not on the basis of an "original characteristic" like race.[35] From

139

this stressing of *historical* and national differences emerged the basic equality of men. Herder had created a synthesis of the universal with the national.[36]

Bildung, to Herder, was education in the ways of development and could only come about through understanding, knowing history. This meant education based on knowledge of reality.[37] Herder had conjured the past to explain what Bismarck later called the "spell" of the word *deutsch*. Fichte, in the same spirit, had called upon Germany to lead mankind, saying: "If Germany falls, so falls mankind without hope of restoration."[38] In the 1920s German Jews called upon Herder and Fichte, gave them new life, reanimated their feelings with a new-old emotion and urge. Contemporary Germans, they said, "could do nothing better than consult the thinkers of the eighteenth century for intellectual growth."[39] It was Herder, the great, classical synthesizer, the advocate of the "greater community of man," whom *"all Germans of today"* should heed.[40] To stand with Herder and with Fichte was to stand on the soil of Germany and mankind.[41]

The third member of this other near-holy patriarchal trinity was Goethe. The year 1932 was Goethe's one-hundredth memorial year. German Jewish Goethe scholars immortalized him: they called his life eternal. Cultural nationalism was Goethe's style of allegiance to Germany. He loved his nation, but not in a chauvinistic sense.[42] For Jews in Germany, "he is our example, our councillor, and our leader."[43] His legacy, wrote Ernst Lissauer in the *CVZ*, was his "lived life," which he devoted to attainment of a "European world community."[44] The following week another article examined the poet's life and avowed that considerations of his thought had to play a major role in Jewish contemporary life.[45]

More important, since it was self-evident that Goethe formed "the great model of German manhood, then it is impossible to doubt that many and strong parts of the most inner essence of *Deutschtum* are tied to Judaism."[46] And the following month, the *CVZ Monthly* plaintively relented: "If only [Goethe] were alive—we *all* should follow his example and find value in the Old Testament." The same article bound him to Herder in his love for Old Testament poetry, ethics, and culture.[47]

Once again German Jews found in Germany's hero Judaism's white knight. He was not anti-Semitic;[48] indeed, he was an admiring student of the Old Testament.[49] In a long correspondence with that other hero, Schiller, Goethe had discussed the talmudic commentaries and interpretations of the Old Testament.[50] He had delivered lengthy panegyrics to Lessing's *Nathan*[51] and had made Faust in the image of Job.[52] In short, he was the model for German Jewish nationalism. His interest in Judaism was historical, aesthetic, and moral. As it had instructed him, so he instructed all Germans who believed in Germany's national and cultural greatness.[53]

Goethe and Herder formed a bridge between the Enlightenment and the Romantic eras. Viewed in retrospect by some German Jewish observers, the transition from one period to another was an easy one because of these two mythical figures. To those observers, smooth, too, was what they considered the imperceptible elision into the *goldene Zeit*, when liberalism was allegedly a major power and the spirit of cooperation ruled Germany.[54] So it seemed to men like Julius Bab, casting furtive, longing glances back to the communal age of 1848 and after, when Christians sought out Jews and took pride in Jewish friendships.[55] To a bewildered *CVZ* editorialist in 1935, the historical emancipation was not only political but "a phenomenon of *Geistgeschichte*," spiritual or intellectual history, the crossing of the German *Geist* with that of antiquity. What a noble act: Goethe's *Iphygenia* repeating the ideal sentiments of Euripides; his *Faust* echoing Job; Humboldt's ethics renewing Judaism's; the nationalism of a proud people directed toward international liberation as seen in the Old Testament, now transposed to the new liberating nation, Germany. Those combinations were born in the eighteenth century and nurtured through the nineteenth century. Coupling references to the "golden age" of the eighteenth century with those of the nineteenth, the article made a desperate plea to Germans not to deny or forget the fruits of that wonderful time and that productive symbiosis.[56]

This recreation of the mythical time, of the Enlightenment, in the Weimar Republic resembles what Thomas Mann called the continual pouring of the past into the present.[57] German Jews claimed that from the first espousal of the *Humanitätsideal* in the Enlightenment, it had been lived more and more visibly in time: 1812, Emancipation, 1848, 1869, 1871 were all landmarks of the rebirth and perpetuation of the ideals in increasingly tangible forms. Emancipation was possible and probable, if not certain, in the nineteenth century, because it grew from the original and eternal ideals of individualism and equality of mankind.[58] It was a challenge in the nineteenth century, "but we all knew it would be realized."[59] Dreams of the German Romantics, and even of later *völkisch*, romantic ideologues like Langbehn and Lagarde, were becoming reality.[60] Those were dreams of "collective living" and "communal existence," of "osmosis and symbiosis of *Deutschtum* and *Judentum*."[61]

Riesser, Bamberger, Lasker, Heine, and the unending list of those proffered by German Jews as German Jewish "greats" demonstrated German Jewish loyalty to the German nation throughout history. But they were revered as German models, reanimations of the original German archetypes. While the *Urzeit* was relived, so, too, were the lives of the *Urmenschen*. Riesser might well have been Moses Mendelssohn or Lessing; Heine was praised with Goethe for his similarities to the greatest of the great German poets; Eva Reichmann later referred to Leo Baeck as the symbol of German Jewry, a man who, she said, "had learnt in the

Goethean manner," the epitome of "all that is true, good, and beautiful" in the German tradition. She called Baeck a "living example" of that tradition.[62] In other words, the living Goethean archetype.

Even Luther's "later" anti-Semitism was explained away, and he was held up as a German founder of German tolerance.[63] Germans like Mommsen and Meinecke were the reborn prototypes of Lessing, Herder, and the Humboldts. All of them were in the true German tradition of the great German *Humanitätsidee.*[64] In 1890 an anti-Semitic petition was circulated by Bernhard Förster and Liebermann von Sonnenberg. It was countered by a petition drive conducted by Mommsen, Droysen, von Gneist, Rudolph Virchow, and some seventy-five others. Mommsen bitterly denounced the "Germanomaniacs" by saying that "racial hatred" would destory "the unity of the nation."[65] Ismar Elbogen's judgment of that confrontation was that the liberal and Enlightenment spirit still lived in Germany.[66]

NOTES

[1]Lévi-Strauss, *Structural Anthropology*, p. 205; Cassirer, *The Philosophy of Symbolic Forms*, II, *Mythical Thought*, 6, 51; Van der Leeuw, "Urzeit und Endzeit"; Rieff, "The Meaning of History and Religion in Freud's Thought."

[2]Virtually all works dealing with myth and mythology discuss this aspect of life in the myth. Perhaps nowhere is it better illustrated or more clearly stated than in Mann's *Joseph* tetralogy. See especially Volume I, *The Tales of Jacob*, "Lunar Syntax," 107–114; cf. Jung, "The Special Phenomenology of the Child Archetype," in "The Psychology of the Child Archetype."

[3]Eliade, *Myths, Dreams*, p. 32.

[4]Ibid.

[5]Jung, *Modern Man in Search*, p. 31; Levy-Bruhl, *The "Soul,"* p. 89; Van der Leeuw, "Urzeit und Endzeit."

[6]Werner Cahnmann, "Deutsche Tradition," *CVZ Monthly*, IV (July 1932).

[7]Ibid.

[8]Elbogen, *Die Geschichte der Juden*, p. 271.

[9]Ludwig Hollander, "Zum Neujahrstage," *CVZ*, I (September 21, 1922), 245–246.

[10]Hollander, *Deutsche-Jüdische Probleme*, p. 6.

[11]*Wir Deutschen Juden*, p. 26; "Die Stellung der Nichtjuden im judischen Schriftum" (report of a lecture by a Rabbi Norden to the Liberal Association for the Concern of the Jewish Community in Berlin), *CVZ*, IX (May 2, 1930).

[12]Hollander, "Zum Neujahrstage"; Ferdinand Lion, "Deutsches und jüdisches Schicksals," *Der Neue Merkur*, V, No. 5 (August 1921), 348–360.

[13]"Die deutsche Adelsgenossenschaft und Wir," *CVZ*, XI (Janury 22, 1932).

[14]Rabbi Lowenstamm, "Menschheit. Zum zehnten Todestag von Hermann Cohen," *CVZ Monthly*, I (May 1928).

[15]Kinkel, "Humanität!"

[16]"1831–1931," *CVZ*, IX (August 7, 1931); Ernst von Aster, "Über allem der Mensch"; "Die Stellung der Nichtjuden in judischen Schriftum"; Cohen, *Die religiösen Bewegung*, p. 24; "Die 'deutschen und christlichen' Grundlagen," *CVZ*, IX (August 22, 1930).

[17]Cf. Reisner, *Die Juden und das deutsche Reich*.

[18]Lion, "Deutsches und jüdisches Schicksals."

[19]Wassermann, *Mein Weg*, p. 119.

[20]Lion, "Deutsches und jüdisches Schicksals."

[21]Levy-Bruhl, The "Soul," p. 50; Eliade, *Cosmos and History*, p. 21.

[22]Hollander, "Was ist deutsch?" *CVZ*, IX (February 7, 1930).

[23]Hermann Funke, "Was ist deutsch?" *CVZ*, IX (February 7, 1930).

[24]Fritz Friedlander, "Irrwege und Wege ins neue Deutschland. Die Überwingung des Nationalsozialismus," *CVZ*, X (July 24, 1931).

[25]Ibid.

[26]Arnold Zweig, "Notiz über Herder" (1921), *Essays*, pp. 39–42.

[27]Zielensiger, "German Jews in the German Economy," *Der Jud ist Schuld*, pp. 225–270.

[28]Eloesser, "Literatur."

[29]Cf. Robinson, *A History of German Literature*, pp. 251, 254, 338.

[30]Cohen, *Die religiösen Bewegung*, pp. 24–25; *Moses Ben Maimon*, p. 65.

[31]Baron, *Deutsche und Juden*, p. 83.

[32]Goldmann, *Der Jude*, pp. 34–35.

[33]Ibid., cf. pp. 45, 54, 56; Baron, *Deutsche und Juden*.

[34]Arendt-Stern, "Aufklärung und Judenfrage."

[35]Ibid.; cf. Iggers, *The German Conception of History*, pp. 29–43.

[36]Zweig, "Notiz über Herder."

[37]Arendt-Stern. "Aufklärung und Judenfrage."

[38]J. Levy, "Erziehung zum Deutschtum," *CVZ*, IV (June 5, 1925); Fichte, *Addresses*, pp. 8, 127, passim.

[39]Karl Aner, "Herders Stellung zur Judenfrage," *CVZ*, I (June 8, 1922), 79–81.

[40]Ibid.

[41]Levy, "Erziehung."

[42]J. Landau, "Wie stehen Sie zu Goethe?" *CVZ*, XI (March 18, 1932).

[43]Ibid.

[44]Ernst Lissauer, "Was bedeutet Goethe dem Menschen von 1932?" *CVZ*, XI (March 18, 1932).

[45]"Nachtrag zum Goethe-Jahr," *CVZ*, XII (March 25, 1933).

[46]Ibid.

[47]Raimund Eberhard, "Das 'Alte Testament' in Goethes Werk," *CVZ Monthly*, IV (April, 1932).

[48]Bab, "War Goethe Antisemit?"

[49]Eberhard, "Das 'Alte Testament.' "

[50]Ibid.

[51]Hans Gober, "Der echte Goethe," *CVZ*, I (January 1, 1922), 157–158; Bab, *Lieben und Tod*, p. 14.

[52]Eberhard, "Das 'Alte Testament.' "

[53]Lissauer, "Was bedeutet Goethe"; Hans Reichmann, "Bilanz," *CVZ*, XI (January 1, 1932).

[54]Fritz Goldschmidt, "Deutschtum und Judentum zu den Grundlagen unseres Seins," *CVZ*, XII (June 8, 1933); Bab, *Lieben und Tod*, p. 35.

[55]In his 11-page chapter "The Liberal Era," Bab, in *Lieben und Tod das deutsches Judentums*, managed to list the names (and contributions) of 67 prominent German Jews of that era. The average number of such names in the book is approximately 5 to 6 per page. See *Lieben und Tod*, pp. 36, 35–44, passim.

[56]Friedlander, "Ein Charakterbild in der Geschichte."

[57]Mann, *Joseph*, III, *Joseph in Egypt*, 144.

[58]"Der deutsche Staatsbürger jüdischen Glaubens," *CVZ*, XII (July 13, 1933).

[59]"Vom Wesen einer neuen Emanzipation," *CVZ*, XII (July 13, 1933).

[60]"Deutschtum und Judentum. Der reichsdeutsche Jude im Dritten Reich," *CVZ*, XII (June 29, 1933). A new column entitled "Deutschtum und Judentum" was begun with this issue. Each week it was to provide examples of the historical symbiosis, with long articles that began to include favorable accounts of men like Langbehn and Lagarde, as Nazi publications referred to them as spiritual precursors.

[61]Ibid.

[62]Eva G. Reichmann, "Symbol of German Jewry," *Leo Baeck Yearbook*, II (London & New York, 1957), 21–26.

[63]Bab, *Lieben und Tod*, p. 19.

[64]Baron, *Deutsche und Jude*; Fritz Friedlander, "Friedrich Meinecke," *CVZ Monthly*, IV (December 1932).

[65]Elbogen, *Die Geschichte der Juden*, p. 265.

[66]Ibid., pp. 262, 266.

145

VIII

The King Never Dies

Heroic individualism is identification with ancestors in a new space and a new time: the new space is the public realm; the new time is history.

NORMAN O. BROWN, *Love's Body*

In the Weimar Republic the German Enlightenment and liberal spirit were described by German Jews as being totally resurrected, the resurrection of an archetypal *Weltanschauung*. In the eyes of German Jews, Germany's potential to be an ideal nation based on the principles of the German *philosophes* was more realized or actualized than ever before. German Jews seemed to argue that, theoretically, nearly all Germans were living the Lessing-like life in the Republic. The "lived life" of the archetypes—life according to their principles and ideals—appeared to have become institutionalized in the Weimar Republic. European liberalism, the protector of German Jews, had been considered the basis for Germans and Jews living together. Weimar brought the movement to fruition, was its highest expression. To German Jews, liberalism once again seemed victorious, honorable, German: "To be known as a liberal and an intellectual was a high honor" in Weimar.[1]

146

Because these beliefs were so firmly held by German Jews, Leo Baeck shocked the newly formed *Reichsvertretung* in March 1933, with the bluntness of his declaration that one thousand years of German Jewish history came to an end with the tragic fall of the Weimar Republic.[2] Some there could still not believe it. It was tragic in the classical sense; that is, a goal had supposedly been achieved, culminated, fulfilled; hopes were brightest; optimism seemed justified—and then came total collapse, failure, and catastrophe.[3] What collapsed with Weimar was both the dream and the opportunity to fulfill the promises of the Enlightenment, the dream of complete, true democracy and freedom of belief.[4] The Republic represented humanity, human value, Herder's idea of "the greater community of man," all the beliefs and values of Lessing and his intellectual, ethical compatriots.[5] Herder or Brecht, "Goethe or Hoffmannsthal, Hölderlin or Rilke . . . they were all contemporaries in the German pantheon."[6]

In 1918 German Jews averred that they had been loyal to Imperial Germany and vowed that they would again be loyal to republican Germany.[7] German patriotism's primary constituent had been defense of Germany in war and in peace. It still remained the same. Heinrich Heine, Ludwig Börne, and Bismarck were symptomatic of Germany and her ideals. They had staunchly defended and served the nation and its values as they had perceived them. Their successors were Ebert, Jakob Wassermann, Hugo Preuss, and Walter Rathenau.[8] Groups like the Organisation des preusszischen Judentums had always been "organically united" with the German community, had professed the teachings of Wilhelm von Humboldt, had stood firmly for the reform of 1812 and against the French, had supported the German unification, and had joined in the efforts of 1848 and 1871. In 1922 they would carry on defending and serving with the same patriotic fervor that had made them good Germans throughout German history.[9]

147

Not only German Jews believed that pre-World War I Germany contained enormous potential for the fulfillment of the great Enlightenment vision. Heinrich Mann, whom many considered Germany's new intellectual leader, as the personification of the new intellectual *Geist*, had also recognized the dormant potential, and after the war he became the embodiment of the new spirit that would actualize that potential. Hermann Hesse called Mann the intellectual and moral leader of the Republic.[10] Arnold Zweig noted that the *New York Times* had called Mann the "representative of a human type in his heights and possibilities."[11] He was honored by the Weimar Republic with the post of President of the Authors' Academy of Prussia.[12] He was honored formally by the Weimar Republic because he was its formal symbol.

What Heinrich Mann symbolized to German Jews and other supporters of the Republic was the brave, human, tolerant, enlightened ideal that they believed would conduct Germany and Europe to a not-so-distant paradise of freedom and humanity. He was the hero of his novels about Henry IV, whose ethics and virtues, at least in Mann's novels, closely conformed to those of Lessing and Herder.[13] Mann was the spirit of the Republic in human form. Weimar was Germany, and to German Jews Mann was its essence, the ineffable German. Germany's noble tradition culminated in him. He was an institution, a collective ideal, a concept.

German Jews esteemed Heinrich Mann as the personification of what they believed was Weimar's spirit, a way of thinking and living that had most clearly overtaken official as well as intellectual Germany. In one of its many encomiums to the Republic, the *CVZ* characterized that spirit of Weimar as German if only because the constitution was the "first to be in the true spirit of Kant's categorical imperative."[14] Through that Kantian constitution lay the road to complete civil equality. A memorial to Friedrich Ebert described "the essence of Weimar" as the great classical tradition of humanity and equality for all, with "roots buried deep in the great age of the German classics." Ebert and the Republic had harmonized the *Humanitätsidee* with the contemporary needs, had updated the heritage of Goethe and Schiller.[15] Universalism was the new path for Europe, and Germany would lead the way. The year 1918 heralded a "return," not a new turn, to ancient truths.

With relentless repetition the *CVZ* editors observed that the bearers of that tradition in Germany had been Lessing and Goethe, and that the bearers of that same tradition in the world at large had been the Jews.[16] Even temperate anti-Semites like Ernst Berg perceived a cultural affinity between the international ideas of German Jews and the national ones of German non-Jews "through Christ."[17]

Section III, Part 2, of the constitution guaranteed freedom to "all the inhabitants of the Federation to enjoy full liberty of faith and conscience."[18] Along with Articles 135–141 assuring religious freedom, Article 148 allegedly typified the "spirit" of the German people . . . that hates authority, *putsches*, violence, and 'rowdies.' "[19] While Article 148 ostensibly dealt with "educational aims," it assumed grave importance to German Jews because, according to it, those "educational aims" were to be "moral training, public spirit . . . and above all, the *cultivation of German national character and of the spirit of international reconciliation.*"[20] German Jews interpreted the injunction "not to wound the susceptibilities of those holding different opinions" as an extension of the constitutional articles dealing with religion. German Jews therefore considered Article 148 to be the quintessence of the constitution that brought the idea and the ideal of Germanness and humanity into practice.[21]

By 1929 German Jews openly celebrated the anniversary of the Republic in religious services with sermons and blessings in praise of Article 148.[22] In praising it, they heralded the Republic and Germany.

Their praise revolved around the belief that any observation of German history would reveal the Weimar Republic as the height of German culture and justice—the height of Germanness. Germanness represented the tie that bound beyond religion. Germanness, as conceived in Article 148, was akin to humanitarianism.[23] Because the contemporary *Zeitgeist* demanded free men,[24] the task of Weimar culture was to educate Germany to that fact, according to German Jewish supporters of the Republic.[25] To ignore that task would be "unpedagogical, un-*German*, and tactless."[26]

German Jews extolled Weimar's institutions for their alleged materializing of the ideals and universal principles of earlier ages. Religious toleration was now law; democracy was enforced in the courts, which adjudicated on the basis of Old Testament ethics—at least theoretically;[27] equality and freedom were at last within the grasp of all Germans because of the new constitution. Those institutions—the courts, the constitution, the Republic itself—represented physical expressions of cultural ideals, goals, values, beliefs, and convictions. Behind important institutional facades was the real stuff of Germany—its spirit.

The steady stream of literature equating true *Deutschtum* with *Judentum*, the insistences upon German Jewish patriotism for centuries, the often-convoluted declarations of spiritual oneness, culminated in the outpourings on the archetypal, edenic nature of Weimar. What agonizing contortions German Jews underwent as they simultaneously rejoiced for the birth of the Republic and grieved for Germany's defeat in Wold War I. Subdued joy mingled with sorrow for Germany and for the German Jewish soldiers dead for a cause doubly tragic for them.[28]

From the depths of defeat, German Jews began to praise the new Germany by calling it the old Germany. In his *Berliner Tageblatt*, Julious Goldstein's entry of December 13, 1918, described his feelings when he returned from the war: he was home—*Home*—in Germany; on German soil; breathing German air; looking at German streets, houses, people. His only emotion: Joy. Even though the banners were not for victory, still, joy. Germany was still his home, he wrote, even if it had a new government. It was "a spiritual homecoming. . . . Now I return to you [Germany] changed, but still the same."[29] The "spiritual home" was the world of the archetypal Germans.

There is symbolic significance in the fact that Peter Gay, historian, insightful commentator, and devotee of Weimar culture, is also the admiring historian of the Enlightenment. He has categorized Weimar Germany's model path as "the way of Goethe and Humboldt . . . truthful, manly . . . cosmopolitan."[30] That description of Weimar culture nearly duplicates Gay's interpretation of the Enlightenment culture as "a program of secularism, humanity, cosmopolitanism, and freedom."[31] Settembrini (Heinrich Mann in shallow disguise) of *The Magic Mountain*, with his belief in Reason, his "deep obligation to the German Enlightenment," seemed to have triumphed in the struggle for Germany's soul.[32] Walter Gropius, like Settembrini, or Heinrich Mann (or Peter Gay), taught "the lesson of Bacon and Descartes and the Enlightenment."[33] Weimar's Jews aspired to the "benign *Humanität* of Goethe," and Carl von Ossietsky acknowledged that "official Germany celebrated Goethe."[34] Privately shunned and isolated, Thomas Mann was officially and publicly invited to speak, and, like Goethe, was praised, celebrated, and honored by the Republic.[35]

What did the Republic mean to German Jews? Eugen Fuchs, then president of the CV, asked and answered that crucial question in March 1919. It meant, he said, the end of militarism and bureaucracy; the end of intolerance by the outdated ruling classes who had for years oppressed Germans and the true German spirit. It meant that "anti-Semitism is . . . under attack by Reason in *all* political parties." It meant that truth would win through education. He was an optimist, he admitted, but with good reason.[36]

151

Weimar meant that Germany's Lessings and Goethes and Schillers were now Ebert, Preuss, and might hypothetically even be a general like Hindenburg. Preuss's constitution and the Democratic Party meant total democratization of public life so that men not generally noted for their enlightened views suddenly were compelled to live the republican life, publicly, at any rate. The Republic meant that Ebert was president because he spoke for most Germans, that he had "Germanness sunk deep in his blood . . . [and] loved Germany more than anything."[37] The Republic meant the realization of the legal and human freedom and equality that had always been the principles of German Jews as well as non-Jews.[38] It had arisen and stood because Germany wanted it. The first elections proved that, and showed that Germany had willed it and had created a positive construction from a negative situation (military defeat).[39]

As if to support such beliefs, non-Jewish critics wrote in German Jewish journals that Alfred Lichtwark and Max Liebermann clearly manifested German character in their art, that they were bearers of Germanness, that they were "leaders of the German future," and that in Liebermann rested "the revelation of the German character."[40] Weimar meant assimilation as the goal of emancipation was at last achieved.

Public institutions, then, were now to express this spirit and these ideals. Strong defense of German institutions had always been the road that aspiring patriots had followed. Patriotism was nothing more (or less) than loyalty and allegiance to a nation's institutions, such as its government and its constitution. What more patriotic Germans could there have been than Jewish Germans in the Weimar Republic? Patriotism now had become loyalty to liberal ideals. German Jews alleged that German patriotism had consisted of such loyalty for 120 years or more, but it had been a subdued, idealistic, wordy, and academic liberalism. Theories were now being practiced in Germany.[41]

It seemed that in 1919 there could be no question that Germany was a republic unequivocally based on and devoted to liberal ideas. Even men who seemed inconsolable in their mourning for the passing of Imperial Germany reluctantly forced themselves to the recognition that they must now uphold the Republic.[42]

Continuity of principles demonstrated the legitimacy of the new government. There could be no thought of an abrupt, radical, and revolutionary break with the past in the public mind. And German Jews, perhaps above all other Germans, could not imagine the need for a violent revolution.[43] That would deny their long-held conception of Germany and *deutsche Tradition*. Bridging the gap with myth, or with history—education—was the game they began in hopeful earnest.

German Jews as republican men, as Germans, held the paradigm of Hugo Preuss before the public. To them he was not the archetypal outsider but the *Kommunalpolitiker*, the German who fought for all Germans and all Germany, past, present, and future. In the eyes of German Jewish scholars, Preuss had synthesized—not unlike Herder—Jewishness and Germanness. Among the memorial speakers for Preuss was a Justice Falk, who celebrated Preuss's "German will, his love of the fatherland, his devotion to *Volk* and land. He was an unquestionably German man ... *Preuss was Germany*."[44]

In that same spirit, Ludo Hartman had demanded that the *Reich* title be retained along with the black-red-gold and the federative articles of the constitution, "as symbols of the *grossdeutschen* idea."[45] German Jews portrayed the Republic as combining nationalism with republican universalism,[46] the old with the new, the two in the one—as Herder and Fichte had combined them.

153

Anti-Semitism in the face of the new official principles of Germany signified more than slander of Jews. It was now treason. To those who linked republicanism with national allegiance, all those who derided the Republic as "Jewish" or *verjudet* were striking at the foundation of official Germany.[47] In Germany, claimed *Im Deutschen Reich*, the "Jewish *Geist*" resided in the homes of most Germans as "Christian *Geist*." Lectures were delivered by Jews and non-Jews in the 1920s arguing that Christ was an archetypal Jew imbued with a Jewish *Geist*.[48] Certainly anti-Semites disregarded the nub of the German *Geist* by avoiding a confrontation with the question of whether *"der deutsche Geist* [ist] *verjudet oder der jüdische Geist verdeutscht."*[49]

Allied anti-German war propaganda had "shocked" most Germans with allegations of German opposition to humanity, morality, and ethics.[50] The Allies had excluded the *Boche* from the community of culture.[51] Bonar Law had called the Germans "the hated of the earth."[52]

The vituperation heaped on Germany accused Germans of barbaric and uncivilized moral codes, of being devoid of a civilized culture and *Geist*. It was a hatred and an isolation, said German Jews, precisely like that which Jews had suffered for ages. Both Germans and Jews, they continued, were falsely accused and both stood for the same civilized principles. *Verjudet* meant *verdeutscht*, especially after defeat and especially in the Republic. Not only were Germans and Jews unified in a community of fate and sorrow but in a community of ideals and principles.

No less a leader of the Jewish community than Alfred Wiener, who, according to one editor, might have been eligible for a "Nobel Prize for Germanness,"[53] called upon all Germans to "Think: is it only Jewish figures . . . that are responsible [for the Republic]?"[54] Goethe and Heine had been alike in their condemnation of despotism.[55] Heine had only extrapolated Goethe's thoughts when from love of

154

Germany he summoned her to conquer the future by means of a republic instead of a Kaiser.[56]

Jewish Germans implored Christian Germans to speak out "for the German future," to fight against anti-Semitism and for the Republic,[57] and to understand that anti-Semitism was dangerous to Christians as well as to Jews in the Weimar Republic.[58] According to this logic, being against anti-Semitism was being for the Republic and Germany; to preach racism and anti-Semitism was to contradict and oppose the constitution and the "Weimar system."[59] The battle against anti-Semitic parties and ideas was no longer the task of German Jews alone because anti-Semitic, *völkisch* electoral successes were threats to *German* culture.[60]

Völkisch parties did level their anti-Semitic tirades against the constitution and against the Republic. From this, German Jews concluded that anti-Semites attacked the civil rights of all Germans and were therefore a danger to all Germany.[61] Consequently, an assault upon a German Jew, such as Rathenau's assassination, warned not only Jewish Germans, but all Germans that *völkisch* anti-Semitism disguised as patriotism concealed subversive activity that threatened the entire nation.[62]

The constitution and, after 1925, President Hindenburg not only guaranteed equal rights for German Jews, but affirmed that they were "through their history, culture ... inextricably bound morally and intellectually to the community of the German *Volk*."[63] In January 1932, as Germany entered the *Entscheidungsjahr* (decisive year), Justice Julius Brodnitz declared at a public meeting that 1932 would bring the verdict on "whether the German Reich can *continue to serve*, as its constitution states in its introduction, in freedom and justice." He concluded by emphasizing that in the battle for Germany's survival "*we are one with all Germans.... Our fate is irrevocably tied to the fate of the German fatherland.*"[64] Conversely, Max Naumann wrote that Jews must not consider anti-Semitic parties as dangerous to themselves as Jews, but that they must oppose any seizure of power by those hostile parties as a danger to Germany.[65] He called upon German Jews to "act . . . not for the supposed interest of the Jews, but for the German *Kultur* and German future."[66]

Toward the opposite extreme of the multiform German Jewish community, *Die Israelit* approached political partisanship by equating the Jewish defense with the republican one: "The struggle for defense of the Jews is a fight for the rights and freedom of all Germany."[67] Defense of the "Weimar spirit" and the constitution was to be taken for granted among German Jews. But all Germans must now join in that struggle because it was now "for the honor of the German Reich."[68] Both Christian and Jewish communities confronted a spiritual and physical crisis posed by anti-Semitic groups. It was incumbent upon all Gemans to answer the call, defend the Republic and themselves "for love and truth" and life.[69]

NOTES

[1]Gay, *Weimar Culture*, p. 135.

[2]Reichmann, "Symbol of German Jewry"; Kurt Jakob Ball-Kadurie, *Das Leben der Juden in Deutschland im Jahre 1933. Ein Zeitbericht* (Frankfurt am Main: Europäische Verlaganstalt, 1963), p. 212.

[3]Eva Reichmann. "Die Lage der Juden in der Weimarer Republik" paper read at the convention of the Evangelische Akademie on "Der Antisemitismus und die deutsche Geschicht," September 18–21, 1957; Karl Buchheim, "Die Tragödie die Weimarer Republik," *Hochland*, XLIX, No. 6 (August 1957).

[4]"Umwälzung und Kriegsende," *Im Deutschen Reich*, XXIV, No. 11 (November 1918), 417–427.

[5]Aner, "Herders Stellung zur Judenfrage."

[6]Gay, *Weimar Culture*, p. 67.

[7]"Umwälzung und Kriegesende."

[8]"Hanns Heinz Ewers gegen Martin Spahn," CVZ, I, No. 7 (June 15, 1922), 85.

⁹Ismar Freund, "Organisation des preusszischen Judentums," *CVZ*, I (June 22, 1922), 101–104.

¹⁰Zweig, "Heinrich Mann, Politischer Scharfblicke und Meisterschaft" (1950), *Essays*, pp. 309–313.

¹¹Ibid.

¹²Ibid.

¹³Zweig, "Heinrich Manns Meisterwerk" (1935), *Essays*, pp. 314–319.

¹⁴Paul Hildebrandt, Gretel Goldstein, Hilde Ephraim, "Lehrer, Mütter und Schüler," *CVZ Monthly*, I (February 1928).

¹⁵Paul Kampffmyer, "For the German People's Leader: Friedrich Ebert," *CVZ*, IV (March 3, 1925).

¹⁶Efraim Frisch, "Jüdische Aufzeichnungen," *Der Neue Merkur*, V, No. 5 (August, 1921), 297–317.

¹⁷Berg, *Wohin treibt Juda?*, p. 17.

¹⁸Heinrich Oppenheimer, *The Constitution of the German Republic* (London: Stevens & Sons, 1923), p. 249; *Dokumente*, III, 148.

¹⁹Karl Severing, "Wie überwindet das deutsche Volk dem Nationalsozialismus?" *CVZ*, IX (Steptember 26, 1930).

²⁰Oppenheimer, *The Constitution*, p. 252; *Dokumente*, III, 150, italics added.

²¹Hildebrandt, "Lehrer, Mütter"; Freund, "Jüdische Gemeinden, Reichsgericht und jüdische Wissenschaft," *CVZ*, XI (January 15, 1932).

²²"Verfassungsfeiern in den Synagogen," *CVZ*, VIII (August 16, 1929).

²³Chaplain F. Rödel, "Mehr Liebe," *CVZ*, IV (March 13, 1925).

²⁴Margarete Holz, "Wie erziehen wir republikanliche Menschen?" *CVZ*, VIII (August 9, 1929).

²⁵Hildebrandt, "Lehrer, Mütter."

²⁶Ibid., italics added.

²⁷"Das Reichsgericht über jüdische Ethik," *CVZ*, I (July 20, 1922), 139.

²⁸Cf. "Umwälzung und Kriegsende."

²⁹Julius Goldstein, "Geistes Heimkehr," excerpt from *Berliner Tageblatt* in *CVZ*, VIII (July 19, 1929).

³⁰Gay, *Weimar Culture*, pp. 1, 11.

³¹Gay, *The Enlightenment*, p. 3.

³²In the battle for Germany's "soul" fought in *The Magic Mountain*, Settembrini represents the humanist "of the old school, an optimist . . . a democrat . . . an idealist who believes that truth, justice, freedom may be reached . . . [through] the enlightenment of man." Roy Pascal, *The German Novel*, p. 83. Settembrini's character is best revealed in his praise of humanists and schoolmasters (educators); Heinrich Mann's hero was Emil Zola, "the enlightened civilian," aptly described by Settembrini. Cf. Thomas Mann, *The Magic Mountain* (New York: Modern Library, 1927), p. 64; and Gay, *Weimar Culture*, p. 73.

³³Gay, *Weimar Culture*, pp. 33–34, 101, 127.

³⁴Ibid., p. 88.

³⁵Cf. Mann, Introduction to *Joseph*.

157

[36]Eugen Fuchs, "Was nun?" *Im Deutschen Reich*, XXV, No. 3 (March, 1919), 103–111.

[37]Kampffmyer, "For the German People's Leader: Ebert"; cf. Erich Eyck, *A History of the Weimar Republic*, 2nd ed., 2 vols. (New York: Atheneum Press, 1970), I, *From the Collapse of the Empire to Hindenburg's Election*, 64–65.

[38]Elbogen, *Die Geschichte der Juden*, p. 286; Stern, *Warum sind wir Deutsche?* p. 7.

[39]Holz, "Wie erziehen wir republikanliche Menschen?"

[40]"The Revelation of the German Character. Lichtwerk and Liebermann," *CVZ*, IV (January 23, 1925).

[41]Willi Lewinsohn, "Ein Blick in unser Inneres. Von den Quellen judenfeindlicher Gefühle," *CVZ*, VIII (August 23, 1929).

[42]Cf. Gay, *Weimar Culture*; Iggers, *The German Conception of History*, pp. 229ff., 272–273.

[43]See Toller, *I Was a German*, pp. 136, passim.

[44]"Dem deutschen Manne, Hugo Preuss," *CVZ*, IV (October 16, 1925).

[45]Carl Misch, "Politik," in Kaznelson, pp. 531–589.

[46]Lewinsohn, "Ein Blick in unser Inneres."

[47]Ibid.

[48]"Rabbiner Dr. Norden spricht über Jesus von Nazareth," *CVZ*, IX (May 19, 1930); Hugo Hahn, "Christliche Forscher über jüdische Quellen der Urchristentums," *CVZ*, IX (May 26, 1930).

[49]Walter Leiser, "Zum 9 November," *Im Deutschen Reich*, XXV, No. 11 (November 1919), 460–468.

[50]"The Jewish Hatred is the Same as the German Hatred," *CVZ Monthly*, IV (January 1932).

[51]Jakob Schenk, "Die 'Schuld' der Juden," *Im Deutschen Reich*, XXV, No. 1 (January 1919), 1–11.

[52]Leiser, "Zum 9 November."

[53]"Die jüdische Abwehr," *Die Israelit*, LXXI, No. 26 (June 26, 1930).

[54]Alfred Wiener in *CVZ*, IV (February 27, 1925).

[55]Arnold Zweig, "Heinrich Heines hunderster Todestag" (1955), *Essays*, pp. 209–211.

[56]Ibid.

[57]Margaret T. Edelheim-Muesham, "Die Haltung der jüdischer Presse gegenüber der nationalsozialistischen Bedrohung."

[58]Wiener, *CVZ*, IV (February 27, 1925).

[59]D. Windfuks, "Der Geist im politischen Kampf," *CVZ Monthly*, IV (October 1932).

[60]"*Völkisch* 'Success' in Lettland. A Threat to the German Culture," *CVZ*, IV (April 3, 1925); M. Spanier, "Nicht nur Hass sehen!" *CVZ Monthly*, IV (October 1932).

[61]"Die jüdische Abwehr," *Der Israelit*, LXXI, No. 26 (June 26, 1930); Windfuks, "Der Geist im politischen Kampf."

[62]"Der Vernichtungskampf gegen das Judentum," CVZ, I (August 3, 1922), 161.

[63]"Die jüdische Abwehr," Die Israelit.

[64]Julius Brodnitz, "1932—das Jahre der Entscheidung," speech delivered at a public meeting on January 16, 1932, reprinted in CVZ, XI (January 22, 1932).

[65]Naumann, Sozialismus, p. 5.

[66]Ibid., p. 15.

[67]"Die jüdische Abwehr," Die Israelit.

[68]Ibid.

[69]Heinrich Hirsch, "Ein offenes Wort," speech on receiving the Goethe Plaque, reported in CVZ Monthly, IV (October 1932).

IX

The Rumor and Reality

If eternal justice then looked down upon the earth, she must have
seen a sorry sight of humilitation, and, what was viler still, of
hypocrisy and self-betrayal.

> HEINRICH MANN, *Henry, King of France*

...jedem Anfang wohnt ein Zauber innen, der uns beschützt,
und der uns hilft zu leben. (Each beginning carries an
illusion in it that protects us and helps us to
live.)

> HERMANN HESSE

Hans Castorp, the hero of Thomas Mann's *The Magic Mountain*, is, like pre-World War I Germany, ensnared by his past and lured into danger and "disease" by his family and German tradition. The agents of opposing ideologies and forces that struggled to dominate Germany in 1924— from the radicals of the right to those of the left—are symbolically represented by characters in the novel who battle for Hans Castorp's mind and soul. He symbolizes Germany and, like Germany, he is seeking a spiritual home and an ideological shelter that will define his own identity. Castorp, like Germany, absorbs the contradictory philosophies of war, struggle, despair, and "grandiloquent humanism." They coexist within him because he cannot wholly reject any of them. Therefore, there are paradoxes at the heart of his ideological identity.

Mann concluded that no single *Weltanschauung* dominated Germany. German Jews, however, saw Germany differently. To them, Settembrini had triumphed: Mann's spokesman of love, tolerance, justice, emancipation, and "grandiloquent humanism" seemed to be the victor of Weimar. Settembrini appeared to mirror their image of a typical German, the image of themselves as Germans. Like them, he was "a humanist of the old school, an optimist . . . a democrat . . . a rationalist who believes that man can be educated by reason and science, an idealist who believes that truth, justice, freedom may be reached."[1] The identification of Settembrini as the typical German corresponded to convictions that Jews in Germany had expressed for years. The myth of the Enlightenment German was alive, and they believed Thomas Mann had reaffirmed it.

Men like Ludwig Hollander, Leo Baeck, Alfred Wiener, Jakob Wassermann, and other leaders of the German Jewish community deeply honored Settembrini's principles and lived their public lives according to those ideals. Along with a few notable non-Jewish liberals, they were the Settembrinis of the Weimar Republic. Thomas Mann portrayed his character, "the unrepentant child of the Enlightenment, well meaning rationalist," as an anachronism in 1924, a symbol of a self-deluding, dying way of life.[2] Unfortunately, "only the Settembrinis did not realize it."[3]

Hannah Arendt has ascribed this blindness to a "dangerous inability . . . to distinguish between friend and foe . . . because they [German Jews] somehow thought that all Gentiles were alike."[4] German Jews' perceptions of Germans were to a great extent projections of their own egos. They projected their own humanist principles onto others and resolved a tension between themselves and a potentially or actually hostile social and political reality.

The tragic "inability to distinguish between friend and foe" was a flaw not only of the Settembrinis among German Jews. Max Naumann, leader of the National deutschen Juden (NdJ) and by no means a Settembrini figure, exhorted German Jews to join with the "national movement." He

161

embraced the NSDAP as an ally of the NdJ in that movement. Having been accused by the CV of supporting National Socialism as the only vehicle for what he termed a
rebirth of true *Deutschtum*, Naumann replied that his devotion was not to the National Socialist Party but to "the
Volksbewegung which may include the Nazi circle but
encompasses far more" than this one party.[5]

Naumann based his praise of National Socialism and
Hitler on their nationalistic enthusiasm and considered the
Nazi ideologues to be "noble idealists" who preached an
idealism with only one "minor error"—anti-Semitism.[6]
Nazism's anti-Semitism, he claimed, was a "regrettable
side effect," a regrettable but minor element of National
Socialism.[7] He denounced talk of Jewish world conspiracy
as fantasy, because such rumors "make us miserable *as
Germans.*"[8] Nevertheless, because he saw the Nazi movement as a whole fighting for the good of Germany, Naumann called upon German Jews to bear with the "error,"
to understand the true value of the thoughts and methods
of these "others" in the national struggle "even if they
behave as *if*: they are our enemies."[9]

As for Hitler, Naumann praised him as a "drummer" to
whom "as a German I am thankful ... even though his
earlier speeches bore hatred against the Jews and in part
still bear it even today [1930]."[10] To Naumann, Hitler
represented a desperate hero trying any means to awaken
Germany from a lethargy of national despair. Anti-Semitism was only a device, used reluctantly, to inspire nationalism. Naumann was convinced that once that national
awakening had begun, anti-Semitism would fall away naturally.

Like another contemporary commentator on the "Jewish
Question," Naumann believed that Germany had assimilated her Jews readily and completely long ago.[11] After the
nineteenth century, however, the "strength of Israel" (religion) was subsumed into the German idea of Reich. Reich
was the goal in the twentieth century, and "one is not a

162

man of the Reich if one calls himself German, but one has the right to call himself German if he is a man of the Reich."[12] To be German was therefore to be a nationalistic supporter of the German Reich, like Naumann and his group—like Hitler and the Nazis.

While Naumann was shunned by the overwhelming majority of German Jews, he nevertheless manifested a faith in Germany and in German nationalism not completely dissimilar to the CV. German Jews proclaimed themselves German because of a national consciousness common to all Germans.[13] Those interminable lists of German Jewish contributions to patriotic causes, testimonies of the cultural effusion of German Jews throughout the nineteenth century, were all proclamations of a true national spirit that resembled Naumann's insistence of German Jewish national allegiance. Even in February 1933, Ludwig Hollander voiced what he said was the common certainty of German Jews, that their "German consciousness ties them *inseparably* to *real* Germans."[14] And again, in April 1933, in the midst of the first Nazi anti-Semitic legislation, the CV repeated that "we cannot believe Germany and Germans will abandon all this [common national goals] and forget us."[15]

This stubborn clinging to identification with Germans, the apparent inability to observe critically and act upon reality, is evidence of a psychological need for security and psychic peace. It was so firmly and deeply rooted in German Jews that most refused to relinquish their identification with German archetypes even after the National Socialist victory of 1933, indeed until 1935 or even 1938. The lead article of the CVZ's first issue after Hitler's seizure of power again spoke of the inseparability of German Jews from other Germans, of German consciousness and the "trust in the final victory of Truth and Reason."[16] In 1935 German Jews generally believed that they would be able to exist within the new order on some sort of restricted basis that would be only a minor, temporary inconvenience.[17]

German Jews wrote about "Our Position in National Socialist Germany," and drafted numerous plans to be submitted to the government on the role of Jews in Germany's new future.[18] Even in 1938 an incredulous Julius Bab, now in exile, continued to write of the "deep ties" of Germans and Jews, and remembered that Jews for centuries had been "*identified* with Germans."[19]

Hugo Bettauer's rich novel of 1921 had portrayed a member of the older generation, Hofrat Spineder, as a hypocrite—seemingly harmless, but still hypocritical.[20] In biting satire, Bettauer described the old patrician as "tolerant, cultured, loving," a self-confessed "democrat through and through, a true servant of the Republic."[21] Yet as he served the new regime, he continued to wear a "Kaiser beard," kept a picture of the Kaiser, with angels around his head, on the wall in a revered place.[22] While he mouthed tolerant slogans and benignly expressed his liking for the Jewish hero and all Jews, Hofrat Spineder nevertheless willingly and happily obeyed and supported the expulsion of the Jews. Not even the hero of the novel recognized that Hofrat Spineder, and all the other Hofrat Spineders of Germany, were fundamentally anti-republican and, if not constitutionally anti-Semitic, opposed Jews as supporters of the new government and destroyers of the old.

Despite the apparent oblivion, despite the excessive patriotic naïveté of Naumann and the NdJ, most German Jews were not impervious to the existence and danger of anti-Semitism in Germany. The events of 1925, 1928, 1930, 1932, and 1933 made it virtually impossible to deny that there was a growing anti-Semitic movement that appealed to a growing number of Germans.

In 1925, even before Hindenburg's election as president of the Republic, the CVZ began devoting most of its space to attacking *völkisch* anti-Semitic theory and practice, the NSDAP, and especially Hitler's speeches.[23] Almost entire issues of the CVZ monthly and weekly were given over to refuting attacks against the Jews. Those articles tacitly acknowledged the increase of anti-Semitism in Germany.

Such attention to anti-Semitic accusations marks a quantitative break with earlier CVZ style and policy. Yet the CV still refused to admit that anti-Semitism was typical or widespread in Germany. The lead article in the CVZ, May 29, 1925, was entitled "Better Times Ahead?" and based its optimistic conclusions on the absolute knowledge that "the majority of Germans are not anti-Semitic, not Nazis."[24] The article added that those few Germans who were anti-Semitic had but to look at the armed and violent Hitler groups and they would be forced by their German tradition and conscience to renounce anti-Semitism.[25] Articles praised Hindenburg as the choice and embodiment of Germany. Because he was truly German, German Jews were to rest assured that Hindenburg would be true to them as Germans.[26]

Anti-Semitism manifested itself in 1925 primarily through verbal propaganda, desecratory acts, and sporadic physical assaults. In 1928, however, although the NSDAP lost seats in the Reichstag, it made some inroads into local, rural areas like Thuringia. Before those elections Alfred Wiener addressed a meeting of the CV executive committee and warned against the stirring Nazi propaganda campaign in such rural districts. The executive committee was unsympathetic to his warning and labeled him a pessimist because he gave a single, isolated campaign such importance. For "Germany as a whole," the committee argued "it was untypical."[27] After the elections the CV began an investigation of the reasons and sources of National Socialist support.[28] They were faced with the incontrovertible fact of at least limited anti-Semitic success.

But because of their firm convictions in what they believed to be the essence of Deutschtum (the Enlightenment myth), German Jews sought rationalizations and explanations for what they considered a twentieth-century deviation from the norm in Germany. The conclusion of the CV

165

investigation was that the Nazi gains were minor, merely another manifestation of a traditional anti-Semitism which German Jews had seen come and go.[29] One German Jewish member of the Reichstag exclaimed: "No! It would be false to take these people [Nazis] seriously politically."[30]

Most German Jews agreed. Anti-Semitism had come and gone before. The evidence of the investigation indicated that these new anti-Semitic advances followed the same pattern of past experiences in Germany: Germans voted rashly out of a sense of disenchantment with the status quo. Anger and frustration had influenced their votes. Because of economic poverty, the electorate of Thuringia (where the Nazis had relative success) had registered a protest vote.[31] The CV seemed certain that the support of the NSDAP would be abandoned after the May 1928 election.

What is of utmost importance in this logic is the retention of the German Jewish perception of Germany as basically not anti-Semitic. German Jews claimed that Germans had voted for the NSDAP not because they opposed Jews, but because they opposed the Republic's economic policies.

By 1930, German Jewish writers regularly linked anti-Semitic outbursts and increasing German support of National Socialism to economic problems. In July of that year a lengthy article in the CVZ repeated the idea that anti-Semitism was not a new phenomenon, but had been intensified by unemployment and economic need.[32] Anti-Semitism could only be countered and reduced, therefore, with an alternative to the völkisch theorists' economic policies.[33] In that same issue of the CVZ appeared an article campaigning for more non-Jews to join the CV.[34] The thrust of the two articles was that together German Jews and German non-Jews could formulate a liberal, successful economic policy that would save Germany and make her great again.

Since the NSDAP successes had been grounded in economics by the CV explanations, the surprising victory of that party in the September 1930 elections was as readily explained as the earlier, localized, and less dramatic "victories" of 1928. Immediately after the 1930 elections Ludwig Hollander wrote: "A great number of Nazi voters—perhaps the greatest part—did *not* support the Nazis for their Jewish enmity, but because they approved of their economic and political solutions to Germany's economic and political troubles. Anti-Semitism did *not* help the National Socialists to victory. Germans did *not* vote against Jews."[35]

Hollander's statement ended with the reaffirmation of the CV policy to refrain from political activity.[36] Only the political parties could combat the economic and political platforms of the NSDAP. Those German Jews who fought in that battle did so as Germans. As spokesman for the CV and for most German Jews, Hollander repeated that German Jews "can never be swayed from our basic belief that we . . . are members of the German *Volk*,"[37] a German *Volk* that had again been proven enlightened and not anti-Semitic.

The CV's apolitical, seemingly obdurate position so clearly enunciated by Hollander elicited a harsh "open letter" in the liberal, non-Jewish journal *Deutsche Republik*.[38] The letter was signed simply "G.H." but was in fact written by Gaston Heymann, an Alsatian Jew. He railed against the CV's persistent theorizing, reasoning, and avoidance of criticism of the German people for supporting anti-Semitism. The German Jewish seeking, proposing, and expecting a better economic situation, the thesis that Germans were anti-Semites only out of what were after all rational economic reasons, he denounced as "ridiculous hopes and dreams."[39]

Despite this warning, while the anti-anti-Semitic campaign became almost exclusively an anti-Nazi operation after the September 1930 elections, it continued to be an undertaking directed toward understanding and explaining the hostility as a derivative of economic and political programs.[40] The campaign was not directed against anti-

167

Semitic Germans. Eva Reichmann-Jungmann responded to Heymann's open letter in a subsequent issue of *Deutsche Republik*.[41] (Both the original letter and the reply were also reprinted in the *CVZ*.) Her reply was bitter but essentially reemphasized the CV line and called upon liberals and the Republic to change the economic and political situation.[42] Albert Einstein, in an eloquent essay, called for solidarity among German Jews themselves. But he made it clear that he firmly believed that the September elections were only a temporary reaction to the present economic situation—a *Kinderkrankheit* of the Weimar Republic.[43] Solidarity among Jews should still be a part of the greater solidarity among Jews and Germans.

Throughout 1931 the CV was resolute in its analysis of the rise of Nazism. The growing support of Hitler was obstinately considered to be a function of Germany's economic predicament.[44] CVZ editorials emphasized that despite economic difficulties, the overwhelming majority of Germans rejected Hitler and anti-Semitism.

Yet in the first issue of the *CVZ* in 1932, virtually every major article attacked the NSDAP, while analyzing its continuing success and growth.[45] The longest article in that issue reasserted that if it were not for "the accident of economic problems" and the split within liberal and leftist political parties, "the majority of German people would stay with the democratic way. If not for the economic situation Hitler would not have been able to win even the number he has."[46] The special educative CV publication, *Wir deutschen Juden, 321–1932*, began with the statement that "hardships and bad times and poverty have shattered the nerves of the German people and forced them to forget they are one people."[47]

By April 1932, an undertone of panic began to creep into *CVZ* articles. Responses to ritual murder accusations, direct replies to the base attacks of *Der Stürmer* multiplied and consumed entire issues.[48] And still these articles contained denials of strong German support for Nazism. Again and again German Jewish authors and journalists resolved that anti-Semitism did not represent the personal feelings of most Germans. Again and again they clung to their perception of Germans as the tolerant and enlightened people of the myth they lived. Their explanations of the rise of Nazism were consistent with these beliefs.

What prompted the multiplication of defensive articles was not only the NSDAP's growth, but also the heightened Nazi propaganda campaign that peaked in 1932, which played such a vital role in that growth. While blaming economic crises for Nazi victories, German Jews were also acutely aware of the effectiveness of anti-Semitic propaganda, of posters and painted walls, of S.A. marches and radio speeches, of leaflets and a bombardment of slogans. Hitler's propaganda effort was partially responsible for his victories and offered German Jews another explanation along with the economic one for German abandonment of the eighteenth-century archetypal German lives.[49]

By 1932 Germans were said to have been misled, duped, and blinded by Nazi propaganda. German Jews explained anti-Semitism as a propaganda tool, used on a German populace vulnerable to what Germans earlier would have seen as bombastic deception, because of a prolonged economic crisis. The propaganda gained the NSDAP votes.[50] And again the German Jewish image of Germans could remain intact—honorable people victimized by evil election campaign lies.

Thus was explained the gradual rise of the NSDAP throughout 1932. In July of that year, the party had polled 37.3 percent of the vote in the Reichstag elections. In April Hitler had received 36.7 percent of the vote in the second presidential election.[51] From March to December Nazi agitators demanded that Germans boycott German Jewish businesses. The various boycotts were dismal failures, and simultaneously the CV won several court cases against perpetra-

169

tors of anti-Semitic propaganda and practice.[52] German Jews decided from this evidence, the economic crisis, and the propaganda campaign waged so effectively by the Nazis, that "the German public in general showed little inclination to comply with the different edicts of the NSDAP followers."[53] In other words, the evidence confirmed their basic belief in Germany.

German Jews did distinguish between friend and foe. But those recognized as enemies were considered hostile only because of economic and political reasons; they were therefore alleged to be enemies of poverty, not of Jews. This position was a logical extension and consequence of the German Jewish belief in the myth of Germans as Lessings, Herders, and Settembrinis. German Jews maintained a sense of security and stability by expounding the myth, and responded to an increasingly hostile physical reality by reaffirming their beliefs. But could that response continue after 1933?

For at least the first year after the Nazi seizure of power, German Jews and many German non-Jews continued to think that anti-Semitism was only an "accidental" symptom of National Socialism.[54] They believed, as Naumann had believed and as Adolf Eichmann later claimed he believed, that Hitler had only used anti-Semitic rhetoric to gain power.[55] They believed Göring when he told them that if German Jews "are loyal and go about their business they have nothing to fear."[56] They believed Papen when he said that "Jewish citizens in Germany can rest assured they will be treated as all good citizens."[57] German Jews were certain that Papen, Hindenburg, Schleicher, and all Germans were victims of fate, history, and circumstances.[58] Since Germans and Germany were spiritually honorable, there was nothing to fear—even with Hitler as chancellor.

Both voluntarily and under duress German Jews continued to express their feelings of patriotism and loyalty to Germany in 1933. Göring visited several leading German

170

Jewish bankers, rabbis, and intellectuals, instructing them to break the European boycott imposed upon Germany.[59] The CV undertook to persuade "friends" in other nations to cease this economic hostility against Germany. On March 30, 1933, the CVZ front page, in bold print, pleaded with the German public to believe that Jews in Germany did not support the boycott: "We do not support the European boycott; we stand with Germany against all foreign attacks. We are, always have been, and can only be true to Germany."[60] In the same issue another editorialist avowed that all attacks on Germany were also attacks on German Jews.[61]

A CV position paper was printed and addressed both to German and foreign newspapers. It declared that all anti-Nazi propaganda was false, that Jewish freedom still lived in Germany, that German Jews were not being mistreated, and that the rumor of German Jews all being forcibly shipped to Geneva was a lie. It went on to say that the CV and all German Jews supported the new regime, which "has begun to fulfill its promises, and Hitler is reponsible for this success." Yes, there was anti-Semitism, it concluded, but no different than before, no stronger than in other European nations, and "we are convinced that the equality of German Jews which they have gained through war and peace, by devotion and blood-service, will not be destroyed, and that just as before, they [German Jews] will be able to work together with all other Germans of good will for the rise of the fatherland—the fatherland to which they are indissolubly bound."[62]

Virtually all other German Jewish journals echoed these sentiments, at least publicly. In an interview with a CVZ reporter, Papen said that German Jews would continue to live as before and that Hitler and Göring agreed with his position.[63] The German Jewish community of Berlin issued a public statement in the CVZ announcing that "German Jews are deeply shaken by the call to boycott the NSDAP."

They denounced the boycott and pledged their allegiance to Germany and all Germans. German Jewish periodicals like *Der Schild*, the *Frankfurter Zeitung*, the *Deutschen Allgemeinen Zeitschrift* all repeated these feelings.[64]

Not surprisingly, the CV led the battle against the boycott. CV representatives went to Holland and London to urge the Dutch and the British to end the boycott.[65] But for the first time, Zionist representatives joined the CV for a common purpose.[66] German Jews were united on this question because it reflected a larger issue: that German Jews were Germans and must therefore remain in Germany.

This basic faith in Germans seemed confirmed after the deceptive failure of the Nazi boycott of Jewish businessmen on April 1. While the fact of a government-decreed and enforced anti-Jewish boycott alarmed many German Jews, they were heartened by the refusals of even conservative German circles to condone such measures.[67] German Jews could conclude from this that in April 1933, the German people still retained their decency, honor, and enlightened outlook.[68]

Optimism was difficult to maintain after April 1, however. On April 7 legislation was enacted prohibiting Jews from the civil service, the legal and medical professions. The initial response to the infamous "Aryan Paragraph" was sorrowful outrage.[69] One *CVZ* editor wrote that the laws transformed religious differences into artificial and arbitrary legal differences between Germans, while another indignantly noted that the new legislation "robs German Jews of a chance to serve Germany and robs Germany of our strength."[70] Yet despite the initial indignation, the final consensus seemed to be that German Jews simply should seek other kinds of employment.[71] Nobel Prize winner J. Franck angrily wrote in a letter to the *CVZ* that he would try to continue to serve Germany, *in* Germany, however he could.[72]

German Jews maintained a precarious position in the

center of a gathering deadly whirlwind. They persisted in their identifications with Germans and in their assertions of German Identity. "No paragraph can take away our relationship with German culture—it is with us, like us, in us as German Jews in Germany's culture," wrote Alfred Hirschberg, spokesman for the CV in the Festschrift *Wille und Weg.*[73] Rather than confronting Nazism as the enemy, Hirschberg turned against Zionism. The year 1933 was not the downfall of Judaism, and for Jews in Germany "to affirm Judaism is still to affirm Germany."[74] Hirschberg emphatically wrote that German Jews were Germans, and must therefore accept whatever the German government said. German Jews, he continued, must say "yes to Germany and no to Zionism." They must wait, not panic; anti-Semitism had come before, and Baal had been struck down. To betray and abandon Germany would be to abandon their true path of Judaism.[75]

As the list of forbidden professions grew, the CVZ reported in an almost clinical fashion precisely what the laws said. Objective explanations and reproduction of laws in detail became the substance of articles dealing with anti-Jewish legislation.[76] Alongside these descriptive accounts, the editorials pleaded for German Jews not to leave Germany. Requests for patience, unity, and settling into a "new pattern of life" accompanied remarkable reports of increased non-Jewish CV membership since May 1.[77]

The book bans seemed to affect and shock German Jews more deeply than the other legislation—the only overtly antigovernment article to appear in the CVZ after April 1 called the policy a "new Inquisition."[78] But the mainstream of the German Jewish periodical literature in 1933 indicated a renewed concern with demonstrating historical unity with Germans, cultural sameness, German Jewish contributions to German culture from art to science, and from Nobel Prize to Olympic Medal winners.[79]

The strong voice of Alfred Wiener, a soothing source of

173

security and knowledge for German Jews, rang more clearly and forcefully than most others in 1933. It is significant that he compared German Jews in 1933 not to Job but to Socrates, "between heaven and earth—helpless."[80] As a member of the CV, Wiener unabashedly spoke for all German Jews.[81] In that capacity he echoed Alfred Hirschberg's demand that German Jews remain on German soil. He echoed, too, the belief that "we want to be subject to the new government" as equal Germans. And he echoed the conviction that German Jews were "*totally* German," "firmly rooted in their German home earth."[82]

There could have been no more eloquent advocate of what most German Jews believed. Wiener's words did not appeal to a Hebrew tradition; they were not abrasive, polemical, or blatantly argumentative (as were Max Naumann's), but calm, assured, and assuring. His words conveyed a self-possession, a deep sense of firm identity, prepared and able to weather the worst assaults and to withstand any denials of that identity. Perhaps no one was more steeped in the beliefs, identified more strongly with the values and lives of Enlightenment Germans—of Settembrini's and Heinrich Mann's Weimar Germany.

By perceiving themselves and all Germans to be endowed with an Enlightenment consciousness, German Jews explained away anti-Semitism. In 1926, as an earlier response to the proliferation of *völkisch* and Nazi anti-Semitic literature, a CV publication included a "Nachwort" to German Jewish youth which read:

> Do not misinterpret the German *Volk*! You are not alone. Look upon not only the enemies but also the host of friends who readily stand by your side to help.
> Do not grow bitter toward your fatherland. . . . You can be both German and Jewish.[83]

Julius Bab considered the statement by Heinrich Treitschke's daughter in February 1933, that "I have lost my fatherland" to be of major symbolic and real importance. She spoke, he said, for the true Germany, "that humanistic Germany, whose spirit had ruled until then [1933]."[84] But even Bab believed that all was not lost in 1933, that Germans continued to hold fast to the *Humanitätsidee* of Lessing, Schiller, and Herder. This was the continuing basis of harmony between German Jews and German non-Jews.

That notion could no longer exist after September 1935. With the Nuremberg Laws of that month, wrote Bab, all possibility of continuing communal life with Germans was ended.[85] Those laws denying German Jews citizenship, finally defining German Jews in racial terms, had a stunning effect upon their victims. German Jews received the news of the alteration of their status, wrote the *CVZ*, with a profound sense of "shattering" *(Erschütterung).*[86] The first commentaries on the Nuremberg Laws appeared in the Rosh-Hashonoh issue of the *CVZ* and deliberately invoked the memory of hardships of Jews in ancient times. For the first time the *CVZ* appealed to Judaism and Jewish history for solace and wrote of the end of an historical epoch in Germany.[87]

No longer was the dominant theme the desire to live in unity with Germans, but rather the desire "only to live in dignity as Jews."[88] They were not the people of the German Enlightenment as it mirrored the universal teachings of the Torah, but only "the people who belong to the Torah";[89] not representatives of German art but of Jewish art;[90] not Jews as Germans in Germany but Jews as Jews everywhere. In October 1935, one *CVZ* editorialist wrote: "The emancipation of German Jews was formally *aufgehoben* on September 15, 1935."[91] His use of *aufgehoben* was perhaps purposeful because of its cryptic, antithetical significations, its double meaning of fulfilled and destroyed. Ironically, with this end of German Jewish emancipation came its new beginning, its preservation and new direction, its turning inward to unity among Jews.

For the first time since the Weimar Republic had begun, the CVZ favorably described those Jews who had left Germany for Palestine.[92] Photographs of the Wailing Wall were placed next to pictures of a synagogue in Berlin.[93] In deep despair, the CV instructed German Jews to live in Germany not joyously, with honor and pride as Germans, but "with the laws—*somehow*."[94] The Jewish community in Germany had been unalterably severed from the German community at large and sought a new solidarity among themselves. "Inner *Jewish* development" was needed and demanded by German Jewish leaders.[95] The voices that for so long had called for cooperation with the Christian German community were dead.

NOTES

[1]Pascal, *The German Novel*, pp. 83–84.
[2]Carl Schorske, "Weimar and the Intellectuals, II," *New York Review of Books*, May 21, 1970.
[3]Ibid.
[4]Arendt, *Eichmann*, p. 11.
[5]Naumann, *Sozialismus*, pp. 8–9.
[6]Ibid.
[7]Ibid., p. 10.
[8]Ibid., p. 8, italics added.
[9]Ibid.
[10]Naumann, "Grüne Frage."
[11]Hubscher, "Reich und Israel," *Klärung*, pp. 33–42.
[12]Ibid.
[13]Heinrich Stern, "Patriotismus," *CVZ*, IX (January 10, 1930).
[14]Hollander, "Die neue Regierung," *CVZ*, XII (February 2, 1933).
[15]"Grenzen des Boykotts," *CVZ*, XII (April 6, 1933).
[16]Hollander, "Die neue Regierung."
[17]Ball-Kaduri, *Das Leben der Juden*, p. 146.
[18]Ibid., pp. 147–148.
[19]Bab, *Lieben und Tod*, p. 7, italics added.

[20]Bettauer, *Stadt ohne Juden*, p. 42.

[21]Ibid.

[22]Ibid., p. 43.

[23]See CVZ, IV; each of the February, March, April, and May issues were filled with articles bearing such titles as "Better Times Ahead?" (May 29), "Völkische Spaltung" (May 8), "National Socialist Resurrection?" (February 5);, "Adolf Hitler's Dream of the Future" (February 20).

[24]"Better Times Ahead?" *CVZ*, IV (May 29, 1925).

[25]Ibid.

[26]Hollander, "The New Reich President," *CVZ*, IV (May 1, 1925); J. Levy, "Erziehung zum Deutschsein," *CVZ*, IV (June 5, 1925).

[27]Paucker, *Der jüdische Abwehrkampf*, p. 27.

[28]Ibid., p. 22.

[29]Werner Mosse, "Der Niedergang der Weimarer Republik."

[30]Ibid.

[31]Ibid.

[32]Karl Löwenstein, "Nationaljuden und Abwehrkampf," *CVZ*, IX (July 11, 1930).

[33]Ibid.

[34]"Freunde des C.V. in Stadt und Land werbt neue Mitglieder!" *CVZ*, IX (July 11, 1930).

[35]Hollander, "Bindet dem Helm fester!" *CVZ*, IX (September 26, 1930).

[36]Ibid.

[37]Ibid.

[38]"Offen Brief am die deutschen Juden," *Deutsche Republik*, IV, No. 39 (1930), 1189–1192.

[39]Ibid.

[40]Edelheim-Muesham, "Die Haltung der jüdische Presse."

[41]Reichman-Jungmann, "Die Selbstwehr der deutschen Juden," *Deutsche Republik*, IV, No. 42 (1930), 1292–1296.

[42]Ibid.

[43]Edelheim-Muesham, "Die Haltung der jüdische Presse."

[44]Werner Mosse, "Der Niedergang der Weimarer Republik."

[45]Reichmann, "Bilanz," *CVZ*, XI (January 1, 1932).

[46]Ibid.

[47]*Wir Deutschen Juden*, p. 1.

[48]"Und noch Ritualmord," "Internationale-Weltherrschaft," *CVZ Monthly*, IV (April 1932); Hans Reichmann, "Dem inneren Frieden. Deutsche 'und' Juden," *CVZ Monthly*, IV (December 1932).

[49]Reichmann, "Dem inneren Frieden."

[50]Ball-Kaduri, *Das Leben der Juden*, p. 30.

[51]Alan Bullock, *Hitler. A Study in Tyranny*, rev. ed. (New York: Harper & Row, 1962), pp. 230–231.

[52]Paucker, *Der jüdische Abwehrkampf*, p. 77.

[53]Ibid.

[54]Reisner, *Die Juden und das deutsche Reich*, pp. 204–205.

[55]Arendt, *Eichmann*, pp. 43, 81; Ball-Kaduri, *Das Leben der Juden*, p. 31.

177

[56]"Göring und Papen über die Judenfrage," *CVZ*, XII (March 9, 1933).

[57]Ibid.

[58]Buchheim, "Die Tragodie der Weimarer Republik."

[59]Bernard Krikler, "Boycotting Nazi Germany," *Wiener Library Bulletin*, XXIII, No. 4 (1969), 26–31; interview with director of Dresden Bank of Berlin, who was one of those directed by Göring to use his influence in breaking the boycott, November 1966.

[60]"Wir 365,000 deutschen Juden legen feurliche Verwahrung ein," *CVZ*, XII (March 30, 1933).

[61]"Unser Kampf für Deutschland. Gegen die Greuelpropaganda im Ausland," *CVZ*, XII (March 30, 1933).

[62]Ibid.

[63]"Die grosse Gegenoffensive. Erklärung von Regierung und Verbanden," *CVZ*, XII (March 30, 1933).

[64]Ibid.; "Boykott-Echo in der Prese," *CVZ*, XII (March 30, 1933).

[65]"Kampf des C.V. gegen die Greuelpropaganda," *CVZ*, XII (April 6, 1933).

[66]Ibid.

[67]Ball-Kaduri, *Das Leben der Juden*, p. 84.

[68]Ibid., p. 89.

[69]"Deutsch-Jüdische Wirklichkeit," *CVZ*, XII (April 13, 1933).

[70]"Die Gesetzgebung der letzten Tage für Beamte und Reichsanwalte," *CVZ*, XII (April 13, 1933).

[71]"Der C.V. gibt Rat," *CVZ*, XII (April 13, 1933).

[72]"Ein Brief des Nobelpreisträger Professor Franck," *CVZ*, XII (April 20, 1933).

[73]Alfred Hirschberg, "Der Centralverein deutscher Staatsbürger jüdischen Glaubens," *Wille und Weg*, pp. 12–29; cf. Karl A. Schleunes, *The Twisted Road to Auschwitz. Nazi Policy toward German Jews 1933–1939* (Urbana, Chicago, London: University of Illinois Press, 1970), pp. 92f.

[74]Hirschberg, "Der Centralverein."

[75]Ibid.

[76]"Der C.V. gibt Rat."

[77]"Unsere Pflicht!" *CVZ*, XII (April 27, 1933); "Die Ungeduldung," *CVZ*, XII (May 18, 1933); "Was tun?" *CVZ*, XII (May 25, 1933); "104 neue Mitglieder in Gross-Berlin seit dem 1. Mai," *CVZ*, XII (May 25, 1933); "Zahlen die beweisen! Jüdische Selbstmorde in dem Jahren 1921 bis 1928," *CVZ*, XII (June 1, 1933); Alfred Wiener, "Zwischen Himmel und Erde," *CVZ*, XII (June 1, 1933).

[78]"Schwarze Liste der deutschen Literatur," *CVZ*, XII (May 4, 1933).

[79]"Jüdische Nobelpreisträges," *CVZ*, XII (May 11, 1933); *Israelitisches Familienblatt*, No. 19, May 11, 1933; "Die Ungeduldung," *CVZ*, XII (May 18, 1933); "Vollarisierung im Sport," and "Juden in der Sportgeschichte," *CVZ*, XII (May 25, 1933).

[80]Wiener, "Zwischen Himmel und Erde."

tions, in other words, do not examine the internal or spiritual assimilation that was so obvious in German Jewish writings of the Weimar period.

For German Jews in the twentieth century it was not enough simply to be aware of past and present hostility of Germans toward Jews. Mere consciousness of anti-Semitism created a tension between external reality and German Jewish internal desires for acceptance, assimilation, and security. The pressures created by this conflict between external and internal reality were relieved by adherence to a myth of Germany and Germans that mentally fulfilled a wish for assimilation into an enlightened German community.

True, Zionists and Marxists offered alternative ideals and myths: land, a new home with ancient roots, revolution, or even violence. They were dismissed by most German Jews because they appeared either unnecessary or opposed to the humanist heritage of the Enlightenment. Without foreseeing the terrible, indeed, unthinkable consequences of German anti-Semitism that would be manifested under the Nazis, the myths of Germans and Germany to which German Jews subscribed *were* functionally adaptive: they allowed life to continue with hope and relative security. Only the pressure, the terror of an unanticipated reality transformed German Jewish assertions into fatally maladaptive myths. Historians can point to the alternatives of other groups like the Zionists and determine that they were more "realistic" and less "illusory," because they would have saved lives, provided new life, more genuine hope, and true security. Yet ex *post facto* judgments fail to recognize the existential validity and significance of beliefs of this sort. Levy-Bruhl, in The *"Soul" of the Primitive,* argued that it was impossible for civilized men to fully penetrate the thought processes and perceptions of "savages"; it is similarly impossible to penetrate the German Jewish perceptions of their world at that moment. Since myth mediates between external pressure and internal desires and needs, the myth of Germany they held was a "true" one—true to them.

E. O. James has suggested that myth is most effective in times of adversity, at critical and dangerous junctures of a people's experience.[3] Under the "pressure of history" people turn to myth because it serves to avert or reverse malign influences and activities by asserting that benevolent forces of the past are still efficacious in the present.[4] Because of their myths, German Jews, like archaic men, could escape the terror, the burden of history, or a harsh historical reality. The "anxiety of man living in [profane] time" was assuaged by living in a reborn mythical time;[5] the anxiety of German Jews living in an increasingly anti-Semitic society was mollified by their mythic view of the Enlightenment and its rebirth in Weimar. For them, the mythic era lived again as the time of the creation of all values, morality, humanitarian beliefs, and actions that were significant to German Jews as a group. Out of the chaos of World War I issued forth the creation of order and life. Belief in the rebirth of Lessing's Germany was the way German Jews overcame the contradictions between their hopes and the political reality that blocked their realization of them.[6]

German Jewish literature of the Weimar years seems obsessed with a memory of the Enlightenment and its heroes: it reveals an overwhelming urge to live as if the past were present and the dead were living. Unconsciously, German Jews substituted a mythical age for an unpleasant, threatening historical present. It was a group belief, which constituted a collective failure to distinguish between mental image (illusion) and objective reality.

In analyzing the relationship between perception and "objective reality," Ernst Cassirer commented that the function of mythical thinking was to transform the world of impressions into expressions; to make inner forms inform reality.[7] The subjective way that myth-believers created reality, he wrote, was the determinant for action.[8] Life lived according to myth, "primitive" or contemporary, is therefore life motivated by a mental process. Although it may appear illusory when compared with the material world, myth is nevertheless psychically real and actual. That psychic actuality is the motivator of action as well.

Therefore, because they shape material existence, myth, fantasy, and illusion are not mere fable.[9] As projects and projections of imagination they have the power to create real effects—fear, security, joy.[10] They can alter fact and make the unreal real—or the real unreal. Jung denied that anything was an "illusion" for the psyche and theorized that psychic actualities such as fantasies or myths "may be for the psyche a most important factor of life—something as indispensable as oxygen."[11] Freud recognized that illusion was not simply "error," even if it caused an individual to disregard reality. He admitted that if illusions could not be proved true, neither could they be proved untrue to the believers.[12] Illusions of a mythical and religious type he called truths, truths that had the power of scientific truths.[13] Among the greatest of Freud's revelations was the realization that psychic reality—fantasy, illusion, hallucination—*"is the determining factor"* in an individual's life.[14]

German Jewish actions become more understandable when viewed as actions of a group totally immersed or assimilated into what they imagined German culture to be —submerged, in short, in their myth of German culture. They could not conceive of themselves as outsiders or strangers. Life within a myth is life lived and experienced as an insider, as a member of a group that shares ideals and values. German Jews presumed that they shared their cultural identity with other Germans. Whether the external facts of that culture corresponded to the German Jewish perception of them was essentially irrelevant.

It has been shown that identification, identity, security, psychic return to an earlier historical epoch, wish fulfillment—all these are characteristics of myth. This ensemble accurately portrays and characterizes German Jewish thoughts and actions as well. German Jews substituted their mythical reality, their illusions of a Germany full of Lessings, for the actuality of growing anti-Semitism. To a great extent their rationalizations regarding the rise of Nazism indicate a refusal to confront real life, a tendency to block out or repress reality. By so doing, German Jews could feel secure. They could live as if their hopes, wishes, idealizations were realized and fulfilled. They shaped the present into a likeness of the past and molded twentieth-century Germans into eighteenth-century *Aufklärer*.

The same characteristics of "shutting out the external world," fixation to the memory of a time past, and illusory wish fulfillment are found in dreams. But it is not simply dreams or myths that are meaningful and effective in analysis of an historical situation. Myths influence action in the external world. They actually are lived by the believers. The memory embodied in the myth is "confused with ordinary [profane] memories, so that the two worlds become mixed."[15] In dreams, where a wish is experienced immediately, there is no physical action. A lived dream, one that corresponds to a lived myth that is acted out in the external world, a waking dream,[16] was Freud's idea of a neurosis.

Of the many similar and congruent traits shared by myth, dreams, and neuroses,[17] the most important for a study of German Jewish motivations are the two mechanisms of repression and projection. These psychological mechanisms in neurosis serve the same functions as myth, the same functions that Freud believed were the fundamental strength of religion and myth: the satisfaction of human wishes and the avoidance of an unpleasant or dangerous reality.[18]

In psychoanalytic terms, the essence of repression is rejecting and keeping something out of consciousness in

184

order to avoid pain.[19] What is repressed in neurosis is real life. Freud believed a neurosis is a means of withdrawal from reality, a "flight from real life."[20] The neurotic turns from a reality that is threatening, painful, unbearable, and frustrating because it does not allow the fulfillment of certain basic wishes.[21]

The counterpart to the loss or repression of reality in neurosis is its substitution of a psychic reality for the material one.[22] Just as a mythic consciousness substitutes in this way, so the neurotic consciousness ignores parts of the real world and substitutes a "new" reality created by inner perceptions, "memory traces, ideas and judgments ... about reality ... by which reality[is] represented in the life of the mind."[23] An earlier historical period that is believed to have fulfilled specific desires is thus substituted for the present.

Neurosis and myth coincide in this characteristic and function. An edenic age, a fantasy or illusion, is substituted for reality, and myth-believer and neurotic alike not only believe in their respective fantasies but live in them. In this respect, the majority of German Jews were both a neurotic and a mythopoetic group. It seems quite clear that while they were aware of the harsh realities around them, they nevertheless ignored parts that could be harmful to their self-images and their perceptions of others. Both neurotics and myth-believers do not completely shut out the external world. Both groups, however, reconcile themselves to reality and adjust reality to their needs.[24] Because of this, German Jews could acknowledge anti-Semitism, address themselves to it, but yet ignore its implications.

It is therefore not only their repression of reality but their projections that constitute the key to German Jewish actions in the Weimar Republic. The projected images of Weimar Germany that German Jews substituted for the real ones provided them defensive protection from psychological unrest. German Jews projected their internal images of Germans outward in the same manner as Cassirer's archaic man and Freud's neurotic man projected their "inner forms" or "hallucinatory material" onto reality.

Jakob Wassermann's autobiography expresses a deep emotional conflict that revolves around his self-image, his identity, and the meaning of assimilation into German society. The famous passage in his book that despaired of the intellectual and moral decline of Germany was attacked by German Jews who could not accept even Wassermann's gentle derision of their so-called promised land and saintly brothers.[25] German Jews avoided Wassermann's psychological dilemma and emotional malaise by reshaping their environment to match their inner world.

Reshaping reality in this way is a defensive, psychological, often unconscious, activity. German Jews seemed to follow a classic psychic pattern of coupling fears or phobias with obsessions.[26] In his earlier papers, and again in his later writings, Freud reduced repression and even neurosis to a "simple method of defense" against a real or imagined threat.[27] German Jewish fear of isolation reached phobic proportions and produced an obsession with the German Enlightenment. Yet if they followed a pattern of substitution or projection characteristic of defensive neuroses,[28] it was not of the usual sort.

When Freud and most psychoanalytic theorists after him discussed projection it was almost always in terms of negative projection: what is projected onto reality or others is evil inner material;[29] unconscious hostility; "everything disagreeable" and objectionable in one's self.[30] German Jews do not fit this pattern.[31] Freud's condemnation of both those who project and those who "withdraw from the community of man,"[32] is not applicable to German Jews.

The psychic motivations of German Jews conform more to a process touched upon by Anna Freud and discussed more fully by Melanie Klein and one of her students, Paula Heimann. Anna Freud described a psychic phenomenon she called "identification with the aggressor."[33] She found some of her child patients not only projecting hostile feelings and fears onto others, but also pretending to be those they feared, identifying with the objects of their projections.[34] Anna Freud's other deviation from classic projection as simply thrusting forth of objectionable ideas and emotions was her concept of "altruistic surrender."[35] Patients who fell under this rubric also identified with the objects of their projections, but—unlike those who identified with the aggressor—they did so only for the purpose of serving those objects and deprecating themselves in the process.[36] To the extent that Anna Freud's formulation encompassed positive feelings and good qualities, it constituted an important break with orthodox theories of projection.

German Jews did not exactly conform to Anna Freud's patterns of projection. Max Naumann may fit the scheme of "identification with the aggressor," but he was an atypical German Jew. And although German Jews projected positive qualities onto other Germans, they did not do it in such a way as to deprecate or punish themselves as in "altruistic surrender."

Theories expounded by Melanie Klein and Paula Heimann provide a more accurate description of German Jewish psychic projection. Following Klein's lead, Heimann theorized that the projection of what is "good and useful," if not as striking, is equally important as the projection of what is "bad and useless."[37] Her description of this procedure and its consequences remarkably reflects the psychological state and dilemma of German Jews:

Good, loving impulses and traits too are projected, and such projection will prove helpful or dangerous according to the character of the object chosen for it, and of the further relations with this object. The danger of projection lies in its obscuring reality; often indeed it leads to serious delusions. To project "good" loving impulses onto a bad object and thus turn it "good" may be no less harmful than to project destructive "bad" impulses onto a loved object and so lose it.[38]

187

Here, then, is the tragic dilemma of German Jews in the Weimar Republic: to accept the "real" world and its hostility, its anti-Semitism, and rejection of them as either an autonomous or unacceptably acculturated group, or to be spared this rejection and isolation by flight into a myth, or a psychic reality, or a neurosis. Even Freud acknowledged that "flight into illness" might be justified if it allowed individuals to function in the external world.[39] In the case of German Jews, the sort of positive projection described by Heimann allowed them to function in the real world not only as Germans but also as Jews.

The unconscious urge in German Jews was to make reality the same as the myth; it meant transforming Germans into archetypal Jews. To be Lessing was to be Nathan. To say, as Jakob Wassermann did, "I am a German, I am a Jew, as much and as completely the one as the other,"[40] was to affirm the equation of identities and the identification of archetypes. When Wassermann described his dream of reflection in a mirror, the mirror images of German and Jew, he betrayed the unconscious belief that Jews were reflected in Germans.[41] The reflection was self-affirming—almost narcissistic. What German Jews loved in their images of Germans was themselves.

As if in response to this tacit conviction, Ernst Berg wrote that "Jews must not take over German culture and mold it in their own image."[42] In that statement by a "moderate" anti-Semite was embedded a perverse, accidental, yet intuitive perception of how German Jews viewed assimilation. Unlike Berg, German Jews did not consider their problem as a choice of being "either German or Jewish" because the one did not preclude the other. Their myth of Germany was built upon the identification of German with Jewish—an identification that, like all narcissism, was an overestimation of both self and other.[43]

German Jews projected their Old Testament intellectual traditions, their ethics and moral values, onto the external world and made a Germany in their own image. That was the substance of their myth of Germany and Germans, a place and a people adhering to the same mythical order as German Jews. German Jewish ego-ideals and archetypes had their roots in Old Testament archetypes. By reliving those archetypal *German* lives, they reaffirmed not only their German identity but their traditional Jewish identity.

In order to exist in Germany, German Jews needed real human objects that were feasible for identification. They found these objects in a German tradition that seemed to mirror their own archaic one. But the identification with the object became too strong; consequently, it blocked out any critical view of reality and thus created a situation analogous to one which Freud had warned would result in "a pathological outcome" in neurotics.[44] To say that German Jews as a group acted in a neurotic, narcissistic manner, or that they were suffering from a group neurosis, is not to condemn them. The negative connotations are called into question by considering the parallels between myth and neurosis, and by examining recent psychoanalytic theories about the meaning and significance of neurosis.

Most scholars of mythology agree that without myth archaic man would have been spiritually and probably physically lost. Myth therefore is unquestionably a positive phenomenon that serves its believers well. To call a shaman or any primitive believer in mythology neurotic at the very least needs considerable qualification and precise contextual definition of "neurotic."[45] Yet with regard to those subject to a modern myth or a group neurosis, the same abeyance of judgment is not observed by many anthropologists, historians, psychologists, or laymen. "Neurotic" implies sick or irresponsible acts that avoid responsible alternatives. While "myth" connotes inner enrichment, "illusion" connotes a self-deception with dangerous historical consequences—like the tragedy of German Jews. But Gershom Scholem's statement that the great illusion German Jews created could only be seen as illusory after 1945 points out again that the negative judgments on illusion are often *ex post facto*, based on historical hindsight.

Such views have been made suspect by analysts like R. D. Laing and Abraham Maslow, who see neurosis as potentially a neutral if not a positive phenomenon.[46] However, they merely elaborate on Freud's notion that without some degree of neurosis, life would be impossible. In *Beyond the Pleasure Principle*, Freud had postulated the concept of a protective shield against external stimuli and, returning to his earlier ideas about the importance of defense mechanisms, wrote that "protection *against* stimuli is . . . almost more important . . . than *reception of* stimuli."[47] In that same work he referred to the illusions men create to bear what Schiller called "the burden of existence."[48] Those illusions that protect, said Freud, were necessary.

These needs were satisfied in some individuals, Freud wrote later, by strict adherence to a *Weltanschauung*, "an intellectual construction which solves all the problems of our existence uniformly on the basis of one overriding hypothesis," thereby creating psychic security and enabling an individual to live.[49] Erik Erikson voiced a similar idea in his formulation of a universal, psychological need for "a system of ideas that provides a convincing world image"—that organizes experience.[50] There are few more succinct descriptions of myth than these two descriptions of neurosis.

Freud believed that all men were neurotic, that the essence of man is neurosis because the essence of man is history.[51] In a penetrating article on Freud's theory of history and religion, Phillip Rieff discussed the relationship of neurosis to history and religion in Freud's system of thought.[52] Through careful exegesis and consideration of Freud's texts, especially *Moses and Monotheism*, Rieff demonstrated that the boundary between "normal" and "neu-

190

rotic" was at best vague, and that all mankind suffers from some sort of neurotic fixation to the past.[53]

It is therefore pointless, according to this view, to condemn or even pity German Jews either for their actions or their lack of political opposition to Nazism before 1933, or for their "neurotic" motivations. The Greeks did not judge Narcissus harshly, but saw him as a tragic victim of his own delusions.[54] If German Jews can be viewed as having suffered from a narcissistic illusion, then they were victims of an inescapable response to a particular condition of existence. Implicit in Freud's thinking was the idea that there are only victims, no villains, partially because illusions are never recognized as illusions until viewed historically.[55] Implicit, too, was the concomitant idea that men are inescapably victims of their own minds and illusions as well as of history and reality.

It is myth that joins illusion with history, fantasy with reality. When the values established by a given mythology are revealed as false, the implicit order collapses. The loss of myth, wrote Joseph Campbell, engenders a loss of meaning in life and the dissolution of social and psychological organization.[56] In other words, when the protective shield of myth is destroyed, the consequence is a traumatic experience.[57] The problem, then, is how men make life bearable, how they escape or buffer themselves against the shock of such an experience, how they "dilute experience to the point where [they] can bear it."[58]

Norman O. Brown has explicitly extended Freud's theories of neurosis to history and all men.[59] By defining sublimation as a neurotic symptom, Brown sees all historical action as neurotic action, as a "search for a lost life," a replaying of a fantasy or myth that is justified because it makes life bearable. Brown has seen the similar functions of certain neuroses and myths. Like Freud, he acknowledged the need for a "protective shield." But, again like

191

Freud, he also considered the neurosis, or history, or myth, a burden as well as a blessing. To sustain a myth or a neurosis may protect individuals from harsh and shocking psychic realities, but it also may foster an ignorance or a neglect of imminent invasion by destructive, external forces. The dilemma is like that which Freud described in *Civilization and Its Discontents:* an inescapable, damning choice where everyone is a victim.

Most German Jews adhered to their myths of Germans as long as possible—until those myths were revealed as empty and untenable, and physical reality invaded their lives and destroyed them. With the loss of myth came loss of meaning in life and a sort of paralyzing, debilitating trauma. The suicide rate among German Jews increased after 1933 and again after the 1935 Nuremberg Laws.[60] The idea that Germans were not like German Jews was crushing, shattering. Narcissistically, German Jews had loved the reflection of their own image in the illusory and deceptive well of the German past. They drowned in that deep pool.

NOTES

[1]M. Wischnitzer, "Jewish Emigration from Germany, 1933–1938," *Jewish Social Studies,* II (1940), 23–44; Lamm, *Über die innere und aussere Entwicklung,* pp. 209, 214; Werner Rosenstock, "Exodus 1933–1939: A Survey of Jewish Emigration from Germany," *Leo Baeck Yearbook,* I, 373–390.

[2]Hilde Ottenheimer, "The Disappearance of Jewish Communities in Germany, 1900–1938," *Jewish Social Studies,* III (1941), 189–206; Hilberg, *The Destruction of the European Jews,* pp. 91, 93–97.

[3]E. O. James, "Myth and Ritual," *Eranos Jahrbuch,* XVII (149), 79–120.

[4]Eliade, *Cosmos and History,* p. 106; James, "Myth and Ritual"; Van der Leeuw, "Urzeit und Endzeit."

[5]Eliade, *Myths, Dreams and Mysteries,* p. 38.

[6]Kluckhohn, "Recurrent Themes in Myth."

[7]Ernst Cassirer, *The Philosophy of Symbolic Forms,* Vol. I, *Language,* 75, 80, 81, 91.

[8]Ibid., p. 91; Johann Huizinga, *Homo Ludens* (Boston: Beacon Press, 1955), p.4.

[9]Levy-Bruhl, The "Soul," p. 52.

[10]Gaston Bachelard, *The Poetics of Space* (Boston: Beacon Press, 1963), p. 132.

[11]Jung, *Modern Man in Search of a Soul,* p. 83.

[12]*Future of an Illusion, Works,* Vol. XXI, pp. 30, 31–32.
[13]*Moses and Monotheism, Works,* Vol. XXIII, pp. 129, 130.
Future of an Illusion, Works, Vol. XXI, p. 30.
[14]*A general Introduction to Psychoanalysis, Works,* Vol. XVI, p. 368.
[15]Campbell, *Primitive Mythology,* p. 79.
[16]Ira Progoff, "Waking Dream and Living Myth," in *Myths, Dreams and Religion,* ed. Joseph Campbell (New York: E. P. Dutton, 1970), pp. 176–195.
[17]Many scholars have recognized the similarities between myths, dreams, and neuroses. Freud often alluded to these similarities; Roheim, and especially Jung, explored the likenesses. Joseph Campbell has dwelled upon them at length; a recent work edited by him is entitled *Myths, Dreams and Religion* (New York: E. P. Dutton, 1970). Roheim's classic account of a primitive tribe and its mythology is entitled *The Eternal Ones of the Dream* (New York, 1945); chap. i of Campbell's now famous *Hero with a Thousand Faces* (New York and Cleveland, Meridian, 1956) is "Myth and Dream," and examples of such couplings are legion. See also Freud's essays: "The Uncanny" (1919), *Collected Papers,* IV 368–407; "Medusa's Head" (1922), *Collected Papers,* V, 105–106; "The Taboo of Virginity" (1918), *Collected Papers,* IV, 217–235; "The Occurrence in Dreams of Material from Fairy Tales" (1913), *Collected Papers,* IV; also Karl Abraham, "Dreams and Myths," *Selected Papers of Karl Abraham* (New York: Basic Books, 1957), pp. 57–63; and Erich Neumann, *The Origins and History of Consciousness,* trans. R. F. Hull (Princeton: Princeton University Press, 1970).
[18]C.P., Vol. II, pp. 25–35.
[19]Freud, "Repression' (1918), *Collected Papers,* IV.
[20]Freud, "The Loss of Reality in Neurosis and Psychosis" (1924), *Collected Papers,* II, 277–282.
[21]Freud, "Formulations Regarding the Two Principles in Mental Functioning" (1911), *Collected Papers,* II.
[22]Freud, "The Loss of Reality in Neurosis and Psychosis."
[23]Ibid.
[24]Slochower, *Mythopoesis,* p. 21.
[25]Wassermann, *Mein Weg,* pp. 122–123.
[26]Freud, "Obsessions and Phobias: Their Psychical Mechanisms and Their Aetiology" (1895), *Collected Papers,* I, 128–137.
[27]Freud, *The Problem of Anxiety,* trans. Henry Alden Bunker (New York: W. W. Norton, 1936) and the Psychoanalytic Press (1936), p. 62; "The Defense Neuro-Psychoses" (1894), *Collected Papers,* I, 59–75; "Further Remarks on the Defense Neuro-Psychoses" (1895), *Collected Papers,* I, 155–182; *Inhibitions, Symptoms and Anxiety;* Anna Freud, *The Ego and the Mechanisms of Defense,* rev. ed. (New York: International Universities Press, 1966), p. 43.
[28]Freud, "The Defense Neuro-Psychoses."
[29]Freud, "Metapsychological Supplement to the Theory of Dreams" (1916), *Collected Papers,* IV.
[30]*Totem and Taboo, Works.* Vol. XIII, pp. 50, 64.
[31]*A General Introduction to Psychoanalysis, Works,* Vol. XVI, p. 273.

[32]*Totem and Taboo, Works.* Vol. XIII, p. 70

[33]Anna Freud, *The Ego and the Mechanisms,* pp. 109–121.

[34]Ibid.

[35]Ibid., p. 123.

[36]Ibid., p. 126.

[37]Melanie Klein, "Notes on Some Schizoid Mechanisms," and Paula Heimann, "Certain Functions of Introjection and Projection in Early Infancy," in Melanie Klein et al., *Developments in Psycho-Analysis* (London: Hogarth Press, 1952), pp. 301, 125.

[38]Paula Heimann, "Notes on the Theory of the Life and Death Instincts," *Developments in Psycho-Analysis,* pp. 326–327.

[39]*A General Introduction to Psychoanalysis, Works,* Vol. XVI, p. 382.

[40]Wassermann, *Mein Weg,* p. 126.

[41]Ibid., p. 119.

[42]Berg, *Wohin treibt Juda?* p. 55.

[43]*A General Introduction to Psychoanalysis, Works,* Vol. XVI, p. 415. C.P., Vol. IV; *An Outline of Psychoanalysis, Works,* Vol. XXIII, pp. 188, 200.

[44]*Ego and Id, Works,* Vol XIX, p. 30.

[45]Eliade, *Myths, Dreams and Mysteries,* p. 61; Roheim, *The Origins and Function of Culture* and "The Evolution of Culture." Roheim, despite his caution, has been criticized for characterizing shamans as neurotic. See also R. D. Laing and A. Esterson, *Sanity, Madness and the Family* (Harmondsworth, England: Penguin Books, 1970), pp. 15–27.

[46]R. D. Laing, *The Politics of Experience* (New York: Ballantine, 1968), and *The Divided Self;* Abraham Maslow, *Toward a Psychology of Being* (New York: D. Van Nostrand Co., 1962).

[47]*Beyond the Pleasure Principle, Works,* Vol. XVIII, p. 27

[48]*Beyond the Pleasure Principle, Works,* Vol. XVIII, p. 45.

[49]*New Introductory Lectures, Works,* Vol. XXII, p. 158.

[50]Erikson, *Identity: Youth and Crisis,* p. 31.

[51]Norman O. Brown, *Life Against Death* (Middletwon: Wesleyan University Press, 1959), p. 82.

[52]Phillip Rieff, "The Meaning of History and Religion in Freud's Thought," in *Psychoanalysis and History,* ed. Bruce Mazlish, rev. ed. (New York: Grosset & Dunlap, 1971).

[53]Ibid.

[54]Ovid, *Metamorphoses,* trans. Mary M. Innes (Harmondsworth, England: Penguin Books, 1955), pp. 83–87. Rose, however, attributes Narcissus' death as punishment for his deliberate cruelty. H. J. Rose, *A Handbook of Greek Mythology* (New York: E. P. Dutton, 1959), p. 169.

[55]Cf. Rieff's introduction to Freud, *Dora: Analysis of a Case of Hysteria.*

[56]Campbell, *The Masks of God,* IV, *Creative Mythology,* 94.

[57]*Beyond the Pleasure Principle, Works,* Vol. XVIII.

[58]*Ibid.,* p. 45.

[59]Brown, *Life Against Death.*

[60]Poliakov, *Harvest of Hate,* p. 12.

APPENDIX A

Dramatis Personae

Hermann Ahlwardt (1846–1914). Virulent anti-Semite who was elected to the Reichstag in 1892. Once rector of a primary school in Berlin, he was dismissed for embezzlement of children's funds and began a career as a professional anti-Semite. His works include the apocalyptic *The Struggle of Despair Between the Aryan Peoples and Judaism*, *The Oath of a Jew*, and *Jew-Rifles*, in which he claimed that arms supplied to German forces by the Jewish manufacturer Loewe were defective because of a Franco-Jewish plot. His theme, like most of the *völkish* theorists, was that the misery of peasants and laborers was due to the Jews and an international Jewish conspiracy.

Julius Bab (1880–1955). Drama critic and literary historian born in Berlin. Founder in 1933 of the Jüdischer Kulturbund, which had its own theatre to maintain cultural life among German Jews and sustain the link between German and Jewish culture. The first play the theatre performed was

Nathan the Wise. His studies included works of Shaw and Shakespeare, but Bab was most prolific as a Goethe scholar.

Leo Baeck (1873–1956). Rabbi, theologian, and historian of Jews and Jewish literature. He became the spiritual leader of reform Jewry, the most famous and prominent member of the CV. He was perhaps the leading spokesman of the German Jewish community in the Weimar Republic. In 1933 the Nazis appointed him head of the Reichsvertretung der Juden in Deutschland. He survived Theresienstadt and continued to devote his life to the study of Judaism. He was among the most eminent scholars who believed that Judaism was supremely compatible with *Deutschtum*, both being expressions of universal morality as he defined it.

Ludwig Bamberger (1823–1899). A participant in the 1848 revolution, he fled to Paris where he became a banker. His loyalty to Germany apparently drew him back and he was subsequently elected to the first Reichstag as a member of the German Liberal Party.

David Gen-Gurion (1886–1973). Zionist labor leader, statesman, architect of Israel as a state, historian and scholar. Born in Russian Poland, he was acutely aware of the problems presented by German Jews in the Zionist movement and of the attraction that Germany held for many Eastern European Jews.

Ludwig Börne (1786–1837). Essayist and poet who rebelled against his traditionalist Jewish background. Forced from his municipal post in Frankfort am Main in 1813, he converted to Christianity in 1818. He became a leading German liberal stylist (in Paris, like Heine) and considered the Jews only as individuals, not as people or even as adherents of a religion.

Joseph Campbell (1904–). Historian of religion, folklore, mythology, and comparative literature. His works on my-

196

thology and psychoanalysis have ranged from the study of archetypal heroes to his famous *A Skeleton Key to Finnegans Wake* (with Henry Morton Robinson). He is an advocate of Jungian theories in the study of comparative religions and mythology, and his *The Masks of God covers primitive, oriental, occidental, and "creative" mythologies.*

Ernst Cassirer (1874–1945). German Jewish philosopher of the Neo-Kantian school. Several of his early essays discuss the epistemological similarities between Kant, Mendelssohn, and Lessing and deal with the parallels between Kantian and Old Testament ethics.

Hermann Cohen (1842–1918). Founder of the Marburg School oᶠ Neo-Kantianism. Around 1880 Cohen began to defend Judaism as a concomitant of Kantianism and argued against anti-Semitism, specifically against Treitschke. He perhaps set the tone for German Jewish intellectuals when he argued for the study and affirmation of Judaism, yet denounced Zionism as reactionary in Germany.

Christian Dohm (1715–1820). Allegedly the first Christian German exponent of Jewish emancipation to publish an explicit argument for it, in his *Über die bürgerliche Verbesserung der Juden* (1781–83). He attacked Christian prejudices and urged equality for Jews through emancipation. It was radical for its day, yet based its argument on a rational pragmatism that often betrayed some of the prejudices it derided.

Alfred Döblin (1878–1956). Author and playwright who attacked Judaism as an ossified religion with archaic ethics and values. After World War I he broke all ties with Judaism and the German Jewish community and devoted his life to social reform. His writings never lost a religious tone, however, and in 1925 Döblin renewed his interest in Judaism. In 1933 he began writing defensively about Jews in Germany.

197

Johan Gustav Droysen (1808–1884). Prussian historian, among the fathers of the Frankfurt constitution. A Prussian nationalist, he was also a liberal and a supporter of Prussian-led German unification. His role in the Frankfurt Parliament made him a prestigious backer of Jewish emancipation, at least on pragmatic grounds.

Friedrich Ebert (1871–1925). An outspoken member of the Social Democratic Party, he urged cooperation among parties in the "revolution" of 1918–19, and because of his less radical leanings, he was elected first president of the Weimar Republic. He served during the turbulent early years and became the target of both left and right. To German Jews, he represented the new liberal spirit of Germany.

Ismar Elbogen (1874–1948). German Jewish scholar, respected, even revered by most German Jewish intellectuals as a peaceful human being who was yet a loyal German. He seemed to combine a faith in Germany with a devout and scholarly belief in Judaism.

Mircea Eliade (1907–). Historian of religion and mythology, anthropologist, who has written extensively on mythology and comparative religions, magic, symbolism, and the like. Perhaps best known for his theory of the "eternal return," he is among the leading authorities in his field(s) at the University of Chicago.

Arthur Eloesser (1870–1937). A leading German drama critic, essayist, and literary historian whose main work was a history of German literature (1930). His German Jewish bias is best seen in the individuals on whom he concentrates in that work and in his essays.

Erik Erikson. (1902–). Psychoanalyst whose major work has been in the area of personality growth and "ego-identity." He had modified Freud's psychosexual theories in light of cultural anthropology, taking into account culturally determined crises and developments in individuals and in groups. He has applied his ideas to historical figures like Luther and Gandhi.

Johann Gottlieb Fichte (1762–1814). Among the first nationalist theorists whose famous *Addresses to the German Nation* were delivered under the eyes of the occupying French police in 1806. A member of the Kant-Schleiermacher-Herder-Hegel group of philosophers, he was an exponent of German idealism, which he applied to state and nation in calls for a "community of mind and body." Among the founders of German nationalism who, like Herder and Schleiermacher, advocated an individualism along with universalism and, also like Herder, he has been accused of "proto-fascism."

Bernhard Förster (1843–1889). Teacher at the Friedrich Gymnasium in Berlin, he was one of the architects of the Anti-Semitic Petition of 1880. The petition attacked Jews as infiltrators of Aryan society and tried to circumscribe their influence and participation in all aspects of life in Germany. Förster, in despair, attempted to establish a "pure" German utopia in Paraguay. He was married to Nietzsche's sister, and Nietzsche despised Förster, his utopia, his ideas, and Paraguay.

Fritz Friedländer. Among the leading CVZ literary critics and essayists. He wrote for numerous journals, both jewish and non-Jewish, including several liberal newspapers like *Die Weltbuhne.* He was a firm believer in the German Enlightenment and the German enlightened spirit. His articles and reviews all speak of one or more of the German *philosophes,* especially Herder and Humboldt.

199

Julius Fürst (1805–1873). Historian, lexicographer, and bibliographer who taught oriental languages at the University of Leipzig, where he founded the scholarly Jewish periodical *Die Orient*. His many publications included a Bible concordance, and his audience included Jews and (primarily liberal) non-Jews.

Eduard Gans (1798–1839). German Jewish jurist who became prominent as a Hegelian legal theorist. He was among the founders (in 1819) and the first president of the Society for Jewish Culture and Learning in which he spoke for a synthesis of Jewish and world culture and a consequent abandonment of "national individuality" on the part of Jews. He converted to Christianity because of failure to achieve an academic position, and was appointed professor of law at Berlin.

Peter Gay (1923–). German Jewish historian who emigrated in 1941. His books perhaps reveal a belief in the values of Enlightenment archetypes and include *The Party of Humanity. Essays on the French Enlightenment; The Dilemma of Democratic Socialism: Eduard Bernstein's Challenge to Marx; Weimar Culture;* and *The Enlightenment.*

Heinrich von Gneist (1816–1895). Moderate and later National Liberal member of parliament and famous professor of law, he spoke against Bismarck in the parliamentary debates. His argument was founded upon his faith in the German people's belief in moral and legal order that created justice and equality. Such faith obviously lent support to Jewish claims in Germany.

Walter Gropius (1883–1969). Director of the Bauhaus in Weimar, he is perhaps the man most responsible for the acceptance of modern architecture and furniture in the twentieth century. Former of the "Bauhaus philosophy," which

200

called for a universal, functional architecture as against a national German one, his politics were left, and he was an integral part and symbol of the Weimar Republic.

Michael Guttmann (1872–1942). Hungarian talmudic scholar whose prestige in talmudic studies made his work *Das Judentum und seine Umwelt*, written as an apologetic treatise advocating assimilation, both popular and respectable.

Karl August von Hardenberg (1758–1882). Prussian chancellor from 1810, instrumental in enacting the Edict of March 3, 1812, concerning the civil status of Prussian Jews. He repudiated the remaining restrictions in the edict, and after 1815 continually opposed the reactionary Prussian administration as it reneged its promises of equality for Jews made during the Napoleonic Wars.

Heinrich Heine (1779–1856). Famous German Jewish poet and journalist who spent much of his life in exile in Paris. He was nevertheless devoted to Germany and was perhaps the greatest and best-known of the Young Germany School. His poems, like "Die Lorelei," became classic German works.

Johann Gottfried von Herder (1744–1803). Philosopher, linguist, historian, among the leading German *philosophes*. He espoused a cultural nationalism that was combined with a humanistic cosmopolitanism based on the toleration of and respect for the dignity of all nationalities, their languages, folk tales, literature, customs, and histories.

Henriette Herz (1764–1847). Prominent German Jewish intellectual whose home was an intellectual center and meeting place for the great German thinkers and authors of the Enlightenment and Romantic eras, for example, Goethe.

201

Along with Rahel Levin's, hers was the most popular of the Berlin salons.

Ludwig Hollander (1877–1936). German Jewish lawyer and president of the CV from 1921 to 1933. He had edited *Im Deutschen Reich*, the CV's organ from 1909 to 1919, and founded the Philo Verlag, which became the official CV publishing house. He was one of the most influential and powerful builders of German Jewish national consciousness, and perhaps more than anyone else defined the CV (and German Jewry's) assimilationist position while helping the CV to become the important organization it was.

Wilhelm von Humboldt (1767–1835). Linguist, historian, and statesman who, along with von Hardenburg, was the architect of the Edict of 1812, which gave Jews in Prussia rights as citizens. He believed that Jews would become loyal, equal, and good German citizens, but only if they gave up their isolation and religion. He tried, for what he considered friendly reasons, to prevent Jewish congregations from uniting and was therefore among the leading and earliest advocates of assimilation.

Adolf Jellinek (1821–1893). Rabbi and scholar, born in Leipzig. He was a "preacher," attracting both Jewish and non-Jewish audiences to his sermons, which dealt with Kabbalah, Jewish philosophy, and medieval history and literature.

Jeorg Jellinek (1851–1911). Son of Adolf Jellinek, he became a prominent jurist and professor of law at Vienna, Heidelberg, and Basle. He converted to Christianity to further his career.

Melanie Klein (1882–1960). Psychoanalyst, disciple of Freud, who made extensive inquiry into the nature of child

202

and infantile experience. Her theories of neurosis and psychosis radically alter Freud's ideas (although she denied this and managed to remain within the fold). Klein's ideas are readily adopted to mythological parallels and are "historical" like Freud's, but reach further into the individual's past, or "pre-history." The questions she raises are of origins—like mythological questions.

R. D. Laing (1927–). Contemporary British psychologist whose work has broken new ground in the study of mental experience. His unusual theories are derivations of Freud's, but in a remote fashion which, like Erikson, Reich, Roheim, and Levi-Strauss, take into serious consideration the cultural environment and its impact on individuals.

Gustav Landauer (1870–1919). Social philosopher and critic, he was a believer in the ethical values of socialism, and saw them in part as derivatives of the ethics of Old Testament Judaism. He held office in the Bavarian Soviet Republic and was brutally slaughtered by anti-revolutionary troops. Toller idolized him.

Eduard Lasker (1829–1884). Participant in the 1848 revolution and member of parliament from 1867. He was an antagonist of Bismarck, and founder and leader of the National Liberal Party. In Prussia he fought for the right of Jews to leave the Jewish community without leaving the religion.

Theodore Lessing (1872–1933). German Jewish social philosopher who, although baptized in his youth, returned to what he termed Judasim in 1900. He was an avowed humanitarian socialist who based his socialism on Old Testament principles and attacked the nationalism of the German government on the same principles. Because of his criticism of Hindenburg he was suspended from his teaching position at the Hanover Technical High School, and a

203

nationalistic movement began in 1926 determined to imprison him. The issue placed the CV in an awkward dilemma of defending Lessing despite their denunciations of his Socialist views, and exposed them to nationalist criticism. He left Germany in 1933 but was killed by the Nazis in Czechoslovakia that same year.

Rahel Levin (1771–1833). A fervent admirer of Goethe, she provided her house as a salon which Goethe and others frequented most often of all the Berlin salons. She was baptized before she married Varnhagen von Ense, a Prussian diplomat.

Claude Lévi-Strauss (1908–). Philosopher and anthropologist who developed the study of "structural anthropology." His work on myths and mythologies and the ways they determine and define cultures and cultural behavior has been of great importance in understanding not only "primitive" peoples, but in shedding light on the human mind, its structure, content, and activity.

Lucien Levy-Bruhl (1857–1939). French anthropologist and philosopher whose studies of the primitive mind or "soul" were incisive, in some ways psychoanalytic, and emphasized the role of the emotions in psychic and physical life. He was a philosopher and student of the sociology of religion, and ultimately he reduced the study of the primitive mind to an analysis of mystic experience.

Ernst Lissauer (1882–1937). German Jewish poet and playwright best remembered as the composer of the "Hymn of Hate" ("Hassgesang gegen England") in 1915, which German troops sang at the front during World War I. From 1924 he lived in Vienna and strongly supported the German nationalists, insisting that the Jewish people were not one and that as a German Jew he had nothing at all in common with East European Jews. He, of course, opposed Zionism and advocated total assimilation.

Raphael Löwenfeld. Berlin Jew whose brochure, *Schtuzjuden oder Staatsbürger?*, produced in January 1893, included six theses that served as the manifesto of the CV, which was founded in March of that year. He was one of the motivating forces in that organization, urging not only its official, organized statement, but determining its policies as well. The "6 Theses" are the briefest and most concise statement of the CV's position as it stood until 1933, and beautifully captured the longings and beliefs of German Jews.

Bronislaw Malinowski (1884–1942). Social anthropologist who originated a "functionalist" approach to the study of culture based on the artifacts, institutions, and other facets of any given culture in terms of the functions they served. His studies of the Trobriand Islanders in 1927 led to a clash with Freud over the universality of the oedipal complex and other psychoanalytic theories which he had used earlier, and Malinowski posited a "Mother Right" situation as a counter to Freud. Despite his later disagreements with Freud and his derivation of culture from man's needs, Malinowski eventually gave precedence to cultural tradition as the primary influence in molding an individual and a group. He never completely rejected the psychoanalytic approach, and the role of myth, magic, religion, and the like continued to be central in his cultural studies.

Heinrich Mann (1871–1950). Author, and brother of Thomas Mann. He was honored as "a visionary of reason" in the Weimar Republic and was to return to Germany as president of the newly organized Academy of the Arts in East Berlin at the time of his death. His works during the Weimar Republic reflected his passionate devotion to intellectual and political freedom and made him "a champion of a new European humanism." He is perhaps best known in America as Settembrini, the liberal humanist in Thomas Mann's *The Magic Mountain.*

Jakob Marcus (1896–). Historian and rabbi. After early works on German Jewry, such as *The Rise and Destiny of the German Jew,* he concentrated on studies of American Jews.

Carl Melchior (1871–1933). Judge and banker in Hamburg who became an important economic adviser to the German government during World War I.

Moses Mendelssohn (1729–1786). The archetypal German Jew. Considered by German Jews of the nineteenth and twentieth centuries to be the first and greatest of assimilated Jews. He was praised by Kant for his philosophical and aesthetic genius and was given the title, "The German Socrates," because of his Platonic style of writing. Mendelssohn persuaded C. W. Dohm to write his work on the Jews, influenced Lessing's thought, collaborated with him, and supposedly became the model for Nathan in Lessing's play. Mendelssohn translated Rousseau's *Discourse on Inequality,* and became a leading German stylist as a result. He was a brilliant intellect and the first Jew in Germany to make his mark as a German scholar in several fields.

Theodore Mommsen (1817–1903). Prussian historian who was among the more eminent spokesmen for liberalism and nationalism. A member of the Progressive Party, founded in 1861, he was an ardent supporter of government by law *(Rechtstaat)* in terms of moral principles of public life under the monarchy. As an advocate of bourgeois, constitutional government, and equality before the law, he campaigned against anti-Semitism and for Jewish emancipation.

George Mosse (1918–). United States historian born in Berlin, whose knowledgeable studies of Nazi culture and German Jewry are informed by a sensitivity to cultural history. His work, *Germans and Jews* (1968), is of particular interest here, and while it has the same excellent qualities of Mosse's other works, is flawed by a particular—if faint—bias regarding German Jews.

Max Naumann. Berlin lawyer and founder of the ultraconservative Union of National German Jews. A rabid nationalist, he was anti-Semitic in his position on East European Jews. He agreed with the radical right's analysis of the Socialists as betrayers, railed against the British and the French as "rapists" of the German people, hated the Russians, and was a sympathizer of Hitler's from 1921 until 1934. In that year he was arrested and put in a concentration camp where he died.

Leonard Nelson (1882–1927). Philosopher of a peculiar brand of Kantianism, which differed from the "Neo-Kantianism" of his associates in its emphasis on psychological method and social action. He was a friend of Franz Oppenheimer, and subscribed to Oppenheimer's sort of moderate socialism.

Franz Oppenheimer (1864–1943). German Jewish economist and sociologist, he developed a theory of "liberal socialism," allegedly in contrast to Marxism. His concern was for agrarian reform and cooperation. As a liberal socialist he was acutely aware of his precarious position as public figure and German Jew.

Karl von Ossietsky (1889–1938). Brilliant, caustic, political polemicist of the Weimar Republic. Along with Kurt Tucholsky and other affiliates of *Die Weltbuhne*, he analyzed, exposed, railed at, and hoped for the Weimar Repub-

207

lic in an extremely liberal, humanitarian, and idealistic fashion.

Franz von Papen. (1879–1969). Member of the right wing of the Center Party, he held a seat in the Prussian Parliament from 1922 to 1932. In 1923 he urged the formation of a dictatorial government and in 1925 supported Hindenburg's candidacy. A reactionary monarchist, he became chancellor of Germany in 1932 (chosen by General Schleicher). The political turmoil and machinations during his and Schleicher's tenure of office led to Hitler's triumph in 1933 under which Papen was vice-chancellor.

Ludwig Philippson (1811–1889). Rabbi and scholar, believer and supporter of liberal ideals. A spokesman for emancipation yet for the maintenance of Jewish tradition and liturgy. Symbolic of his views is his translation of the Bible into German.

Hugo Preuss (1860–1925). Professor of law at the Berlin Institute of Commerce, having been refused a teaching position at the University of Berlin because of his Jewish background and liberal views. He became Minister of the Interior in 1918 and headed the committee that prepared the first draft of the Weimar Constitution. He resigned in 1919 because of opposition to the Versailles Treaty. An avid anti-Zionist and not active in Jewish affairs in Germany, he was nevertheless highly regarded by almost all German Jews.

Walter Rathenau (1867–1922). German Jewish economist, engineer, philosopher, and statesman. A successful industrialist, he was appointed Minister of Reconstruction in 1921 and Foreign Minister in 1922. In both capacities he strove for Franco-German rapprochement. He was a self-effacing Jew who quietly accepted—almost masochistically—anti-Semitic abuses. He was assassinated by right-wing anti-Semites in 1922.

208

Wilhelm Reich (1897–1957). Member of the psychoanalytic movement in its early days and, until 1932, a close associate of Freud. His theories of character analysis, identification, defense mechanisms, among others finally culminated in his "orgone vegotherapy" ideology. His perceptiveness in analysis of character was demonstrated in his work, *The Mass Psychology of Facism*, and he has been unfairly derogated because of his later bizarre ideas and his affiliation with socialism and Soviet Communism.

Eva Reichmann-Jungmann. Prominent member of the CV and a frequent contributor to the CVZ. She spoke out firmly for the Germanness of German Jews and for their useful role in German society. Like most of the CV spokesmen, she emphasized reason and rationalism over emotion and passion, and used methods appropriate to these beliefs. She emigrated to England in or around 1938.

Gabriel Riesser (1806–1863). Long-time advocate of Jewish emancipation. After being denied permission to practice law because of his Jewishness, he wrote a series of articles calling for civic emancipation. He was elected vice-president to the Frankfurt Parliament in 1848 and became the first Jewish judge in Germany.

Geza Roheim (1891–1953). Cultural anthropologist who came under the influence of Freud and applied psychoanalytic concepts to his study of culture, mythology, and folklore. He broke with Freud (although neither acknowledged it) over the importance of the oedipal complex. His studies were most important in the realm of understanding the unconscious basis of myth, legend, religion, and all aspects of culture.

Kurt von Schleicher (1882–1934). Prussian general who became politically active as an extreme reactionary. He believed he could "tame" and use the SA and the Nazis. Schleicher was made chancellor after Papen, but his political intrigues and devious bargains brought Hitler to power. He was murdered during the Rohm purge of June 1934.

Friedrich Schleiermacher (1768–1835). Theologian, philosopher who is among those, like Herder, Fichte and Goethe, considered a transitional figure from the Enlightenment to the Romantic era in Germany. He addressed the problem of religion, its definition, its relationship to morality, human motivation, reason, community, history, and nationality in 1799. His views on God, religion, the state, the church, and Christ were among the most significant in Germany because of their uniqueness, the redefinition of all of them, and the application to nationalistic ideas.

Gershom Scholem (1897–). Scholar of Jewish mysticism and of German Jews by virtue of his birth in Germany. His work has contributed to a new, historical interpretation of the Kabbalah and other forms of Jewish mysticism, yet he is a respected scholar in Jewish studies at Hebrew University in Jerusalem.

Baron Karl von Stein (1757–1831). Prussian statesman whose ordinance of 1808 granted municipal citizenship to Jews. He nevertheless opposed political emancipation as it was granted during and after the French Revolution. He was an intransigent anti-Semite who was responsible for numerous restrictive measures against the "harmful" Jewish population of Germany.

Adolf Stöcker (1835–1909). German anti-Semite and founder, in 1878, of the Christian Social Workers Party to fight socialism and the Jews, whom he claimed were undermining religion and morality. His ideas were disseminated through the Society of German Students into intellectual circles. Stöcker stimulated small groups of liberal Christian intellectuals to respond to anti-Semitism, and his popularity is partially responsible for the founding of the CV.

Christian Thomasius (1655–1728). Jurist, philosopher, and theologian who was among the founders of the University of Halle in 1694. As Thomasius left Pietism, Halle became the first school of the German Enlightenment. His friends and colleagues included Leibniz, Christian Wolff, and Pufendorf, and he especially fought against superstition, intolerance, and for more egalitarian administrative reforms.

Ernst Toller (1893–1939). Playwright, poet, and revolutionary. Born in Samotschin, Prussia, into a family that prided itself as representative of German culture in the midst of Poles, he was active in the 1919 Bavarian Soviet Republic, briefly led it after the assassination of Kurt Eisner, and was imprisoned for five years after it collapsed. His revolutionary, expressionist plays, *Die Wandlung* and *Masse Mensch*, were published while he was in prison and he was labeled, despite his renunciation of his Jewish background, as a Jewish revolutionary by German conservatives. Part of his abandonment of Judaism was what he believed to be its inseparability from German nationalism.

Moritz Veit (1808–1864). Publisher, politician, and leader of the Berlin Jewish community. Veit published works by Fichte and Ranke among other nationalist theorists. Although he argued for Jewish emancipation in the 1848 parliament, he was nevertheless both a Prussian and a Jewish traditionalist and conservative.

Rudolf Virchow (1821–1902). Eminent scientist and liberal deputy, he was one of the founders of the Progressive Party. Virchow stood firmly on the principles of constitutional government but remained loyal to the Prussian monarchy. He added prominence to the list of Prussian patriots who supported Jewish emancipation and assimilation.

Max Warburg (1867–1946). German Jewish banker, among the major financiers of the Kaiser and of Germany's war effort in World War I. He was appointed delegate to the Versailles Peace Conference.

Jacob Wassermann (1873–1934). German Jewish novelist who gradually became disillusioned with the idea of total assimilation. Perhaps the first and most passionate articulator of the tragic realization of the dilemma of German Jews in the twentieth century.

Robert Weltsch (1891–). Zionist editor and journalist. He became editor of the German Zionist organ, *Die Jüdische Rundschau*, and determined much of German Zionist policy. Weltsch retained his editorial post until 1938. He and the Zionist movement became stronger in Germany after 1933, and Weltsch asserted more influence on German Jews after that point as he shifted what had largely been a laissez-faire view in Germany regarding German Jews and Zionism.

Alfred Wiener (1885–1964). Leading member of the German Jewish community, secretary-general of the CV, which he joined after World War I. He was co-founder of the Jewish Central Information Office in Amsterdam in 1933, which in 1939 was moved to London as the Wiener Library.

Christian Wolff (1679–1754). Considered the greatest German philosopher of the eighteenth century by thinkers of that century, including Kant. Another of the Halle philosophers who came out of Pietism, he developed a German prose that was "suitable for philosophizing," called for the reform of social conditions and education, and defended the

212

greatness and autonomy of reason. Were he better known (he was pushed from prominence by Kant), he would probably have been more often considered by German Jews and German liberals in the nineteenth and twentieth centuries.

Arnold Zweig (1887–1968). German Jewish novelist and literary critic. His most famous novel was *The Case of Sergeant Grischa* (1927), but he dealt with Jewish culture in his essays and other works. Exiled by the Nazis in 1933, he lived in Palestine but returned to East Berlin after World War II.

APPENDIX B

Bibliographical Essay

Several areas of interest that are relevant to a study of German Jews in the Weimar Republic have not been discussed in this book. They are: the political and social milieu within which German Jewry functioned; the growth, changes, and development of German anti-Semitism; the relationships between East European Jews and German Jews, between Zionists and anti-Zionists in Germany; the politics of individual Jews and of some organizations. Some of the following books may be of interest in considering these areas. The purpose of including them here is to provide a selective, complementary bibliography to the thesis.

Political developments in the Weimar Republic were, of course, crucial to the lives of German Jews. Erich Eyck, *A History of the Weimar Republic* (New York, 1970), and William Halperin, *Germany Tried Democracy* (New York, 1965) are among the best political surveys and are particularly good in describing the reasons for the strength of right-wing political parties and movements after 1925.

Karl Dietrich Bracher, *Die Auflösung der Weimarer Repub-lik* (Villingen, 1955), is a massive, incisive account of the rise and fall of the Republic. He argues well that the "dilemma of democracy in the nineteenth century" and the German defeat in World War I led to the compromise government of Weimar that was beset with problems from the start. Bracher's *Die Enstehung der Weimarer Verfassung* (1963) is indispensable for an understanding of the Weimar Constitution, and the two books together comprise the convincing thesis that a compromise between old and new was doomed from 1919. Ernst Niekisch's little book, *Die Legende von der Weimarer Republik* (Koln, 1965), is a devastating, left-wing attack on the Republic as an illusion of liberalism, and complements Bracher's larger works. Niekisch also sees the Constitution as the deluding factor whose ideals were noble but in practice benefited only the middle and upper classes, a thesis, despite its doctrinaire Marxism, complemented by H. E. Hannover, *Politsche Jus-tiz, 1918–1933* (1966). A good general survey of party politics in the Weimar Republic is Sigmund Neumann, *Die Parteien der Weimarer Republik* (1932). Hajo Herbell, *Staatsbürger in Uniform 1789–1961* (Berlin, 1969), deals with the failure of German liberal politics, in terms of a liberalized military system, to overcome conservative, mili-taristic traditions and opposition. The failures of the politi-cal and intellectual left are examined in Istvan Deak, *Wei-mar Germany's Left-Wing Intellectuals* (Berkeley and Los Angeles, 1968), and a fine article by Gordon Craig, "Engage-ment or Neutrality," *Journal of Contemporary History*, II, No. 2 (1967). Harold L. Poor's biography of Kurt Tucholsky, *Kurt Tucholsky and the Ordeal of Germany 1914–1935* (New York, 1968), follows Deak's thesis and is a good analysis of the reasons for the failure of Tucholsky and the other leftist critics of the Republic. Friedrich Meinecke's classic, *The German Catastrophe*, and Friedrich Sell, *Die Tragodie des deutschen Liberalismus*, both analyze the

215

reasons for the failure of liberalism, the Republic, and the victory of National Socialism.

The conservative tradition in Germany is discussed by most political, intellectual, and social surveys, but is the specific topic of many historians. Among the best of such studies is George Mosse, *The Crisis of German Ideology* (New York, 1965), a brilliant treatment of the impact of *völkisch* thought on twentieth-century German life and politics. Fritz Stern, *The Politics of Cultural Despair*, traces the developmentof the *völksich*, conservative, and usually anti-Semitic ideology through three of its leading exponents and examines the socioeconomic and intellectual origins of that ideology; Hans Kohn, *The Mind of Germany* (New York, 1960), and Peter Viereck, *Metapolitics* (New York, 1941), both assert that the thrust of German history from at least the eighteenth century was toward National Socialism, and both provide provocative arguments for what they consider the dominant trend in German intellectual and political history. A. J. P. Taylor, *The Course of German History* (New York, 1962), develops a similar theme and gives an interesting analysis of the failure of liberalism in Germany and the idea that the concept of the Republic was more an anomaly than a logical consequence of German history and was never, not even briefly, realized. John Weiss, *The Fascist Tradition* (New York, 1967), and Eugen Weber's essay on the radical right in Germany in *The European Right* (1966) trace the conservative tradition as it led to fascism.

Kurt Sontheimer, *Anti-Demokratische Denken in der Weimarer Republik* (München, 1962), is among the best surveys of conservative and anti-Semitic groups and ideologies in the Weimer Republic. Robert Ernst Curtius, *Deutsche Geist in Gefahr* (1932), is a German non-Jew's statement that the noble German tradition of reason and humanity was being assaulted and subverted by rightist forces in Weimar. Part I of E. B. Wheaton's *The Nazi Revolution, 1933—1935: Prelude to Calamity* (Garden City, 1968) as well as Alan Bullock, *Hitler. A Study in Tyranny*, are good accounts of the anti-republican forces in Weimar. An interesting account of the social and economic conservatism that seemed to coexist with the political liberalism of the Republic is Herman Lebovics, *Social Conservatism and the Middle Classes in Germany 1914–1933* (Princeton, 1969).

The political affiliations of Jews in Germany, both in thought and action, are thoroughly documented by Jacob Toury in *Die politischen Orientierung der Juden in Deutschland* (Tübingen, 1966). Toury shows that after 1870 nearly 90 percent of German Jews who were politically conscious identified themselves with liberal parties. Elenore Sterling, *Judenhass* (Frankfurt, a.M., 1969), follows Toury's thesis and explores the origins of political anti-Semitism in the nineteenth century as an outgrowth of the conservative–liberal struggle. Werner Mosse, "The Conflict of Liberalism and Nationalism and Its Effect on German Jewry," *Leo Baeck Yearbook*, XV (1970), describes the dilemma of German Jews active in German politics in the 1860s and 1870s with the rise of conservative nationalism, and argues that those German Jewish liberals were the true patriots who might have rescued Germany from the defeat and humiliation of 1918. Werner Sombart, *The Jews and Modern Capitalism*, while exaggerated and jaded, does illustrate the capitalist identity of German Jews. The early chapters of Karl A. Schleunes, *The Twisted Road to Auschwitz. Nazi Policy Toward German Jews, 1933–1939* (Urbana, Chicago, London, 1970), show that Jews were linked with liberals and liberalism from the Second Reich through the Weimar Republic. A valuable counter to the assertions that anti-Semitism was a purely conservative phenomenon is Hans-Helmuth Knütter, *Die Juden und die deutsche Linke in der*

217

Weimarer Republik (Düsseldorf, 1971), and his "Die Links-parteien," in *Entscheidungsjahr 1932*. Knütter points out the anti-capitalist basis for socialist anti-Semitism.

Knütter's and Schleunes' theses lead to the economic and political and social bases for anti-Semitism. Eva Reich-mann, *Hostages of Civilization*, is a particularly good analysis of the social preconditions for anti-Semitism in Germany. P. W. Massing, *Rehearsal for Destruction*, examines the political history of anti-Semitism in Germany in the nineteenth century. An excellent study of the connections between the socioeconomic, political, and psychological foundations of anti-Semitism is Adolf Leschnitzer, *The Magic Background of Modern Anti-Semitism. An Analysis of the German Jewish Relationship* (New York, 1956). Equally good, although not as apropos to German Jews, is Norman Cohn, *Warrant for Genocide* (London, 1967), the last chapter of which is an interesting resurrection of Freud's theory of anti-Semitism developed in *Moses and Monotheism* and augmented by Cohn with his analysis of the history of *The Protocols of the Elders of Zion*. "The Economic and Social Background of Modern Antisemi-tism" by Bernard D. Weinreyb, "Some Remarks on the Psychology of Antisemitism" by I. S. Wechsler, and "An-tisemitism in Modern Germany" by Waldemar Gurian are all essays in *Essays on Antisemitism*, ed. Koppel S. Pinson (New York, 1946), that are relevant to a study of German Jews and their environment. Ernst Simmel's anthology, *Anti-Semitism: A Social Disease* (New York, 1946), also contains some pertinent essays: Simmel, "Anti-Semitism and Mass Psychopathology," T. W. Adorno, "Anti-Semi-tism and Fascist Propaganda," Otto Fenichel, "Elements of a Psychoanalytic Theory of Anti-Semitism."

Almost all the histories of the Jews in modern times include major sections on German Jewry. While it is diffi-cult to find a thorough history of the Jews that does not have a particular bias, generally Zionist, some are more reliable than others. Salo Baron, *The Social and Religious History of the Jews* is perhaps the most comprehensive in its detail and narrative style. His treatment of the history of Jews in Germany is matter-of-fact and deals primarily with the advances in emancipation. Howard Sachar, *The Course of Modern Jewish History*, is another good if somewhat biased survey, which argues implicitly that a history of the Jews is a history of anti-Semitism. The classic histories are those of S. Dubnow, *Weltgeschichte des jüdischen Volkes* (Berlin, 1925–29), and H. Graetz, *History of the Jews* (1900) (the latter goes only to 1848). Jacob Katz, *Tradition and Crisis. Jewish Society at the End of the Middle Ages* (New York, 1961), centers on Central and Eastern Europe and describes Jewish participation in the Enlightenment as contributing to the disintegration of traditional Jewish society. Julius Guttmann, *Philosophies of Judaism*, is a good general introduction to the major thinkers of Jewish history from Maimonides to Franz Rosenzweig and includes sections on Hermann Cohen and Leo Baeck, as does Arthur Cohen, *The Natural and the Supernatural Jew*. Hermann Schwab, *A World in Ruins* (London, 1946), is a rather philosemitic work that covers the contributions of Jews to German culture until 1933 with what Schwab believes was the destruction of German culture. Solomon Lipitzin, *Germany's Stepchildren*, is a study of famous German Jews from the eighteenth to the twentieth century and includes Börne, Heine, Rathenau, Buber and Wassermann. Gershom Scholem, *The Kaballah and Its Symbolism* (New York, 1969), adds a different and fascinating dimension to the history of Jewish thought and communities.

A comprehensive bibliography of German Jewry is the Wiener Library Catalogue entitled *German Jewry, Its History, Life and Culture*. Some works concerned specifically with Jews in the Weimar Republic are Walter Gross, "Das politische Schicksal der Juden in der Weimarer Republik," in Hans Tramer, ed., *In Zwei Welten* (Tel Aviv, 1962), and some personal accounts such as Rahel Strauss, *Wir lebten in Deutschland: Erinnerungen einer deutschen Jüdin, 1880 –1933* (Stuttgart, 1962); Margarete Susman, *Ich habe viele gelebt: Erinnerungen* (Stuttgart, 1964); Hans Joachim Schoeps, *Bereit für Deutschland!* and *Die letzten dreissig Jahre;* Heinemann Stern, *Warum hassen sieuns eigentlich?* An indispensable book for studying the position of Jews in Germany after 1933 is Helmut Genschel, *Die Verdrängung der Juden aus der Wirtschaft im Dritten Reich* (Berlin, Frankfurt, Zurich, 1966). Klauss J. Hermann, *Das Dritte Reich und die deutsche-jüdischen Organisationen, 1933– 1934* (Koln, 1969), is a valuable little collection of documents, correspondence between leaders of the various organizations and Nazi officials including Hitler, legislation, orders, minutes of meetings. There is a considerable amount of material concerning Max Naumann, and more from and about Leo Baeck. Leon Poliakov and J. Wulf, *Der Dritte Reich und die Juden* (1959), is a more complete collection of Nazi documents dealing with Jews in and out of Germany. *The Jews in Nazi Germany. The Factual Record of Their Persecution by the National Socialists,* ed. American Jewish Committee (New York, 1933), is a collection and commentary of articles, letters, and legislation that is interesting for its innocent and unsuspecting outrage.

Reiner Bernstein, *Zwischen Emanzipation und Anti-semitismus* (Berlin, 1969), is a thorough history of the CV and the CVZ with good, well-documented sections on the organization's positions on Zionism and National Socialism. Indispensable for any work dealing with German Jewish organizations after 1933 is Hans Lamm, *Uber die innere und aüssere Entwicklung des deutschen Judentums im Dritten Reich* (München, 1951). S. Adler-Rudel, *Ostjuden in Deutschland* (Tübingen, 1959), is the most comprehensive study of Eastern European Jewish immigration into Germany. Contemporary accounts (Weimar) of the interaction or antagonism between German and other Jews are *Ostjuden, Süddeutsche Monatshefte,* XIII, No. 5 (February, 1916); *Ostjuden in Deutschland* (Berlin, 1921); Paul Nathan, *Das Problem der Ostjuden* (Berlin, 1926).

Finally, there is, of course, an unlimited number of anthropological and psychological material that can help to supplement the works of those disciplines used in this thesis. Robert J. Lifton, "Psychohistory," *Partisan Review* (1970), and his book *Death in Life* (New York, 1967) are good examples of one type of psychohistory. Erik Erikson's now-classic *Young Man Luther* (New York, 1958) is still one of the outstanding works of this kind. Both Erikson and Lifton have succeeded in integrating Freudian conceptions of biologically rooted drives with a concern for interaction between the development of an individual and his culture. Other worthwhile psychohistorical works include Stanley Elkins, *Slavery: A Problem in American Institutional and Intellectual Life* (Chicago, 1959); Arthur Mitzman, *The Iron Cage* (New York, 1970); Winthrop Jordan, *White Over Black: American Attitudes Toward the Negro, 1550–1812* (Chapel Hill, 1968); Frantz Fanon, *Black Skins, White Masks* (among the only historical works that explicitly uses Jungian theory). Philip Slater, *The Glory of Hera: Greek Mythology and Greek Family (Boston, 1968), is a brilliant work that integrates history, anthropology, psychology and mythology. Bruce Mazlish, Psychoanalysis and History* (New York, 1971), is an excellent collection of essays on the application of psychoanalysis to history. Herbert Marcuse, *Eros and Civilization* (Boston, 1955), and N. O. Brown, *Life Against Death,* contain excellent sections on Freud and his relationship to history, religion and myth. Philip Rieff, *Freud: The Mind of the Moralist* (New York, 1959), and the essays in his *The Triumph of the Therapeutic (New York, 1966) are excellent studies of psychoanalytic theories and their effect on Western culture. The most outstanding re-*

221

cent work on Freud and Freudian theories and their crucial importance for modern culture is Paul Ricoeur, *Freud and Philosophy* (New Haven, 1970).

The more specialized combinations of psychoanalytic anthropology include W. Beck, "Culture and Neurosis," *American Sociology Review* (April 1936), an elaboration of Freud's theories of culture as sublimation; and Geza Roheim, "the Psycho-Analytic Interpretation of Culture," *International Journal of Psychoanalysis* (1943), and "Freud and Cultural Anthropology," *Psychoanalytic Quarterly* (1940). Along with these are studies of culture and myth such as A. Kroeber and C. Kluckhohn, *Culture: A Critical Review of Concepts and Definitions* (Cambridge, 1952), and W. Muensterberger, ed., *Man and His Culture. Psychoanalytic Anthropology after "Totem and Taboo"* (New York, 1970). Paul Ricoeur, *The Symbolism of Evil* (Boston, 1969), is a fascinating book that adds to an understanding of myth and its attraction and enormous power. Joseph Campbell, *The Hero with a Thousand Faces* (Cleveland, 1956), is becoming a standard companion to his four-volume work *(The Masks of God)*, and one of the more recent works with a psychohistorical orientation is G. S. Kirk, *Myth: Its Meaning and Functions in Ancient and Other Cultures* (Cambridge, Berkeley, Los Angeles, 1970). Among the many studies that link myth with the unconscious and psychoanalysis are M. S. Bergman, "The . .Impact of Ego Psychology on the Study of Myth," *American Imago* (1966); Dorothy Eggan, "The Personal Use of Myth in Dreams," *Myth: A symposium, Journal of American Folklore* (1955); Roheim, "Super-Ego and Group Ideal," *International Journal of Psychoanalysis* (1932).

Selected Bibliography

Abraham, Karl. "Dreams and Myths." *Clinical Papers and Essays on Psychoanalysis.* New York: Basic Books, 1955.

Adler, H. G. *Die Juden in Deutschland. Von der Aufklärung bis zum Nationalsozialismus.* München: Kösel-Verlag, 1960.

Anti-Anti: Tatsachen zur Judenfrage. Edited by the C. V. Berlin, 1932.

Arendt, Hannah. *Eichmann in Jerusalem: A Report on the Banality of Evil.* New York: Viking Press, 1965.

――――. *The Origins of Totalitarianism.* Cleveland & New York: World Publishing Co., 1958.

Arendt-Stern, Hannah. "Aufklärung und Judenfrage." *Zeitschrift für Geschichte der Juden in Deutschland,* IV (1932), 65–77.

Bab, Julius. *Goethe und die Juden.* Berlin: Philo-Verlag, 1926.

――――. *Lieben und Tod des deutschen Judentums.* Paris, 1938.

Bachelard, Gaston. *The Poetics of Space.* Boston: Beacon Press, 1963.

――――. *The Psychoanalysis of Fire.* Boston: Beacon Press, 1964.

Ball-Kaduri, Kurt Jakob. *Das Leben der Juden in Deutschland im Jahre 1933. Ein Zeitbericht.* Frankfurt am Main: Europäische Verlaganstalt, 1963.

223

Baron, Salo W. "The Jewish Communal Crisis in 1848." *Jewish Social Studies*, XIV (1952), 99–144.

———. *Nationalism and Religion*. New York: Harper & Row, 1947.

———. *A Social and Religious History of the Jews*. 3 vols. New York: Columbia University Press, 1937.

Becker, Werner. "Die Rolle der liberalen Presse." *Deutsches Judentum in Krieg und Revolution, 1916–1923*. Edited by Werner E. Mosse. Tübingen: J. C. B. Mohr (Paul Siebeck), 1971.

Berg, Ernst. *Wohin treibt Juda?* Leipzig: Diskus-Verlag Emil Krug, 1926.

Behr, Stefan. *Der Bevölkerungsrückgang der deutschen Juden*. Frankfurt am Main: J. Kauffmann Verlag, 1932.

Bennathan, Esra. "Die demographische und wirtschaftliche Struktur der Juden." *Entscheidungsjahr 1932*. Tübingen: J. C. B. Mohr (Paul Siebeck), 1965.

Bettauer, Hugo. *Die Stadt ohne Juden. Ein Roman von übermorgen*. Wien: Gloriette-Verlag, 1922.

Bieber, Hugo. "Jews and Jewish Problems in German Literature." *The Jewish People Past and Present*. 3 vols. New York: Jewish Encyclopedic Handbooks, 1952.

Blütlugen. Marchen und Tatsachen. Edited by the C.V. Berlin: Philo-Verlag, 1929.

Borman, Thorleif. *Hebrew Thought Compared with Greek* New York: W. W. Norton, 1970.

Brecht, Arnold. "Walter Rathenau and the Germans." *Journal of Politics*, X (February 1948), 20–48.

Brown, Norman O. *Life Against Death. The Psychoanalytical Meaning of History*. Middletown, Conn.: Wesleyan University Press, 1959.

———. *Love's Body*. New York: Vintage Books, 1966.

Buchheim, Karl. "Die Tragödie der Weimarer Republik." *Hochland*, XLIX, No. 6 (August 1957).

Butler, E. M. *The Tyranny of Greece over Germany. A Study of the Influence Exercised by Greek Art and Poetry over the Great German Writers of the Eighteenth, Nineteenth and Twentieth Centuries*. Boston: Beacon Press, 1958.

Cahnman, Werner J. "The Three Regions of German-Jewish History." *Jubilee Volume Dedicated to Curt C. Silberman*. Edited by Herbert A. Strauss and Hanns G. Reissner. New York: American Federation of Jews from Central Europe, 1969.

Campbell, Joseph. *The Masks of God*. Vol. I: *Primitive Mythology*. Vol. IV: *Creative Mythology*. New York: Viking Press, 1959.

224

Caro, Leopold. *Die Judenfrage: Eine ethische Frage*. Leipzig: Grunow, 1892.

Cassirer, Ernst. "Die Idee der Religion bei Lessing und Mendelssohn." *Festgabe zum zehnjahrigen Bestehen der Akademie für die Wissenschaft des Judentums, 1919–1929*. Berlin: Akademie Verlag, 1929.

————. *Language and Myth*. Translated by Susanne K. Langer. New York: Dover Publications, 1946.

————. *The Philosophy of Symbolic Forms*. Vol. I: *Language*. Vol. II: *Mythical Thought*. New Haven & London: Yale University Press, 1970.

C. V. Zeitung. Blätter für Deutschtum und Judentum. Organ des C.V. Vols. I-XIV. Berlin, 1922–35.

C.V. Zeitung. Montausgabe. Vols. I–IV. Berlin, 1928–32.

Civis Germanus Sum. Von Einem Juden deutscher Nation. Berlin. Verlag von Richard Wilhelm, 1891.

Cohen, Arthur. *The Natural and the Supernatural Jew*. New York: Pantheon Books, 1962.

Cohen, Hermann. *Die Bedeutung des Judentums für den religiösen Fortschritt der Menschkeit*. Berlin-Schöneberg: Protestantischer Schriftenvertrieb, 1910.

————. *Deutschtum und Judentum*. Giessen: Töpelmann, 1923.

————. *Moses Ben Maimon*. 2 vols. Leipzig: Buchhandlung Gustav Fock, 1908.

————. *Die religiösen Bewegungen der Gegenwart*. Leipzig: Buchhandlung Gustav Fock, 1914.

Dawson, Jerry F. *Friedrich Schleiermacher, the Evolution of a Nationalist*. Austin & London: University of Texas Press, 1966.

Diringer, David. *The Alphabet. A Key to the History of Mankind*. 3rd ed., rev. with the collaboration of Reinhold Regensburger. 2 vols. London: Alden & Mowbray, 1968.

Dohm, Wilhelm Christian. *Über die bürgerliche Verbesserung der Juden. Anhang: Manasseh Ben Israel: Rettung der Juden. Nebst einer Vorrede von Moses Mendelssohn*. Berlin, Stettin: Nicolai, 1781–83.

Dokumente zur deutschen Verfassungsgeschichte. Edited by Ernst Rudolf Huber. 3 vols. Stuttgart: W. Kohlhammer Verlag, 1961.

Edelheim-Muehsam, Margaret T. "Die Haltung der jüdischen Presse gegenüber der Nationalsozialistischen Bedrohung." *Deutsches Judentum: Aufsteig und Krise*. Edited by Robert Weltsch. Stuttgart: Leo Baeck Institut, 1963.

Eliade, Mircea. *Cosmos and History: The Myth of the Eternal Return.* Translated by Willard R. Trask. New York: Harper & Row, 1959.

──────. *Myth and Reality.* Translated by Willard R. Trask. New York: Harper & Row, 1963.

──────. *Myths, Dreams and Mysteries. The Encounter Between Contemporary Faiths and Archaic Realities.* Translated by Philip Mairet. New York: Harper & Row, 1960.

──────. "The Yearning for Paradise in Primitive Tradition." *Myth and Mythmaking.* Edited by Henry A. Murray. Boston: Beacon Press, 1959.

Elbogen, Ismar. *Die Geschichte der Juden in Deutschland.* Revised by Elenore Sterling. Frankfurt am Main: Europäische Verlaganstalt, 1966.

──────. "Wanderungen der Juden." *Süddeutsche Monatschefte,* XVII (September, 1930), 802–809.

Eloesser, Arthur. *Das bürgerliche Drama.* Berlin, 1898.

Engelman, Bernt. *Deutschland ohne Juden. Eine Bilanz.* München: Franz Schneekluth Verlag, 1970.

Erasmus, Siegfried. *Die Juden in der ersten deutschen Nationalversammlung 1848–1849.* Weimar: Fink, 1941.

Erikson, Erik. *Childhood and Society.* 2nd ed. New York: W. W. Norton, 1963.

──────. *Identity: Youth and Crisis.* New York: W. W. Norton, 1968.

Frankfort, Henry, and Frankfort, Mrs. Henry A. "Myth and Reality." *Before Philosophy. The Intellectual Adventure of Ancient Man.* Edited by Henry A. Frankfort and Mrs. Henry A. Frankfort. Baltimore: Penguin Books, 1949.

Frazer, James George. *The Golden Bough. A Study in Magic and Religion.* London: Macmillan & Co., 1970.

Freud, Anna. *The Ego and the Mechanisms of Defense.* Rev. ed. New York: International Universities Press, 1966.

Freud, Sigmund. " 'The Antithetical Sense of Primary Words' " (1910). *Collected Papers,* IV. Translated by Joan Riviere. 5 vols. London: Hogarth Press & Institute of Psycho-Analysis, 1949–50.

──────. *Beyond the Pleasure Principle* (1920). *The Standard Edition of the Complete Psychological Works of Sigmund Freud,* ed. James Strachey, Anna Freud, Alix Strachey, & Alan Tyson. [24] Vols. London; Hogarth Press and The Institute of Psycho-Analysis, 1954–   , XVIII.

──────. *Civilization and Its Discontents* (1930). *Works,* Vol XXI.

──────. "The Defense Neuro-Psychoses" (1894). *Collected Papers,* I.

———. "The Economic Problem in Masochism" (1924). *Collected Papers*, II.

———. *The Ego and the Id* (1923). Works, XIX.

———. "Formulations Regarding the Two Principles in Mental Functioning" (1911). *Collected Papers*, IV.

———. "Further Remarks on the Defense Neuro-Psychoses" (1896). *Collected Papers*, I.

———. *The Future of an Illusion*. Works, XXI.

———. *A General Introduction to Psychoanalysis*. Works, XVI.

———. *Group Psychology and the Analysis of the Ego*. Works, XVIII.

———. *The Interpretation of Dreams* (1900). Works, IV.

———. "Instincts and Their Vicissitudes" (1915). *Collected Papers*, IV.

———. "The Loss of Reality in Neurosis and Psychosis" (1924). *Collected Papers*, II.

———. "Metapsychological Supplement to the Theory of Dreams" (1916). *Collected Papers*, IV.

———. *Moses and Monotheism*. Works, XXIII

———. "Negation" (1925). *Collected Papers*, V.

———. "Neurosis and Psychosis" (1924). *Collected Papers*, II.

———. *New Introductory Lectures on Psychoanalysis* (1933). Works, XXII.

———. "A Note upon the Mystic Writing Pad" (1925). *Collected Papers*, V.

———. "Obsessive Acts and Religious Practices" (1907). *Collected Papers*, II.

———. "Obsessions and Phobias; Their Psychical Mechanisms and Their Aetiology" (1895). *Collected Papers*, I.

———. "The Occurrence in Dreams of Material from Fairy-Tales" (1913). *Collected Papers*, IV.

———. "On Narcissism: an Introduction" (1914). *Collected Papers*, IV.

———. "On the Psychical Mechanisms of Hysterical Phenomena" (1893). *Collected Papers*, I.

———. *An Outline of Psycho-Analysis*. Works, XXIII.

———. *The Problem of Anxiety*. Translated by Henry Alden. New York: W. W. Norton & Psychoanalytic Quarterly Press, 1936.

———. "Psycho-Analysis and Religious Origins" (1919). *Collected Papers*, V.

———. "Repression" (1915). *Collected Papers*, IV.

———. "Splitting of the Ego in the Defensive Process" (1938). *Collected Papers*, V.

227

————. *Totem and Taboo* (1913). Works, XIII.

————. "The Uncanny" (1919). *Collected Papers*, IV.

Friedlander, Saul. "Die politischen Veränderungen der Kriegszeit und ihre Auswirkungen auf die Judenfrage." *Deutsches Judentum in Krieg und Revolution, 1916–1923*. Edited by Werner E. Mosse. Tübingen: J. C. B. Mohr (Paul Siebeck), 1971.

Friedman, Philip. "Aspects of Jewish Communal Crisis in the Period of the Nazi Regime in Germany, Austria, and Czechoslovakia." *Essays on Jewish Life and Thought*. Edited by Joseph L. Blau, et al. New York: Columbia University Press, 1959.

Frisch, Efraim. "Judische Aufzeichnungen." *Der Neue Merkur*, V, No. 5 (August 1921), 297–317.

Flake, Otto. "Zum jüdischen Problem." *Der Neue Merkur*, V No. 5 (August 1921), 318–328.

Fritsch, Theodor. "Zur Geschichte der Antisemitischen Bewegung." *Süddeutsche Monatshefte*, XXVII (September 1930), 852–856.

Fuchs, Eugen. *Um Deutschtum und Judentum*. Frankfurt am Main: Verlag von J. Kauffmann, 1919.

Garland, H. B. *Lessing. The Founder of Modern German Literature*. London: Macmillan & Co., 1962.

Gaster, Theodore H. *Myth, Legend and Custom in the Old Testament*. New York: Harper & Row, 1969.

Gay, Peter, *The Enlightenment: An Interpretation. The Rise of Modern Paganism*. New York: Alfred A. Knopf, 1966.

————. *Weimar Culture. The Outsider as Insider*. New York: Harper & Row, 1968.

Geiger, Ludwig. "Herder und das Judentum." *Die deutsche Literatur und die Juden*. Berlin: Reimer Verlag, 1910.

————. "Schiller und Juden." *Die deutsche Literatur und die Juden*. Berlin: Reimer Verlag, 1910.

Goldmann, Felix, *Der Jude im deutschen Kulturkreise. Ein Beitrag zum Wesen des Nationalismus*. Leipzig: Philo-Verlag, 1930.

Goldmann, Nahum, *et al. Deutsche und Juden*. Frankfurt am Main: Suhrkamp Verlag, 1967.

Goldstein, Julius. *Deutsche Volksidee oder deutschvölkische Idee*. Berlin: Philo-Verlag, 1927.

Gordon, Cyrus H. *The Common Background of Greek and Hebrew Civilizations*. New York: W. W. Norton, 1965.

Greunwald, Max. "Der Anfang der Reichsvertretung." *Deutsches Judentum: Aufsteig und Krise*. Stuttgart: Leo Baeck Institut, Deutsche Verlags-Anstalt, 1963.

Guttmann, Michael. *Das Judentum und seine Umwelt. Eine Darstellung der religiösen und rechtlichen Beziehungen zwischen Juden und Nichtjuden mit besonderer Berucksichtung der talmudisch-rabbinischen Quellens.* Berlin: Philo-Verlag, 1927.

Guttmann, Julius. *Kant und das Judentum.* Leipzig: Gustav Fock, 1908.

Hamerow, Theodore S. *Restoration, Revolution, Reaction. Economics and Politics in Germany, 1815–1871.* Princeton: Princeton University Press, 1958.

Heimann, Paula. "Certain Functions of Introjection and Projection in Early Infancy." In Melanie Klein, et al., *Developments in Psycho-Analysis.* London: Hogarth Press, 1952.

———. "Notes on the Theory of the Life and Death Instincts." In Melanie Klein, et al., *Developments in Psycho-Analysis.* London: Hogarth Press, 1952.

Heinz, Friedrich Wilhelm. "Die Ursachen des Antisemitismus." *Klärung. 12 Autoren, Politiker über die Judenfrage.* Berlin: Verlag Tradition Wilhelm Kolk, 1932.

Holborn, Hajo. *A History of Modern Germany.* 3 vols. New York: Alfred A. Knopf, 1959–69.

Holdheim, Gerhard. "Der Zionismus in Deutschland." *Süddeutsche Monatshefte,* XXVII (September 1930), 814–817.

Hollander, Ludwig. *Deutsche-Jüdische Probleme der Gegenwart. Eine Auseinanderung über die Grundfragen des Central-Vereins deutscher Staatsbürger jüdischen Glaubens.* Berlin: Philo-Verlag, 1929.

Huizinga, Johan. *Homo Ludens. A Study of the Play Element in Culture.* Boston: Beacon Press, 1955.

Hübscher, Friedrich. "Reich und Israel." *Klärung. 12 Autoren, Politiker über die Judenfrage.* Berlin: Verlag Tradition Wilhelm Kolk, 1932.

Iggers, Georg. *The German Conception of History. The National Tradition of Historical Thought from Herder to the Present.* Middletown, Conn.: Wesleyan University Press, 1968.

Im Deutschen Reich. Zeitschrift des Central-Vereins deutscher Staatsbürger jüdischen Glaubens. Vols. XXIV–XXVII. Berlin, 1918–21.

Israelitisches Familienblatt. Vol. XXXV, No. 19 (May 11, 1933).

James, E. O. "Myth and Ritual." *Eranos Jahrbuch,* XVII (1949), 79–120.

Johannsen, Ernst. "Über den Antisemitismus als gegebene Tatsache." *Klärung. 12 Autoren, Politiker über die Judenfrage.* Berlin: Verlag Tradition Wilhelm Kolk, 1932.

Joll, James. *Three Intellectuals in Politics.* New York: Random House, 1960.

Jones, Ernest. "Mother-Right and the Sexual Ignorance of Savages" *International Journal of Psychoanalysis,* VI, Part 2 (April 1925), 109–130.

Der Jud ist Schuld . . .? Diskussionsbuch über die Judenfrage. Basel, Berlin: Zinnen-Verlag, 1932.

"Die jüdische Abwehr." *Der Israelit,* LXXI, No. 26 (June 26, 1930).

Jung, Carl Gustav. *Aion. Collected Works.* Vol. IX, Part 2: *The Archetypes and the Collective Unconscious.* Edited by Sir Herbert Read, *et al.* 14 vols. Princeton: Princeton University Press, 1956.

———. *Man and His Symbols.* Garden City: Doubleday & Co., 1964.

———. *Modern Man in Search of a Soul.* Translated by W. S. Dell and Cary F. Baynes. London: Kegan Paul, Trench, Trubner & Co., 1933.

———. "The Phenomenology of the Spirit in Fairy Tales." *Collected Works.* Vol. IX, Part 1: *The Archetypes and the Collective Unconscious.*

———. "The Psychology of the Child Archetype." *Collected Works.* Vol. IX, Part 2: *The Archetypes and the Collective Unconscious.*

Kaulla, Rudolf. *Der Liberalismus und die deutschen Juden. Das Judentum als konservatives Element.* Leipzig: Verlag von Duncker und Humboldt, 1928.

Kaznelson, Siegmund, ed. *Juden im deutschen Kulturbereich. Ein Sammelwerk.* Berlin: Judischer Verlag, 1959.

Kerenyi, C. "Prolegomena." In C. Kerenyi and C. G. Jung, *Essays on a Science of Mythology.* Translated by R. F. C. Hull. Princeton: Princeton University Press, 1959.

Klein, Bernard. "The Judenrat." *Jewish Social Studies,* XXII (1960), 27–42.

Klein, Melanie. "Notes on Some Schizoid Mechanisms." *Developments in Psycho-Analysis.* London: Hogarth Press, 1952.

———. "Some Theoretical Conclusions Regarding the Emotional Life of the Infant." *Developments in Psycho-Analysis.* London: Hogarth Press, 1952.

Kober, Adolf. "Die Geschichte deutschen Juden in der historischen Forschung der letzten 35 Jahre." *Zeitschrift für die Geschichte die Juden in Deutschland,* I (1929), 13–23.

———. "Jewish Communities in Germany from the Age of the Enlightenment to Their Destruction by the Nazis." *Jewish Social Studies,* IX (1947), 195–238.

Kobler, Franz, ed. *Juden und Judentum in deutschen Briefen aus drei Jahrhunderten*. Vienna: Saturn-Verlag, 1935.

Koch, Franz. "Goethe und die Juden." *Schriften des Reichsinstituts für Geschichte des neuen Deutschlands*. Vol. II; *Forschugen zur Judenfrage*. 8 Vols. Hamburg: Hanseatische Verlaganstalt, 1937.

Kohn, Hans. *The Idea of Nationalism: A Study in Its Origins and Background*. New York: Macmillan & Co., 1943.

Krihler, Bernard. "Boycotting Nazi Germany." *The Wiener Library Bulletin*, XXIII, No. 4 (1969), 26–31.

Kroeber, A. L. "Totem and Taboo in Retrospect." *American Journal of Sociology*, XLV, No. 3 (November, 1939), 446–451.

Lamm. Hans. *Über die innere and aüssere Entwicklung des deutschen Judentums im Dritten Reich. Innaugural Dissertation, Friedrich-Alexander Universität*. Erlangen, 1951.

Laswell, Harold D. "A Hypothesis Rooted in the Preconceptions of a Single Civilization Tested by Bronislaw Malinowski." *Methods in Social Science*. Edited by Stuart A. Rice. Chicago: University of Chicago Press, 1931.

Layard, John. "Identification with the Sacrificial Animal." *Eranos Jahrbuch*, XXIV (1955). 341–406.

Layton, Roland V. "The *Völkischer Beobachter*, 1920–1933: The Nazi Party Newspaper in the Weimar Era." *Central European History*, III, No. 4 (December 1970), 353–382.

Van der Leeuw, G. "Urzeit und Endzeit." *Eranos, Jahrbuch*, XVII (1949), 11–51.

Lessing, Gotthold Effraim. *Die Erziehung des Menschengeschlechts. Gesammelte Werke*. Vo. VIII. Edited by Paul Rilla. 10 vols. Berlin: Aufbau Verlag, 1956.

———, *Nathan the Wise*. Translated by W. A. Steel. London: J. M. Dent & Sons, 1930.

Lessing, Theodore. *Deutschland und seine Juden*. Prague: Neumann & Co., 1933.

Lévi-Strauss, Claude. "Story of Asdiwal." *The Structural Study of Myth and Totemism*. Edited by Edmund Leach. London: Tanistack Publications, 1967.

———. *The Raw and the Cooked. Introduction to a Science of Mythology*. Vol. I. New York: Harper & Row, 1969.

———. *Structural Anthropology*. Garden City: Doubleday & Co., 1967.

Levy-Bruhl, Lucien. *The "Soul" of the Primitive*. Translated by Lilian A. Claire. London: George Allen & Unwin, 1965.

231

Lewin, Kurt. *Resolving Social Conflicts: Selected Papers on Group Dynamics*. New York: Harper & Row, 1948.

Lion, Ferdinand, "Deutsches und jüdisches Schicksals." *Der Neue Merkur*, V, No. 5 (August, 1921), 348–360.

Loew, Cornelius. *Myth, Sacred History, and Philosophy. The Pre-Christian Religious Heritage of the West*. New York: Harcourt, Brace & World, 1967.

Landauer, George. "Zur Geschichte der Judenrechtswissenschaft." *Zeitschrift für die Geschichte die Juden in Deutschland*, II (1930), 255–261.

Lowenthal, E. G. "Die Juden im öffentlichen Leben." *Entscheidungsjahr 1932*. Tübingen: J. C. B. Mohr (Paul Siebeck), 1965.

Lowenthal, Marvin. *The Jews of Germany*. New York: Longmans, Green, 1936.

Löwenfeld, Raphael. *Schutzjuden oder Staatsbürger?* Berlin: Schweitzer & Mohr, 1893.

Löwenstein, Leo. "Des Linie des Reichsbundes jüdischer Frontsoldaten." *Wille und Weg des deutschen Judentums*. Berlin: Vortrupp Verlag, 1935.

Malinowski, Bronislaw. *Magic, Science and Religion, and Other Essays*. Garden City: Doubleday & Co., 1954.

——. *A Scientific Theory of Culture, and Other Essays*. Chapel Hill: University of North Carolina Press, 1944.

——. *Sex, Culture, and Myth*. New York: Harcourt, Brace & Wrod, 1962.

Mann, Thomas. "Freud and the Future." *Essays of Three Decades*. Translated by H. T. Lowe-Porder. New York: Alfred A. Knopf, 1948.

—— "Lessing." *Essays of Three Decades*. Translated by H. T. Lowe-Porter. New York: Alfred A. Knopf, 1948.

——. *Joseph and His Brothers*. Translated by H. T. Lowe-Porder. 4 vols. London: Sphere Books, 1968.

——. *The Magic Mountain*. New York: Modern Library, 1927.

Marcus, Jacob. *The Rise and Destiny of the German Jew*. Cincinnati: Union of American Hebrew Congregations, 1934.

Meisels, Samuel. *Deutsche Klassiker im Ghetto*. Wien: Verlag die Neuzeit, 1922.

——. *Goethe im Ghetto*. Wien: Verlag die Neuzeit, 1932.

Myerson, Abraham, and Goldberg, Issac. *The German Jew. His Share in Modern Culture*. New York: Alfred A. Knopf, 1933.

Mosse, George L. "Die deutsche Recht und die Juden." Entscheidungsjahr 1932. Tübingen: J. C. B. Mohr (Paul Siebeck), 1965.

———. Germans and Jews. The Right, the Left, and the Search for a "Third Force" in Pre-Nazi Germany. New York: Howard Fertig, 1970.

Mosse, Werner. "Die Krise der europäischen Bourgeoisie und das deutsche Judentum." Deutsches Judentum in Krieg und Revolution, 1916–1923. Edited by Werner E. Mosse. Tübingen: J. C. B. Mohr (Paul Siebeck), 1971.

———. "Der Niedergang der Weimarer Republik und die Juden." Entscheidungsjahr 1932. Tübingen: J. C. B. Mohr (Paul Siebeck), 1965.

Myth and Mythmaking. Edited by Henry A. Murray. Boston: Beacon Press, 1959.

Naumann, Max. "Grüne Fragen und gelbe Antworten." Klärung. 12 Autoren, Politiker über die Judenfrage. Berlin: Verlag Tradition Wilhelm Kolk, 1932.

———. "Nationaldeutsches Judentum." Süddeutsche Monatshefte, XXVII (September, 1930), 824–848.

———. Sozialismus, Nationalsozialismus und national-deutsches Judentum. Berlin: Manuscript, 1932.

Nazi Conspiracy and Aggression. "Heydrich Schnellbrief on Jewish Councils." Vol. VI. Washington: U. S. Government Printing Office, 1946.

Nisbet, Robert A. The Quest for Community. New York: Oxford University Press, 1953.

"Norman O. Brown's Body: A Conversation Between Brown and Warren Bennis." Psychology Today (August, 1970), pp. 42–47.

"Offen Brief am die deutschen Juden." Deutsche Republik, IV, No. 39 (1930), 1189–1192.

Oppenheimer, Franz. Erlebtes, Erstrebtes, Erreichtes. Erinnerungen von Franz Oppenheimer. Berlin: Welt-Verlag, 1932.

Oppenheimer, Heinrich. The Constitution of the German Republic. London: Stevens & Sons, 1923.

Osborne, Sidney. Germany and Her Jews. London: Soncino Press, 1939.

Ottenheimer, Hilde. "The Disappearance of Jewish Communities in Germany, 1900–1938." Jewish Social Studies, III (1941), 189–206.

Pascal, Roy. The German Novel. London: Methuen & Co., 1956.

Paucker, Arnold. "Der jüdische Abwehrkampf." Entscheidungsjahr 1932. Tübingen: J. C. B. Mohr (Paul Siebeck), 1965.

233

————. *Der jüdische Abwehrkampf gegen Antisemitismus und Nationalsozialismus in den letzten Jahren der Weimarer Republik.* Hamburg: Leibniz Verlag, 1969.

Pinson, Koppel. *Modern Germany. Its History and Civilization.* 2nd ed. New York & London: Macmillan & Co., 1966.

————. *Pietism as a Factor in the Rise of German Nationalism.* New York: Octagon Books, 1968.

Poliakov, Leon. *Harvest of Hate.* Syracuse: Syracuse University Press, 1954.

Poll, B. "Jüdische Presse in Deutschland von den Anfängen bis November, 1938." *Joodse Pers in de Nederlanden en in Duitsland, 1674–1940. Jüdische Presse in den Niederlander und in Deutschland, 1674–1940.* Amsterdam, 1969.

Pulzer, Peter G. J. *The Rise of Political Anti-Semitism in Germany and Austria.* New York, London, Sydney: John Wiley & Sons, 1964.

Reich, Wilhelm. *The Mass Psychology of Fascism.* Translated by Vincent R. Carfagno. New York: Farrar, Straus & Giroux, 1971.

Reichmann, Eva. "Die Lage der Juden in der Weimarer Republik." In *Evangelische Akademie: Loecum.* Speech delivered at the convention on "Der Antisemitismus und die deutsche Geschichte," September 18–21, 1957. Reprint in Wiener Library, London.

————. "Symbol of German Jewry." *Leo Baeck Yearbook,* VII (1957), 21–26.

Reichmann-Jungmann, Eva. "Der Centralverein deutsche Staatsbürger jüdischer Glaubens." *Süddeutsche Monatshefte,* XXVII (September 1930), 818—824.

Reisner Erwin. *Die Juden und das deutsche Reich.* Erlenback-Zürich & Stuttgart: Eugen Rentsch Verlag, 1966.

Reventlow, Graf Ernst. "Deutsche—Juden." *Süddeutsche Monatshefte,* XXVII (September 1930), 846–852.

Robertson, J. G. *A History of German Literature.* Edited by Edna Pardie. 3rd ed. Edinburgh & London: William Blackwood & Sons, 1959.

Robinson, Jacob. *And the Crooked Shall Be Made Straight. The Eichmann Trial, the Jewish Catastrophe, and Hannah Arendt's Narrative.* New York & London: Macmillan & Co., 1965.

Roheim, Geza. "The Evolution of Culture." *International Journal of Psychoanalysis,* XV, No. 4 (October 1934), 387–418.

————. *The Origin and Function of Culture.* Garden City: Doubleday & Co., 1971.

234

―――. *Psychoanalysis and Anthropology: Culture, Personality and the Unconscious*. New York: International Universities Press, 1950.

Rose, William. *Men Myths and Movements in German Literature*. London: Allen & Unwin, 1932.

Rosenthal, Erich. "Trends in the Jewish Population of Germany, 1910–1939." *Jewish Social Studies, VI (1944), 233–274.*

Rosenzweig, Franz. *Briefe*, Berlin: Schocken Verlag, 1935.

Ruppin, Arthur. *The Jews in the Modern World*. London: Macmillan & Co., 1934.

Sachar, Howard Morley. *The Course of Modern Jewish History*. New York: Schocken Books, 1958.

Salfeld, Siegmund. "Welt und Haus des deutschen Juden in Mittelalter." *Jahrbuch für jüdische Geschichte und Literatur*, XXIII (1920), 61–85.

Schay, Rudolf. *Juden in der deutschen Politik*. Berlin: Welt-Verlag, 1929.

Schiller, Friedrich. *Die Braut von Messalina*. Stuttgart: Philipp Reclam, 1964.

―――. *Don Carlos. The Classic Theatre*. Vol. II. Edited by Eric Bentley. Garden City: Anchor Books, 1959.

―――. *Kabale und Liebe*. Edited by Elizabeth M. Wilkinson and L. A. Willoughby. Oxford: Basil Blackwell, 1968.

Schleiermacher, Friedrick. *On Religion. Speeches to Its Cultured Despisers*. Translated by John Oman. New York: Harper & Row, 1958.

Schleunes, Karl A. *The Twisted Road to Auschwitz. Nazi Policy Toward German Jews 1933–1939*. Urbana, Chicago, London: University of Illinois Press, 1970.

Scholem, Gershom. "Jews and Germans." *Commentary*, XLII (November 1966), 32–38.

Schorer, Mark. "The Necessity of Myth." *Myth and Myth-making*. Edited by Henry A. Murray. Boston: Beacon Press, 1959.

Schorske, Carl. "Weimar and the Intellectuals: I." *New York Review of Books*, XIV, No. 9 (May 7, 1970), 22–27.

―――. "Weimar and the Intellectuals: II." *New York Review of Books*, XIV, No. 10 (May 21, 1970), 20–25.

Shafer, Boyd C. *Nationalism: Myth and Reality*. New York: Harcourt, Brace & World, 1955.

Shelley, Percey Bysshe. *Percey Bysshe Shelley: Selected Poetry and Prose*. Edited by Kenneth Neill Cameron. New York: Holt, Rinehart & Winston, 1963.

Slochower, Harry. *Mythopoesis. Mythic Patterns in the Literary Classics.* Detroit: Wayne State University Press, 1970.

Sorel, Georges. *Reflections on Violence.* Translated by T. E Hulme and J. Roth. New York: Collier Books, 1961

Stahl, Rudolph. "Vocational Retraining of Jews in Nazi Germany, 1933–1938." *Jewish Social Studies*, I (1939), 169–194.

Stern, Heinrich. *Warum sind wir Deutsche? Sechs Aufsätze für die deutsche–jüdische Jugend.* Berlin: C. V. Landesverband Ostwestfalen und Nachbargebiete, 1926.

Stern,Täubler, Selma. "The First Generation of Emancipated Jews." *Leo Baeck Yearbook*, XV (1970), 3–40.

Stillmann, Ernst, and Rosenstock, Werner. "Vom Jüdischen Angestellten." *Von deutsch–jüdischer Jugend*, VII, No. 1 (June 17, 1931).

Stonehill, C. A., ed. *The Jewish Contribution to Civilization.* London: C. A. Stonehill, 1940.

Teweles, Heinrich. *Goethe und die Juden.* Hamburg: Gente Verlag, 1925.

Theilhaber, Felix A. *Der Untergang der deutschen Juden. Eine Volkswirtschaftliche Studie.* 2nd ed. Berlin: Jüdischer Verlag, 1921.

Toller, Ernst. *Briefe vom Gefangnis.* 1935.

———. *I Was a German.* Translated by Edward Crankshaw. London: John Lane, The Bodley Head, 1934.

Toury, Jacob. *Die politischen Orientierungen der Juden von Jena bis Weimar.* Tübingen: J. C. B. Mohr (Paul Siebeck), 1966.

———. " 'The Jewish Question'—A Semantic Approach." *Leo Baeck Yearbook*, XI. Edited by Robert Weltsch. London: Horovitz Publishing Co., 1966.

Tramer, Hans. "Der Beitrag der Juden zu Geist und Kultur." *Deutsches Judentum in Krieg und Revolution, 1916–1923.* Edited by Werner E. Mosse. Tübingen: J. C. B. Mohr (Paul Siebeck), 1971.

Treue, Wilhelm. "Zur Frage der wirtschaftlichen Motive in deutscher Antisemitismus." *Deutsches Judentum in Krieg und Revolution, 1916–1923.* Tübingen: J. C. B. Mohr (Paul Siebeck), 1971.

Wassermann, Jakob. *Mein Weg als Deutscher und Jude.* Berlin: S. Fischer Verlag, 1921.

Weil, Bruno. *Der Weg der deutschen Juden.* Berlin, 1934.

Wiener, Alfred. *Das deutsche Judentum in politischer, wirtschaftlicher und kultureller Hinsicht.* Berlin: Philo-Verlag, 1924.

Wiener, Max. "Moses Mendelssohn und die religiösen Gestaltung des Judentums im 19 Jahrhundert." *Zeitschrift für die Geschichte der Juden in Deutschland*, I (1929), 201–212.

Wir Deutschen Juden, 321–1932. Edited by the C.V. Berlin, 1933.

Wischnitzer, M. "Jewish Emigration from Germany, 1933–1938." *Jewish Social Studies*, II (1940), 23–44.

Wordsworth, William. *William Wordsworth. Selected Poetry.* Edited by Mark Van Doren. New York: Modern Library, 1950.

Wundt, Max. "Das Judentum in der Philosophie." *Schriften des Reichsinstituts für Geschichte des neuen Deutschlands.* Vol. II: *Forschungen zur Judenfrage.* 8 vols. Hamburg: Hanseatische Verlaganstalt, 1937.

Zucker, Stanley. "Ludwig Bamberger and the Rise of Anti-Semitism in Germany, 1848–1893." *Central European History*, III, No. 4 (December 1970), 332–352.

Zur Ritualmordbeschuldigung. Edited by the C.V. Berlin; Philo-Verlag, 1934.

Zweig, Arnold. *Bilanz der deutschen Judenheit 1933.* Amsterdam: Querido, 1934.

——. *Essays.* Vol. I: *Literatur und Theater.* Berlin: Aufbau-Verlag, 1959.

ADDENDA:

Blake, William. *The Portable Blake.* Introduction by Alfred Kazin. New York: Viking Press, 1968.

Böckmann, Paul. "Die innere Form in Schillers Jugenddramen." *Dichtung und Volkstum*, XXXV (1934).

Bramsted, Ernest K. *Aristocracy and the Middle–Classes in Germany. Social Types in German Literature 1830–1900.* Řev. ed. Chicago & London: University of Chicago Press, 1964.

Brown, Norman O. *Hermes the Thief. The Evolution of a Myth.* New York: Vintage Books, 1969.

Coleridge, Samuel Taylor. *Coleridge. Selected Poetry and Prose.* Edited by Elisabeth Schneider. 6th ed. New York: Holt, Rinehart & Winston, 1962.

Diesel, Eugen. *Germany and the Germans.* Translated by W. D. Robson-Scott. New York: Macmillan & Co., 1931.

Fichte, Johann Gottlieb. *Addresses to the German Nation.* Translated by R. F. Jones and G. H. Turnbull. Chicago & London: Open Court Publishing Co., 1922.

Hayes, Carlton J. H. *Nationalism: A Religion.* New York: Macmillan & Co., 1960.

Hegel, Georg Wilhelm Friedrich. *The Philosophy of History.* Translated by J. Sibree. New York: Dover Publications, 1956.

Herder, Johann Gottfried. *God, Some Conversations.* Translated by Frederick H. Burckhardt. Indianapolis & New York: Bobbs-Merrill Co., 1940.

Hesse, Hermann. *Demian.* Translated by Michael Roloff and Michael Lebeck. New York: Bantam Books, 1968.

Kienitz, Werner. "Die Zeit der Weimarer Republik." *Monumenta Judaica. 2000 Jahre Geschichte und Kultur der Juden am Rhein.* Edited by Konrad Schilling. Koln, 1963.

Klinkenberg, Hans Martin. "Zwischen Liberalismus und Nationalismus." *Monumenta Judaica. 2000 Jahre Geschichte und Kultur der Juden am Rhein.* Edited by Konrad Schilling. Köln, 1963.

Kluckhohn, Clyde. "Recurrent Themes in Myth and Mythmaking." *Myth and Mythmaking.* Edited by Henry A. Murray. Boston: Beacon Press, 1959.

Laing, R. D. *The Divided Self.* Harmondsworth, Middlesex, England: Penguin Books, 1965.

————. *The Politcs of Experience.* New York: Ballantine Books, 1968.

————. and Esterson, A. *Sanity, Madness and the Family.* Harmondsworth, Middlesex, England: Penguin Books, 1970.

Malinowski, Bronislaw. "Culture." *Encyclopaedia of the Social Sciences.* New York, 1935.

Progoff, Ira. "Waking Dream and Living Myth." *Myths, Dreams, and Religion.* Edited by Joseph Campbell. New York: E. P. Dutton & Co., 1970.

Schorsch, Ismar. *Jewish Reactions to German Anti–Semitism, 1870–1914.* New York: Columbia University Press, 1972.

Index

239

243

245